Fall Classics

Fall Classics

THE BEST WRITING
ABOUT THE WORLD SERIES'
FIRST 100 YEARS

BILL LITTLEFIELD
RICHARD A. JOHNSON

CROWN PUBLISHERS

NEW YORK

Published by Crown Publishers, New York, New York.

Member of the Crown Publishing Group,

a division of Random House, Inc.

www.crownpublishing.com

CROWN is a trademark and the Crown colophon is a registered trademark
of Random House, Inc.

Please see page 275 for permission acknowledgments.

Printed in the United States of America

DESIGN BY LENNY HENDERSON

Library of Congress Cataloging-in-Publication Data

Fall classics : the best writing about the World Series' first 100 years /
[edited by] Bill Littlefield and Richard A. Johnson.— 1st ed.

p. cm.

ISBN 1-4000-4899-0 (Hardcover)

1. World Series (Baseball)—History. 2. Baseball—United States—History.
I. Littlefield, Bill. II. Johnson, Richard A. III. Title.

GV878.4.F35 2003

796.357'646—dc21

2003011603

10 9 8 7 6 5 4 3 2 1

First Edition

To the writers who've chronicled the World Series
for the past one hundred years.
Thanks for sharing the fun you've found in your work.
—B.L.

To Mary, Brave and True
—R.J.

Roster

INTRODUCTION *1*

1903 Pittsburgh a Winner in the First Clash

    Tim Murnane *5*

1905 Giants Champions, the Score, 2–0

    New York Times *12*

1911 Philadelphia Athletics 4, New York Giants 2

    Lloyd Lewis *22*

1912 Snodgrass, Speaker, and Smoky Joe

    Christy Mathewson, Heinie Wagner, and Tris Speaker *28*

1919 From Eight Men Out

    Eliot Asinof *38*

1919 I'm Forever Blowing Ball Games

    Ring Lardner *51*

1919 Dispatches from the World Serious

    Ring Lardner *52*

1919 From Blue Ruin

    Brendan Boyd. *70*

1923 New York Giants 5, New York Yankees 4

    Damon Runyon *73*

1923 From Damon Runyon

    Jimmy Breslin. *84*

1923 New York Yankees 4, New York Giants 2

    Heywood Broun *88*

1924 Washington Senators 4, New York Giants 3

    Bill Corum. *94*

1926 Boy Regains Health as Ruth Hits Homers

    New York Times *100*

1932 Chicago Isn't Like New York

    Marshall Smelser. *102*

1934 St. Louis Cardinals 11, Detroit Tigers 0

    John Drebinger *112*

1941 Winning by Striking Out

    Red Smith *119*

1942 From Catching Dreams

    Frazier "Slow" Robinson with Paul Bauer. *123*

1945 Tiger Triumph

    Jimmy Powers. *134*

1947 Brooklyn Dodgers 3, New York Yankees 2

    Dick Young *140*

1948 From Maybe I'll Pitch Forever

    Satchel Paige *146*

1954 From Willie's Time

    Charles Einstein *154*

1955 Paradise at Last

    Joe Trimble. *160*

1956 Sal Maglie . . . A Gracious Man

    Murray Kempton *166*

CONTENTS

1960 "Dad Would Have Loved It"

Will Grimsley 171

1962 Tension and Torment

Arnold Hano 173

1963 The Last Shovel (World Series Game IV)

Jerry Izenberg 186

1967 The Knot-Hole Gang Goes Climbing

Bud Collins 189

1969 Defying Belief

Arthur Daley 192

The World Turned Upside Down: The Last Five Series

of the 1960s

Luke Salisbury 195

1973 The Game They Invented for Willie

Red Smith 202

1975 The Sixth Game

Peter Gammons. 205

1977 The Right-Field Sign Says "REG-GIE,

REG-GIE, REG-GIE"

Thomas Boswell 223

1981 Brooklyn No Longer Place to Be When Dodgers Win

Joe Soucheray 227

1985 In the World Series, Any Buddy Can Be a Hero

Tony Kornheiser 231

1986 Game Six, World Series

Roger Angell. 235

1988 It's Never Happened Before in the World Series

    Thomas Boswell *246*

1991 As Series Go, '91 Is One to Remember

    Dave Kindred *251*

1994 Game Is Too Young to Die

    Jim Murray *255*

2000 Roger & Out

    Tom Verducci *259*

2001 New York Stories

    Glenn Stout *266*

ACKNOWLEDGMENTS *273*

CREDITS *275*

ABOUT THE EDITORS *281*

ABOUT THE CONTRIBUTORS *283*

Fall Classics

Introduction

Ⓣ HE RUTH IS MIGHTY and shall prevail."

Heywood Broun wrote that sentence to begin his account of the second game of the 1923 World Series between the New York Yankees and the New York Giants.

How did he write the next line? How did he do it?

You can ask how any pitcher ever works up the nerve to throw a strike to Barry Bonds, or how any hitter convinces himself to stand in against Randy Johnson. Me, I'm still wondering how Heywood Broun found strength and discipline enough to remain seated and typing after he tapped out that lead.

How could he not have been afraid he'd ruin it?

The material in this book is characterized by great first lines. There are plenty of great last lines, too, and some sustained passages so lyrical that when you read them, you may find yourself imagining an unlikely muse . . . one partial to cramped spaces and cigar smoke.

Of course, not everything in the collection was written in the press box. Roger Angell is only the most recent excellent writer to have figured out that although it's terrific to be there, and that writers who wrestle deadlines to submission are admirable, the World Series recollected in tranquillity works pretty well as a subject, too.

* * *

Any competition lasting one hundred years is bound to give us heroes, and they are here. Don Larson, Reggie Jackson, Bill Mazeroski, Kirk Gibson, Willie Mays, and so on. There have also been goats, of course, and the World Series has also provided us the sweet sentiment of Walter Johnson finally winning, the terrible irony of Ted Williams failing in the only shot he got, and the unlikely tales over the years of a couple dozen guys you'd never have heard of if they hadn't punched a single through the infield or snatched a ball out of the air when everybody was watching. (Consider Tony Kornheiser's piece on the 1985 World Series. It begins: "Biancalana.")

And the World Serious, as Ring Lardner liked to call it, has given us more. Though the point of baseball is supposed to be scoring more runs than the other guys, the most fascinating Series in terms of the stories it produced was one in which at least six and perhaps as many as eight players on the White Sox were working to make sure their team didn't fall ahead of the Reds. Ah, America. If there had never been a World Series in which the greed and penuriousness of an owner drove bitter, gullible workers to sabotage the product at the urging of duplicitous gamblers who escaped persecution while tyrannous, arbitrary authority crushed the workers despite their vindication by the courts, surely somebody (Nelson Algren? Philip Roth?) would have invented one.

Long before there was the Super Bowl, the NBA Championship, the Final Four, or the World Cup, there was the World Series. That matters, too. When it began, men in derby hats sat—sometimes on the grass in the outfield so that the take would be greater—and marveled at the genius of John McGraw. When the Boston Red Sox made the Series (five times between 1903 and 1918), the mayor of the city led a hooting and tooting musical aggregation calling itself the Royal Rooters through the city's streets and into the ball yard. Back in the days when the Series was played on weekday afternoons, the event was a license to skip school or smuggle a transistor radio into class. Generations of fans recall October afternoons when favorite teachers put aside lesson plans and invited everybody to watch the Series on the black-and-white TV temporarily resting between the microscopes on the scarred, black table in the science lab.

Many regard the good old days as better in every respect, but in terms of the World Series, it's a shaky case. Sure, the owners and the players manifested sufficient distrust and loathing to abort the 1994 World Series, a circumstance so vile that some hysterics maintained then that the game would never recover. But back in 1904, after just one edition of the "modern" World Series had transpired, the aforementioned John McGraw demonstrated his contempt for the American League by refusing to allow his Giants to play its champion, so there was no World Series that year, either. Though baseball fans of the late twentieth and early twenty-first centuries may not be able to conceive of lucre poisoning the pastime before their own baseball days, there were even whispers that money (and the ways and means of apportioning it) might have figured in Mr. McGraw's decision. The following season McGraw relented and the Giants, clad in brilliant new uniforms made for the occasion, met the Philadelphia Athletics. On that occasion, the players reportedly agreed beforehand to split the profits of the Series 50-50—a sensible, democratic, and gentlemanly arrangement that would have each player on both clubs banned for life were it to occur today.

So much for the good old days.

Baseball fans of a certain age are as likely to have a favorite World Series as they are to have a favorite team and a favorite player. As a writer, I especially appreciated the 1986 edition, because game six gave us one of those story lines no novelist writing for anybody over the age of eight would have dared to invent. I liked the 1993 World Series a lot, too, because when the Blue Jays, known as a scientifically constructed and especially disciplined team, met the Phils, considered by some a collection of beer-bellied rejects, it gave me the opportunity to write:

The fans of the Jays—many of them—speak Spanish
And French, also Latin and Greek;
The fans of the Phils can sometimes manage English,
That is, those of them who can speak.

Most of them only grunt on their most vocal days,
Scratch themselves, spit, and paw at the ground,
While the Jays fans play classical music and chess
And pass pâté de foie gras around.

During the process of reviewing the material for this collection, I found many more reasons for treasuring Series past. I revisited the novel *Blue Ruin* and was amazed all over again at what Brendon Boyd had done with Sport Sullivan, who got so much less than he thought he might have gotten out of his role in fixing the 1919 World Series. I read Murray Kempton again, and Jimmy Breslin, and Damon Runyon and felt lasting gratitude to the World Series for being a big enough deal to draw the attention of writers of such genius. I hope this collection will be as much fun to read as it was to assemble.

Bill Littlefield

1903

Pittsburgh a Winner
in the First Clash

TIM MURNANE

BOSTON BEATEN BY A SCORE OF 7 TO 3

"CY" YOUNG IS OFF EDGE AND IS BUMPED HARD

MORE THAN 16,000 PERSONS SEE OPENING CONTEST

BOSTON THE FAVORITE IN THE GAME

SCHEDULED FOR TODAY

W ITH CY YOUNG IN THE BOX AND more than 16,000 persons looking on, the Pittsburgh club won from Boston by a score of 7 to 3 in the first game in the series for the world's championship at the Huntington Avenue grounds yesterday.

The crowd, which encircled the field, was held well back by ropes and a small army of policemen, and the best of order prevailed. Both teams received liberal applause for good work.

The Boston players evidently were a little nervous, as is usually the case with teams on the home grounds in an important series. As the game progressed, however, Collins' boys got into their stride, and played grand ball when it was too late to overtake the Pirates.

Cy Young was hit hard. He fell considerably short of his best work, lacking speed, his winning ingredient. With Young off edge, the home players were carrying a big handicap.

Phillippe was in rare good form, but weakened perceptibly as the game drew out, withering under a brace of triples by Freeman and Parent, and finishing at a much slower clip than the one at which he started, although he had no trouble with O'Brien and Farrell, who were sent in to bat for the Boston battery in the ninth when there were two men on bases.

Pittsburgh had all the luck and a shade the better of the umpiring, as Connolly favored Phillippe on strikes, while O'Day had no close plays on the bases.

The Boston infield outplayed Pittsburgh's. Ferris, after making two bad fumbles and giving the visitors four runs at the start, pulled himself together, and, with Collins and Parent, put up a superb article of baseball.

Criger, who's probably the greatest catcher living, had a bad day, making two poor throws to second and having a passed ball on a third strike.

But for the misplays of Ferris and Criger and the bad piece of fielding by Freeman in allowing a line hit to pass under him for three bases, the Pittsburgh men would have another story to send home.

Because the Boston boys failed to play up to their natural gait from start to finish, and slipped a shoe in the first game, it need not be assumed that it will occur again.

Fred Clarke carried off the honors of the day in left field. He covered ground like a cyclone, and three times pulled in line drives that were marked for three bases. His marvelous work cut off at least three runs, and the chances are that not another man playing ball today would have connected with any one of the three great running catches made by him. It was ground covering with a vengeance. He was off with the swing of the bat besides pretty nearly calling the turn on the batsman.

Beaumont and Stahl made clever catches, but outside this work of Clarke and Beaumont, and two pretty plays by Ritchey the visitors were not offering anything sensational in the way of fielding.

Ferris, Parent and Collins played fast ball, one play by Criger to Ferris and back to the plate, where they got their man was a classic.

Phillippe apparently took things easy, as he well might, with the start of four runs in the first inning. These runs were started after two men were out and Cy had two strikes on Tommy Leach. The latter and Sebring did the hitting for the Burgers, the little third base man clipping off four safe ones, which is pretty good work for a light batsman.

Sebring got in one clean hit and two lucky ones. LaChance failing to go out and stop his first grounder, and his home run coming from a Texas leaguer; Stahl thinking the ball would roll into the crowd and failing to go after it, thus making a gift of a run.

The crowd had little chance to cheer until "Buck" Freeman lined one up against the right fence in the seventh, and Parent followed with one into the crowd in left field for three bases. The cheering was like the roll of thunder, and was tuned up for business when shut off by one of Clarke's great running catches clear over in center field.

After the game one club looked just as good as the other, the difference yesterday was in the pitchers' box, and it's not often that Uncle Cyrus fails to send the money, even if he is a bit fat.

INTO THE CROWD—THREE BASES

After making ground rules, giving three bases for balls hit into the crowd on fair ground, Tommy Connolly took his place behind the bat and Hank O'Day on the bases. Here was a pair of umpires who know their business, and the players never undertook to question their decisions.

Cy Young started off by disposing of the clever Beaumont on a fly to Stahl. He then forced Fred Clarke to pop up a weak fly to Criger. Leach was in for two strikes and then cast one of Young's straight ones past Freeman for three bases. Wagner threw his bat at the wide-out curve and sent it safe to left, Leach scoring. On the first ball pitched the Pittsburgh man was off for second like a shot and landed safely, as Criger was a bit slow and Ferris was very much surprised.

It was evident that the visitors were going to force Criger to show his speed, and by so doing they made the Boston man look like a fur overcoat in July.

Bransfield hit a merry grounder at Ferris, and after evading several stabs the ball rolled up Hobe's sleeve, while Bransfield was safe at first. Bransfield went down to second, and Criger threw the ball out to center, Wagner scoring and Bransfield going to third. Ritchey drew a pass, and off he went to second. This time Criger made a bluff to throw down and turn the ball to Collins, but Bransfield was hugging the base. Sebring came in with a timely line single to left, and two runs were scored. Phelps struck out, but got first on Criger's passed ball. Phillippe, the ninth man up, fanned, and the home team started in on a big contract.

Dougherty and Collins struck out. Stahl scratched a single to left, and Freeman flied out to right.

BEAUMONT STRIKES OUT

Beaumont opened the second inning with a strikeout. Clarke hit one down the left line and was thrown out by Dougherty while trying for two bases. Leach flied out to left.

Phillippe got a round of applause by striking out Parent, LaChance and Ferris, the only men who went to bat in Boston's half.

In the third Collins made a fine catch of Wagner's fly.

Bransfield lined one to right that Freeman came in for and then allowed to go through him to the crowd for the three bases. Bransfield scored on Sebring's single past LaChance.

Boston went out in order.

Beaumont opened the fourth with a grounder that was fumbled by Ferris. Clarke and Leach singled, scoring Beaumont. Wagner flied out to Parent, and Bransfield forced a man at second, Ferris making a clever running assist.

Collins hit a ball into the crowd along the left line but was called back and then hit a fierce liner that Clarke made a grand catch of. Stahl flied out to center. Freeman hit one too warm for Bransfield. Parent hit to Leach and the ball was thrown wild, but luckily for Pittsburgh it hit the fence back of first base. LaChance flied out to Ritchey.

In the fifth Collins made two fine assists to first. Phelps singled; then Phillippe flied out to Ferris.

Boston went out in order.

With two out in the sixth Leach singled and Wagner drew on base on balls only to be forced by Bransfield, Ferris making another fine assist. For the fourth time, Boston went out in order.

In the seventh Parent made a pretty assist off Ritchey.

Sebring hit a weak fly over Ferris that rolled nearly to the ropes, the Boston outfielders taking their time in fielding it and permitting a home run.

Freeman hit the fence in right for three bases and scored on Parent's drive into the crowd in left for three sacks. LaChance made a fine bid for a hit, but Clarke was there for a great catch. Ferris was hit by a pitched ball. Then the Boston battery turned in a double strikeout.

Parent made a grand assist of Beaumont in the eighth. Clarke flied out to Freeman. Leach hit for three bases and Wagner drew a pass. Then the best play of the game took place. Wagner started for second and Criger drove the ball to Parent but Ferris saw Leach start for home and intercepted the ball and lined it back to Criger for an out.

Boston went out in order.

BRIEF RALLY IN THE NINTH

The visitors went out in order in their half of the ninth.

For Boston, Freeman was safe on Wagner's fumble. Parent singled. LaChance made one more fine try for business, but Clarke again came across the field like a flash and took the ball over his head. Ferris dropped one safe and center and Freeman scored. O'Brien was sent up for Criger, and struck out. Farrell hit the ball to the pitcher and was thrown out at first, and the game was over.

The crowd gathered on the field and many good-sized bets were paid over.

The Pittsburgh players were surrounded by their friends and escorted to their carriages, a well pleased lot of ball players, while the Boston men looked anything by discouraged over the loss of game number one. The score:

PITTSBURGH	AB	R	BH	TB	PO	A	E
Beaumont cf	5	1	0	0	4	0	0
Clarke lf	5	0	2	2	3	0	0
Leach 3b	5	1	4	8	0	1	1
Wagner ss	3	1	1	1	1	2	1
Bransfield 1b	5	2	1	3	7	0	0
Ritchey 2b	4	1	0	0	1	2	0
Sebring rf	5	1	3	7	1	0	0
Phelps c	4	0	1	1	10	0	0
Phillippe p	4	0	0	0	0	2	0
Totals:	40	7	12	22	27	7	2

BOSTON							
Dougherty 1b	4	0	0	0	1	1	0
Collins 3b	4	0	0	0	2	4	0

C. Stahl cf	4	0	1	1	2	0	0
Freeman rf	4	2	2	4	2	0	0
Parent ss	4	1	2	4	4	2	0
LaChance 1b	4	0	0	0	8	0	0
Ferris 2b	3	0	1	1	2	4	2
Criger c	3	0	0	0	6	1	2
Young p	3	0	0	0	0	1	0
*O'Brien	1	0	0	0	0	0	0
†Farrell	1	0	0	0	0	0	0
Totals:	35	3	6	10	27	13	4

*Batted for Criger in the ninth. †Batted for Young in the ninth.

INNINGS	1	2	3	4	5	6	7	8	9
Pittsburgh	4	0	1	1	0	0	1	0	0–7
Boston	0	0	0	0	0	0	2	0	1–3

Home run, Sebring. Three base hits, Leach 2, Bransfield, Sebring, Freeman, Parent. Stolen bases, Wagner, Bransfield, Ritchey. Bases on balls off Young, Wagner 2, Ritchey. Struck out by Young, Beaumont, Clarke, Ritchey, Phelps, Phillippe. By Phillippe, Dougherty, Collins, Stahl, Parent, LaChance, Ferris 2, Criger, Young, O'Brien. Hit by pitched ball by Phillippe, Ferris. Umpires, O'Day and Connolly. Attendance: 16,242.

1905

Giants Champions, the Score, 2–0

New York Times

MATHEWSON'S SUPERB WORK ENDS

THE INTER-LEAGUE SERIES.

CROWD GOES WILD WITH JOY

MCGRAW'S MEN BESIEGED IN THEIR CLUBHOUSE

BY 10,000 CHEERING ADMIRERS.

TWO NEATLY DRESSED, RUDDY FACED, athletic looking young men, grinning broadly; one a giant in contrast to the squattiness of the other, walked along the veranda of the clubhouse at the Polo Grounds about 5 o'clock yesterday afternoon. Below them was a sea of 10,000 faces, wildly emitting a thundrous eruption of enthusiasm. The two young men looked down upon the reverberating ocean of humanity for a moment, and then walked to a point directly in front of the plaza, where they were in view of all. The ten thousand throats bellowed forth a tribute that would have almost drowned a broadside of twelve-inch guns.

The two smiling athletes stopped, one of them drew forth a long sheet of yellow paper rolled under his arm. As the crowd pushed and fought and cheered he unwrapped an impromptu banner and let it flutter on the breeze. The multitude pressed forward like a wave to read this inscription:

THE GIANTS, WORLD'S CHAMPIONS, 1905.

Geological records show that Vesuvius disturbs the earth and that seismic demonstrations are felt by the greater number. But if that doctrine had been promulgated in the vicinity of the Polo Grounds yesterday, as Christie Mathewson and Roger Bresnahan of the New York Baseball Club unfurled their victorious banner, it would have been minimized. For, as volcanoes assert themselves upon the earth's surface surely must that deafening, reverberating roar have lifted Manhattan's soil from its base.

The Giants, the most intelligent, the quickest, strongest, and grittiest combination of baseball players that have ever represented this city in any league, demonstrated beyond opportunity for quibble or claim their paramount superiority over anything extant in diamond life of today by winning the fourth and deciding game of the world's championship series by the score of 2 to 0.

The victory meant an honor which has not hitherto fallen to the lot of New York through any other team, and by the victory of yesterday the Giants may hold up their heads in the athletic world as being the one collection of peerless ball tossers.

The crowd, in the neighborhood of 27,000 people, saw the battle, and a battle it was, to cheer the baseball heart and satisfy the innermost cravings of the rooter's mind. It was a fight of slow stages, but at no time during the contest were the Giants in danger, and at all times were they masters. It settled the question so often propounded whether the National or the American League offers the better brand of baseball. The championship decree of yesterday, to be accepted as final, lays at rest all doubt and demonstrates the transcendent superiority of the National brand and the indisputable invulnerability of the Giants.

And be it recorded right here that New York possesses the pitching marvel of the century. Christie Mathewson, the giant slabman, who made the world's championship possible for New York, may be legitimately designated as the premier pitching wonder of all baseball records. The diamond has known its Clarkson, its Keefe, and its Caruthers. Their records radiate. But to Mathewson belongs the palm, for his almost superhuman accomplishment during the series which closed yesterday will stand as a mark for all pitchers of the future.

MATHEWSON'S GREAT RECORD.

Figures show best just what Mathewson accomplished. In the three victories over which he presided he twirled twenty-seven innings. During that series he allowed not a single run; not an Athletic even reached third base. He was touched for only a total of fifteen hits, and by men who are reckoned as the American League's strongest batters; he allowed only one pass to first, hit only a single batsman, and struck out sixteen men. The record is a classic. Baseball New York appreciates this work. That fact was amply demonstrated yesterday, when it gave Mathewson a marvelous vocal panegyric and placed upon his modest brow a bellowed wreath that evoked only a half-suppressed smile and bow.

The game yesterday was one of giants—clean, fast, and decisive. Both teams were keyed to the point of desperation, for to the Giants it meant rosy conquest and to the Athletics a saving clause which would offer them yet a chance to redeem themselves. But the Giants were not to be repulsed. They went at the ball in the first inning with a we-never-can-lose expression of dogged determination, and there was not a minute during play in which that spirit didn't manifest itself. Philadelphia tried its best, but, strive as hard as it did, it was only a shadow reflecting the masterful Mathewson's will. He bestrode the field like a mighty Colossus, and the Athletics peeped about the diamond like pigmies who struggled gallantly for their lives, but in vain.

Bender, the much favored brave from the Carlisle reservation, sought to repeat his scalping bee of Tuesday, but the Spartan McGraw laconically expressed the situation when at the beginning of the game he remarked good-naturedly to the Athletics' pitcher:

"It will be off the warpath for you today, Chief." The stolid, phlegmatic copper-colored man only smiled grimly.

"It's uncertain," he replied, "but I did it once, and I'm going to do my best to do it again."

Analyzed in the statistical point the twirling features of the game shows little advantage to either side, but when weighed in parts Mathewson had by far the advantage. Five hits were all that the Giants could register off Bender, while the Athletics rang up for a total of six against Mathewson. Mathewson fanned only three to Bender's five, but the Indian gave three passes. Mathewson proved a surprise to his admirers by poorly fielding his position. He made two errors, but they luckily resulted in nothing harmful in the net result.

GIANTS GET $1,141 EACH.

The Giants were well rewarded for their hard work in defeating the Athletics, for by the week's labor each man to-day has a check in his wallet for $1,141.41. That is the share of each of the eighteen Giants for the series. The figures given out officially yesterday show the receipts of the first four games, from which the players derive their profit, to have been $50,730.50. The share for which the two teams struggled amounted to $27,394. Seventy-five per cent of that amount was divided among the Giants. The remainder went in equal shares to the Athletics.

The crowd which saw yesterday's game was immense, exceeding by a small margin that of Tuesday. All the stands were filled, while men and women stood in a line ten deep back of the ropes from the right to the left field bleachers. Men hung on the fence and sat on the grandstand roof, and some peered at the game through glasses from distant poles and housetops. The crowd was there to cheer its idols, and every move was followed by a roar.

The New York management had a band on the field to enliven things until play began, and it was kept busy as the players walked to the field and started practice. As McGraw appeared on the diamond, coming from the clubhouse, he was met with a volley of applause and was obliged to lift his hat in response.

"Clinch it to-day, Mac," yelled the crowd. "Nothing but the championship will suit us now."

"That's what you'll get," he responded smilingly.

While McGraw was walking across the field the Athletics appeared from the clubhouse with Bender in the lead.

"Back to the tepee for yours," hooted a rooter. "Giants grab heap much wampum," yelled another, giving an imitation Indian yell. Bender looked at his foes in stolid silence, but smiled widely as the running fire of comments continued. James J. Corbett, with an eye for all public opportunities, walked onto the field with the Giants and helped the players to warm up. He was subjected to a good deal of bantering. Just before play was called Corbett and Bresnahan posed with an Irish flag between them and were snapped by a photographer. Mathewson was the last to arrive on the scene and got a magnificent reception. He was applauded for a full minute and the crowd yelled for him to doff his cap. Instead of doing so, however, he walked over to McGinnity, the conqueror of yesterday, and ostentatiously removed Joe's headgear. McGinnity returned the compliment.

"Shake 'em up, Matty. Go after 'em," screamed the bleachers. Mathewson waved his arm as though he would do his utmost. As McGraw went to the plate to bat out in practice the band began to play:

We'll all get stone blind.

Johnnie go fill up the bowl

The crowd cheered, and a half dozen men went through the grandstand offering to bet 100 to 75 that the Giants would win the game. There were no takers.

COULDN'T RATTLE BENDER.

Time and again Bender was yelled at, for the crowd wanted to rattle him, but its noise might as well have been directed at a steamboat, for he was impassive and cool at all stages. In one inning he gave two bases on balls in succession and the crowd jumped to its feet in glee. Bender was thunderously informed that at that particular stage he was booked for the soap factory, but stuck grimly to his task. At another time two bunts were made in succession. Again the crowd rose in its might and expressed itself as of the opinion that the chief would surely go to the happy hunting grounds, but he refused to die and stood gamely and quietly to the end.

Danny McGann was again a target for the Bender brand of curves, and added to his strike-out performance of Tuesday, when he slashed the air in a way that was distressing. The first time up yesterday McGann, with his strike-out record fresh in the minds of the fans, was cautioned to be wary and smash the ball to the earth's ends.

"Look out, Danny, the Heap-Much-Kill-'em-Giants man'll get you. Lace it out of the lot."

McGann's face bespoke ill for the future of the ball, but, much to the chagrin of the rooters, he was called out on strikes. As McGann walked toward the home bench the crowd raised a hiss of protest at Sheridan. McGraw, Dahlen, Bresnahan, and Clark had heart-to-heart talks with the indicator, but they were shooed away.

As the game proceeded the crowd saw that it was to be a magnificent pitching struggle, and both twirlers were cheered. After the fourth, when Bender had acquitted himself by retiring the Giants in one, two, three order, he was heartily applauded.

"You're the real thing: kangaroo out of the American and come to us next season," howled one fan. Bender lifted his cap in acknowledgment.

Philadelphia had men on bases in the first, second, third, fifth, and sixth innings, but couldn't get one past the second sack. In the fifth inning they came close to pushing a man to third, but Mathewson, evidently intent upon keeping his record intact, interfered. Powers had made a two-base hit to left. Bender, the next man up, lined one to Mathewson. There were two out, and by the ordinary rules of baseball the batter should have been retired. Powers started off for third, however, and Mathewson, seeing him approaching the bag, took the insult to heart. He threw quickly to Devlin, who touched the runner before he could put his spikes upon the bag.

New York made its runs in the fifth and eighth. In the fifth inning Mertes got a pass and Dahlen followed suit by passing four bad ones. With two on bases the crowd, keen for an opportunity to root, stood up and roared for Devlin to drive in a run.

"Show 'em the way to the clubhouse, Arthur," shouted Clark, who stood upon the coaching line. Devlin, however, had his orders and bunted. He sacrificed the runners to third and second, respectively and as the men chased down the line the crowd nearly yelled itself hoarse.

BESIEGED BY THE ROOTERS.

"Come on, Gilbert, you can do it!" roared the stands. Then came a volley of taunts to Bender, who viewed the situation with absolute imperturbability and wound up his pitching arm for New York's second baseman. But Gilbert was equal to the occasion, for he caught one of Bender's twists on the end of his bat and sent the sphere to deep left. Hartzel got under the base and caught it, but Mertes on third raced home with the first tally of the game. Then the crowd went wild and cheered everything and everybody.

In the eighth the Giants rolled up another. After Gilbert had flied to Lord, Mathewson went to the bag amid a storm of yells. He passed four bad ones, and walked. Bresnahan put an extra coat of dust upon his hands as he stalked to the plate and carefully inspected the business end of his bat. The crowd yelled for him to "Swat it off the earth!"

"Put it in a balloon, Roger, and send it away for good!" screamed the fans. Roger did the next best thing by driving the ball on a straight line to the left field bleachers. Ordinarily it would have counted for a home run, but under the ground rules he was allowed only two bases. Even Matty was enamored of the coup, for as he trotted around to third he paused, under the ground rule allowance, and clapped his hands with satisfaction. Browne, the next up, did his best to imitate Bresnahan, and swung viciously at one of Bender's curves. It went like a shot straight for the Indian. Bender grabbed at the leather, and it struck his right hand, caroming off to Murphy, who retired Browne. Matty, however, jumped across the rubber and registered a second tally.

The Giants also came within an ace of scoring in the sixth. Mathewson went out to Lord on a high fly, to be followed by Bresnahan who bunted safely along the third-base line. The crowd wanted blood in this round, and told as much to Browne, who followed.

"Once more, boys," yelled McGraw, who was standing on the coaching line. "Let's get at the Indian here and fix 'em."

Browne was equal to the occasion and put one exactly where Roger had sent it. Donlin walked to the plate with the air of a man capable of great things.

"I'm sorry, old Pitch-Em-Heap," he remarked to Bender jokingly, "but here's where you go back to the reservation."

"Is that so?" answered Bender sarcastically. "Your conclusion, Mr. Donlin, is right in this immediate vicinity." Donlin went out to Lord, and McGann, who followed, cut off three slices of air, and walked away a heart-broken man.

The score:

PHILADELPHIA	R	1B	PO	A	E
Hartsel, lf	0	2	4	1	0
Lord, cf	0	0	3	0	0
Davis, 1b	0	1	10	0	0
L. Cross, 3b	0	0	1	1	0
Seybold, rf	0	1	0	0	0
Murphy, 2b	0	0	0	0	0
M. Cross, ss	0	1	1	5	0
Powers, c	0	1	5	1	0
Bender, p	0	0	0	5	0
Total	0	6	24	13	0

NEW YORK	R	1B	PO	A	E
Bresn'h'n, c	0	2	5	2	0
Browne, rf	0	1	0	0	0
Donlin, cf	0	0	1	0	0
M'Gann, 1b	0	0	12	1	0
Mertes, lf	1	1	1	0	0
Dahlen, ss	0	0	3	4	0
Devlin, 3b	0	0	1	4	0
Gilbert, 2b	0	1	3	6	0
M'th'son, p	1	0	1	3	1
Total	2	5	27	20	1

PHILADELPHIA

0	0	0	0	0	0	0	0	0	0

NEW YORK

0	0	0	0	1	0	0	1	–	2

First base on errors—Philadelphia, 1. Bases on balls—Off Bender, 3. Struck out—By Mathewson, 4; by Bender, 4. Left on bases—New York, 4; Philadelphia, 6. Two-base Two-base hits—Powers, Bresnahan. Sacrifice hits—Devlin, Mathewson. Double plays—Dahlen, Gilbert, and McGann; Hartsel, M. Cross, and L. Cross. Umpires—Messrs. Sheridan and O'Day. Time of game—One hour and twenty-eight minutes. Attendance—24,187.

1911

Philadelphia Athletics 4, New York Giants 2

Lloyd Lewis

WHEN THE BLEACHER GATES at Shibe Park in Philadelphia were thrown open on the morning of Oct. 24, 1911, I was in the mob that went whooping toward the front seats. I got one, partly because the right-field crowd was smaller than the one in left, partly because most Philadelphians wanted to sit close to their worshiped Athletics, for the World Series at that moment stood two games to one for Connie Mack against John McGraw, and Philadelphia was loud and passionate in the confidence that now they would get revenge for the bitter dose—four games to one, three shutouts—the Giants had given them six years before.

Me, I wanted to get as close to the Giants as possible, and found a place at the rail close to the empty chairs which would that afternoon become the Giants' bull pen. My whole adolescence had been devoted, so far as baseball went—and it went a long way to an Indiana farm boy—to the Giants and to their kingly pitcher, "Big Six," the great, the incomparable Christy Mathewson. I hadn't had the courage to cut classes in the nearby college and go to the first game of the series at Shibe Park. But today I had. Things were desperate. Up in New York's Polo Grounds to start this, the World Series, Mathewson had won—2 to 1—giving but five hits and demonstrating that with 12 years of herculean toil behind him he was practically as invincible as when in 1905 he had shut out these same Athletics three times.

It had looked like 1905 over again; then, in the second game, the A's long, lean yokel third baseman J. Franklin Baker had suddenly and incredibly knocked a home run off Rube Marquard, the Giants' amazing young pitcher. Baker, who had hit only nine homers all season, had tagged the 22-year-old Giant and two runs had come in—and the final had stood 3 to 1.

The papers which I read, as the morning wore on, were still full of that home run and its aftermath.

From the start of the series the newspapers had been publishing syndicated articles signed by Giant and Athletic stars—the real start of the "ghost writers" whose spurious trade flourished so long but which the better papers in time eliminated. And in the article signed by Mathewson the day after Marquard's disaster it had been said that Rube had lost the game by failing to obey orders. The article rebuked the boy for throwing Baker the high outside pitch he liked, instead of the low fast one he didn't like and which McGraw had ordered.

The rebuke had been a sensation which grew in the third game when Baker had hit another homer off Mathewson himself, and had been the main wrecker of the great man's long sway over the A's. Up in the ninth inning of that third game Matty had kept command. Always when the Athletics had got men on bases he had turned on his magic. As he went to the bench at the end of the eighth, New York had risen and given him a tremendous ovation, for in 44 innings of World Series play, 1905 and 1911, he had allowed the Mack-men exactly one run—and the A's were hitters, indeed. Their season's average for 1911 had been .297.

Then in the ninth, Eddie Collins had gone out, and only two men had stood between Matty and his fifth series victory over his victims. Up had come Baker with the American League fans begging him to do to Matty what he had done to Marquard—and, incredible as it seemed, he had done this.

As home runs go, it hadn't been much more than a long fly

that sailed into the convenient right-field stand at the Polo Grounds, but it had gone far enough to tie the score and give Baker a nickname for life—"Home Run" Baker.

Snodgrass, the Giants' center fielder, one of the smartest and greatest of base runners, had ripped Baker's trousers almost off him, sliding into third in the first of the 10th inning. With McGraw snarling, railing, jeering from the coaching line, the Giants made no secret of their hatred of Baker. To them he was merely a lucky lout, a greenhorn who had by sheer accident homered off the two top pitchers of the season.

But Baker had hit again, a scratch single in the 11th, which had been part of the making of the run which had won, and Marquard in his "ghosted" article had quipped at Mathewson's advice.

All that was in everybody's mind—and mine—as on Oct. 24 the fourth game came up. The papers had had time to chew the sensation over and over, for it had rained for a week after the third game and now, with seven days' rest, Mathewson was to try again—this time in Shibe Park.

The long delay hadn't cooled excitement. The press box was still as crowded as at the opening game. This was the first World Series to be handled in the modern publicity fashion—the first to have as many as 50 telegraphers on the job—the first to wire the game by play-by-play to points as distant as Havana, Cuba—the first to which newspapers in the Far West and South sent their own writers. And though the A's now had a lead of two games to one, the threat of the Giants was still great enough to keep fever high.

It was a little after one o'clock when my long vigil ended. Onto the field came the Giants with their immemorial swagger, chips still on their shoulders—the cocky, ornery, defiant men of Muggsy McGraw—the rip-roaring demons who had that season of 1911 set a record of 347 stolen bases—a record which would stand for another 31 years without any other club ever coming nearer to it than the Senators' 288 in 1913.

And here at long last they were! I knew them from their pictures as, clad in dangerous black, they came strutting across toward their dugout. McGraw had dressed his men in black, back in 1905 when he had humbled the Athletics, and he was playing hunches now.

Muggsy was first—stocky, hard-eyed. Behind him came slim, handsome Snodgrass, striding as became a genius at getting hit by pitched balls and in scaring infielders with his flashing spikes. Then came swart, ominous Larry Doyle; lantern-jawed Art Fletcher; Buck Herzog, whose nose curved like a scimitar; lithe little Josh Devore; burly Otis Crandall; flat-faced, mahogany-colored Chief Meyers, the full-blooded Indian; Fred Merkle, all muscles even in his jaws, a lion-heart living down the most awful bonehead blunder ever made in baseball.

Then came Marquard, 6 feet 3, his sharp face and slitlike eyes smiling—his head tilting to the left at the top of a long wry neck— Marquard the meteoric! At 19 years of age he had been bought at a record price from Indianapolis and had immediately flopped two straight years for McGraw, becoming the nationally goatish "$11,000 lemon." Then, this 1911, he had flamed out, won 24 games, and become the "$11,000 beauty."

As the Giants began to toss the ball around, I couldn't see my hero, the Mathewson whom I had come to see, the great one who from the time I was nine I had pretended I was, playing ball in the Indiana cow pasture, throwing his famous "fadeaway" which, for me, never came off. Then, suddenly, there he was, warming up and growling "Who am I working for, the Giants or the photographers," as the cameramen, not 20 feet from my popeyed head, begged him for poses.

I was let down for a minute. He didn't speak like a demigod but as I stared, he looked it, all the same. He held his head high, and his eye with slow, lordly contempt swept the Athletics as they warmed up across the field. He was 31, all bone and muscle and princely poise. Surely he would get those Athletics today and put the Giants back in the running. Surely his unique "fadeaway," the curve that broke backward, his speed, his snapping curve, his fabulous brain, couldn't be stopped. It had been luck that had beaten him in the last game. Now he'd get them.

My eye never left him till the bell rang and he strode, hard but easy, with the swing of the aristocrat, into the dugout and little Josh Devore went up to hit.

Josh singled, Doyle tripled, Snodgrass scored Larry with a long fly. Black figures were flying everywhere. The big copper-colored Chief Bender on Mack's mound was wobbling, and when the side was finally out he practically ran for the dugout. Later, we learned, he had run in to cut off bandages from his ribs, tape from a recent injury. After that he was to be unbeatable.

Up came the Athletics. Matty, as though in princely disdain, fanned the first two men. The third man, Eddie Collins, singled. Here came Baker, his sun-tanned face tense, his bat flailing—the air thick with one word from 25,000 throats, "Homer! Homer!"

Matty studied him as a scientist contemplates a beetle, then struck him out! What I yelled I don't know. All I remember is standing there bellowing and paying no heed to the wadded newspapers the Athletic fans around me threw. It was wonderful.

In the fourth, Baker came up to start it and doubled. Dannie Murphy doubled. Harry Davis doubled. Ira Thomas hit a sacrifice fly—three runs. It couldn't be. Up came Baker again in the fifth with Collins on first and another double boomed across the diamond. I saw Snodgrass eventually stop it, but he didn't really have it in his glove at all. It had stuck in my gullet.

Right in front of me an unthinkable thing happened. Hooks Wiltse, the southpaw, began warming up for the Giants. Was Matty knocked out? Another figure rose from the bull pen. Rube Marquard. He didn't warm up, he only strolled up and down, a great sardonic grin on his face. The fans around me were screaming at him, "You're even with Matty now, Rube! He won't tell you what to pitch any more!" etc., etc. Rube smirked at them.

Matty got by without more scores, but in the seventh with a man on third Christy walked Baker on four intentional balls, and

Shibe Park's walls waved in a cyclone of boos. I wished I were dead.

The eighth. A pinch hitter went up for Mathewson. I was sorry I hadn't died in the seventh.

Finally it was all over.

I walked out through 25,000 of the most loathsome individuals ever created—all jeering at Mathewson, all howling Baker's virtues. I dragged my feet this way and that trying to escape the currents of fans. At the end of a dolorous mile I stopped at a saloon. I had never had a drink. Now was the time.

"Beer," I said, in the voice of Poe's raven.

"You ain't 21," the bartender rasped. Then he took a second look, saw that I was 100 years old, and splashed a great stein in front of me.

I took one swallow. It was bitter, just as bitter as everything else in the world. I laid down a nickel and walked out. Every step of the way downtown I kept telling myself that in my coffin, some day, there'd be only room for one thing besides myself—my hatred of the Athletics.

But what I started out to tell was about my greatest day in baseball. That came three years later, Oct. 9, 1914, when the lowly, despised Boston Braves wallowed, humbled, trampled, laughed at the lofty Athletics to the tune of 7 to 1. Hoarse and happy, I came out of Shibe Park, spent hours hunting that same saloon, but I couldn't find it. It had to be that one. What I wanted to do was to walk in all alone—find nobody else in there—order two beers, and when the bartender looked inquiringly at the extra one, say to him in a condescending voice, "Oh, that? That's for Mathewson."

1912

Snodgrass, Speaker,
and Smoky Joe

CHRISTY MATHEWSON, HEINIE WAGNER, AND TRIS SPEAKER

The 1912 World Series was played amid much fanfare and more than
lived up to its advance billing. The series produced five one-run games,
a tie played in the darkness of the Polo Grounds, and a decisive eighth
game that took ten innings and an immortal error by Giants centerfielder Fred Snodgrass to give the Red Sox their second world championship in as many tries.

The reporting of the series dominated the sixteen dailies of both
cities and the national press as well. Included in the coverage was a
genre of World Series writing that continues to serve as a staple of
sports pages to this day, namely the ghost-written articles allegedly
penned by players. In all likelihood the articles by Mathewson, Speaker,
and Wagner describing the eighth and final game were virtual tran-
scripts of interviews, polished by writers to read like the efforts of the
players themselves, though the college-educated Mathewson and
Speaker may well have written at least part of their columns.

BY CHRISTY MATHEWSON

FANS ARE PROBABLY WONDERING how I feel about that
defeat.

Let it be distinctly understood that I do not blame any one.
Least of all do I blame Snodgrass, who muffed Engle's fly in the
10th. We are all liable to make errors.

There are several things about the game and the series that I
want the public to know. In the first place, it was one of the

cleanest, yet hardest played, series that I have ever been in. I don't remember hearing a cuss word used during any of the games, and yet there was lots of fight shown by the two teams. Opposing players frequently said to each other, "O, we'll get you yet." But there was no dirty work and no bad language. It spoke well for baseball and for the players.

PROBABLY HIS FAREWELL

Then there is another thing I would like to say, if the ego can be pardoned. Few pitchers in their big league careers are picked to pitch such a game as that one yesterday, and I appreciate the confidence McGraw had in me in sending me into that game. If the Giants get into the World Series next year, and, if by any chance the battle should run to the seventh game, I shall probably not be selected to pitch. I am getting old.

I am glad that I had this honor while I was in baseball. McGraw walked out and met me as I came to the bench after the 10th inning, and he shook hands with me. "Matty," he said, "I am glad that I sent you in. If I had the same thing to do over again, it would be you."

That made me feel good, and it evened up some for the disappointment in losing the game. Fans know and I know that after a man has been pitching in the big league for 13 years, as I have, he probably will never have the chance again that I had today. It was a great honor.

NO BLAME FOR SNODGRASS

Doubtless many persons wonder whether I blame Snodgrass. His name is on every one's lips, and adherents of the Giants censured him severely. The newspaper men will probably criticise him, but the members of the team do not. I have seen Hans Wagner make the same kind of an error on an easy pop fly to the infield, and he has been called the greatest player of all time. I can forgive the error that Snodgrass made easier than I can one where players do not get together on the ball, as he and Fletcher failed to do in the seventh inning when Boston made its first run, or in the 10th, when Merkle and Meyers balled up Speaker's foul fly. That was the play which really broke our backs.

Then again, I was guilty of a mistake in the 10th inning myself, which proved costly. I passed Yerkes, trying to get him to bat at bad balls, and in that way put the winning run on the bases. It was not because I lacked control.

GOOD WORD FOR BEDIENT

The Boston players deserve great credit for their work in the games. I want to compliment particularly young Hugh Bedient, who started yesterday's game against us and who pitched wonderful ball, with everything depending upon him. We tried in every way to get to him, but we could not hit the ball hard. Once, when it looked as if we had him going, a sensational catch by Hooper saved him.

In the seventh inning a young fellow stepped into the limelight who should be highly recommended. Stahl sent Henriksen to the bat, cold from the bench, without a chance to warm up. He is only a kid, and he came up with men on first and second bases and two out.

HENRIKSEN LOOKED EASY

The first ball I pitched to Henriksen, O'Loughlin called a strike, and it looked like a bad strike to me. It was the only one that looked bad in the series that an umpire has given me. The next ball was a bad ball and Henriksen struck at it and missed it. That put him in the hole right away and I thought that I had him sure.

Then he refused to strike at a bad ball and let two pass him when I was trying to get him to bite at bad ones. I figured on giving him a curve over the outside corner of the plate, so that if he, being a left-hand batter, hit it anywhere the ball would go to left field, and Murray could probably throw the runner from second out at the plate.

Then Henriksen hit the ball and hit it the only place where he could hit that kind of a ball and score the run. He smashed it over third base, the ball bounding off the bag. He deserves great credit for his coolness and nerve.

GAME LOST IN TWO MIXUPS

The game was lost by the Giants on two plays. I am not counting the error that Snodgrass made. In the seventh inning, with one out, Stahl raised an easy fly back of second base. On account of the shouting of the crowd the players could not hear one another yell, and Fletcher thought that Snodgrass was playing the ball all the way and Snodgrass thought Fletcher had it. The ball dropped safe.

The players did not get together on the ball. That missed fly resulted in the first run of the Red Sox for Stahl scored on Henriksen's hit.

After Snodgrass had dropped the fly in the 10th inning, putting Engle on second base, he caught Hooper's hard hit. Then I walked Yerkes, trying to get him to strike at a bad ball. Speaker then pushed up a little foul that Merkle could have caught, but Meyers went after it, too, and they both lost it. That play broke our backs. Speaker made a hit and scored Engle. With one out, the game and series were over then.

BY HEINIE WAGNER

CAPTAIN OF THE RED SOX

Well, it's all over now and there are no more excuses to make—no more things to explain. We have won a world's championship and everybody is happy. And every man on the team deserves all the credit you can hand him for keeping his head and helping to win.

I want, however, to give especial credit to Olaf Henriksen. You cannot say too much for the part he took in the contest—for the way he put us in the game. If it hadn't been for his timely clout we might have been feeling like McGraw and Matty are feeling now. And there's an awful difference in being a winner instead of a loser.

Henriksen had about the toughest proposition put up to him that ever was presented to a player in a world's championship game. Any pinch hitter who goes into the game without any previous preparation and against such a wonderful twirler as Mathewson has everything against him.

On Henriksen the fate of the Red Sox depended and on that two-base hit a world's championship hung. If it hadn't been for that fine hit the chances are we might not have scored off Matty at all. For the regulars in the line-up weren't doing much with him when a hit would have meant something, and Henriksen's gameness is all the more wonderful in consequence.

SHOOK THE GIANTS' NERVE

That two-base hit, sending in the tieing run, shook the nerve of the Giants and put us in the game. After we tied the score we never had any doubt of winning. And you can see that the run scored in the 10th by New York failed to take our nerve away.

You've got to hand it to Bedient, too. It was too bad that we were forced to take him out after pitching so splendidly. But that was the only way we could have done. It was the only thing to do. His performance in this series has been wonderful. Only for that base on balls he gave Devore New York wouldn't have tallied off him.

Then there's Harry Hooper. He didn't win the game, but he

certainly saved it. I have never seen a more wonderful catch than the one he pulled off Doyle in the fifth. He ran far back, whirled into the face of the sun and grabbed that tremendous drive at full speed and while still off his balance. If the ball had ever got by him it would have gone for a home run. You can't say too much in Hooper's praise. His work has been sensational in the extreme ever since the series opened, and even the fans cannot appreciate the work that he has done for us.

AND SPEAKER CAME THROUGH

Speaker came through as we have been wishing and hoping for all along. It is singular that he should have been the one to turn the tide of battle in the 10th. He got his chance to distinguish himself at the eleventh hour, and he made good, as we knew he could. That hit of his settled the game without anything else, for while Gardner's drive let Yerkes come home with the winning run, it was Speaker's drive that robbed Mathewson of his last bit of confidence.

Yerkes played splendidly and he has been one of the strongest points in our defence. So have Cady and Gardner, and although Larry acted a bit nervous at the start of the game, he certainly rounded to with a rush right afterwards. The whole Red Sox team and old reliable Clyde Engle, who had his wits about him in that 10th, were full of fight and fire.

PAY TRIBUTE TO MATHEWSON

I want to pay a deserved tribute to Mathewson. It was rather tough for him to lose out after showing such wonderful form. His support defeated him yesterday and I can sympathize with him, for if ever a man deserved a better fate it is the same old "Big Six." He lost, but defeat cannot be laid at his door in any way.

Snodgrass and Merkle, perhaps Meyers, must bear the burden

of blame. Snodgrass looked pretty bad out there in centre field. I think that Snodgrass must have lost his nerve completely. That's the only way I can account for his awful muff of Engle's fly ball.

That foul fly that dropped between Meyers and Merkle cost Matty dear. If Meyers had kept away and allowed Merkle to take it neither of them would be under the necessity for furnishing the alibis that are sure to follow this defeat. It was an easy fly to get and it was Merkle's ball. The chief should have stayed away. But he crossed Merkle, nobody yelled and the ball was allowed to drop between them. Then came Speaker's hit and disaster.

NO TRUTH IN TROUBLE RUMOR

I want to deny with emphasis that rumor that has been travelling about town concerning an alleged inside fight on the Boston club. Any such story as that is a malicious lie. The report claims that Wood and O'Brien are at swords' points and that they had a personal mixup after Buck lost the game last Monday. This is a downright lie and the men never even exchanged words after Buck lost.

I think that this story must have originated from the trouble that occurred in the New York team. It's a well known fact that several members of the club are at swords' points.

I'm glad to say that we won the world's championship and I want to thank the Royal Rooters for the game way in which they stuck to us through victory and defeat.

BY TRIS SPEAKER

The Red Sox won the deciding game in a remarkable series. Of course every member of the team is glad that we did so, and it would have been a great disappointment and a big surprise if we had not.

There is not a man on the team, however, who will not say that Christy Mathewson pitched a great game, and a hard one to have decided against him. His performance was up to the grand reputation he enjoys and deserves.

The breaks were against him, just as they have been against some of our own men in this series and so the great pitcher has to stand for the loss of the game. Everybody sympathizes with him on this account, as it was his supreme effort, and a grand one.

MCGRAW A HARD, CLEAN FIGHTER

After the game was over Manager McGraw came to the dressing room and congratulated Manager Stahl of the Boston team on the great fight it had made. I want to say right here that McGraw is to be congratulated on the wonderful fight that he put up. He has shown himself to be a great baseball manager and a general of the first rank. He kept his team playing ball from the beginning of the series to the very end.

At some stages the fight appeared to be going hopelessly against him, but he never let up, or seemed to lose heart. His example must have inspired the players working under his direction and made them fight all the harder.

All through the series under the varying conditions McGraw's conduct was irreproachable. It never aroused antagonism and as a result there was no friction or ill feeling between the players on the opposing team. I cannot fully express my appreciation of McGraw as a baseball manager and as a man.

PRAISE FOR BEDIENT AND HENRIKSEN

The last game in the series was the most fiercely contested of the eight, not excepting the one which resulted in a tie.

Bedient deserves great praise for his magnificent work.

Undoubtedly he would have gone through the game and continued his good work, but a situation arose in the seventh inning which tactically gave Manager Stahl an opportunity to make use of a pinch hitter, as one run was needed to tie. Henriksen was thrown into the breach, and after being put in the hole for two strikes delivered the single which brought home the run that tied. This young player showed wonderful nerve in the emergency, and it was he who put the Boston club in a position to make the fight it did and gave it an opportunity to win the game, which went into extra innings.

WOOD'S STOP ON MEYERS SAVES GAME

Joe Wood went in to do the pitching after Bedient had withdrawn from the game. Too much credit cannot be given him for his wonderful work, especially as it was done on nerve alone. He had a lame arm, which bothered him greatly and made his work almost agonizing.

The spectators who watched him little knew what a handicap he was working under, and probably supposed that he was as fit as he ever had been during the season.

The hot liner from Meyers' bat, which he stopped with his bare hand in the 10th inning, saved the game. The Giants were one run in the lead at the time, and if Meyers' hit had got away from Wood it would have meant another run and the game.

HOOPER'S CATCH WITHOUT AN EQUAL

Previous to this another great play was made, the greatest, I believe, that I ever saw, and that was the catch by Harry Hooper off Doyle's hit in the fifth. Other players on the Boston and New York teams told me that they had never seen its equal. Had Hooper failed to make the catch the hit would have resulted in a home run and probably would have won the game.

Larry Gardner's great wallop which brought in the winning run certainly looked good to me.

I sympathize with Snodgrass, whose error in the 10th gave Boston its chance. Nine hundred and ninety-nine times out of a thousand Snodgrass would make the catch, but he failed this time on the easy chance and his error certainly proved costly for his team.

"REMEMBER, SNODGRASS SAVED ONE GAME!"

It ought to be remembered, however, that in a previous game he made an almost impossible catch and saved his team from defeat thereby. That great play is probably forgotten in view of his slipup in this last game.

Doyle and Fletcher pulled off a phenomenal play in the second inning, when they forced Gardner on Stahl's hit, and Meyers, Mathewson and Herzog did clever work when they caught Yerkes off third in the sixth inning on a bluff throw to second when Lewis went down. Every movement had to be perfect, with not a false motion made by any of the three men to make the out, and they made it.

Herzog's batting and fielding were one of the striking features of these games.

I believe this series just ended to have been the most remarkable played since the post-season contests began.

1919

From *Eight Men Out*

ELIOT ASINOF

Of all the big league cities one
Is easy to get lost in.
I hardly need to tell you that
The one I mean is Boston.

RING LARDNER

EXACTLY THREE WEEKS before the World Series was to begin, a tall, beefy, red-faced man in a white suit and bright bow tie stepped out of a taxi and walked into Boston's Hotel Buckminster. His name was Joseph "Sport" Sullivan. His occupation: book-maker and gambler.

He moved through the musty lobby to the front desk, picked up the house phone, and asked to be connected with Mr. Arnold "Chick" Gandil. As he waited, he surveyed the subdued, conser-vative, old-lady atmosphere. Although he had lived in Boston all the forty-four years of his life, he could not remember when he had been here last. In his profession, he seldom did business with subdued, conservative old ladies. There was something ludicrous about the Chicago White Sox Baseball Club staying here instead of at the Somerset or the Buckingham, more commercially cen-tered and alive. Sullivan knew the reason for the change. He made it his business to know everything about the club.

During an earlier visit to Boston, there had been some trouble. These White Sox boys were an especially volatile, spirited bunch, a club loaded with bitterness and tension. There had been an excessive amount of drinking one night, and before the party was over, they had made wrecks of the furniture. Chairs, lamps, tables, even beds had been dumped out of the windows into the court-yard below. The hotel management thereupon had advised the Chicago organization that its patronage was no longer solicited. Harry Grabiner, Secretary of the Club, decided that a more subdued atmosphere might influence the boys. The Hotel Buckminster was the result. . . .

Sullivan's ear was suddenly jarred by Gandil's loud greeting. Having identified himself to the ballplayer, Sullivan was immedi-ately asked to come up. He had sensed that something special was in the air when they had spoken earlier in the day. Now the ten-sion in Gandil's voice confirmed his hunch. Sullivan liked to rely on his ear. It was said of him that he could tell what a man was about to say by the first few seconds of his speech. That Gandil had called him was in itself certainly not surprising. He had known the first baseman for eight or nine years and, as a result, knew all about him:

Chick Gandil was as tough as they come. He was thirty-one years old. He stood six feet, two inches tall; a broad, powerful 197 pounds. This was his fourteenth year in baseball. He had started at the age of seventeen after running away from home in St. Paul, Minnesota. He had hopped a freight bound for Amarillo, Texas, where he'd heard he could get a job playing semipro ball. Later, he caught on with an outlaw team in Cananea, Mexico, just across the Arizona border. Cananea was a wide-open mining town, con-genial to his wild, rough temperament. Gandil not only played ball; he became a heavy-weight fighter, taking in $150 a fight, far more money than he had ever seen before. In the off season, he worked as a boilermaker in the local copper mines. Back in Texas, at nineteen, he met the girl who became his wife. If the marriage had gratified him, it was because he was permitted to remain a roughhouse character.

He played minor-league ball until 1910 when he was picked up by the Chicago White Sox. He was sold to the Washington Senators, then to Cleveland in 1916, then back to Chicago. He was a reliable .280 hitter and an exceptionally strong first baseman, whose extraordinary hands were his greatest asset. It was said that he was the only first baseman around who didn't need a glove.

It was while Gandil was with Washington that Sullivan met him at a Boston pool hall. In typically gracious manner, he made friends with the big ballplayer immediately, buying him drinks, handing him good cigars. And also, before long, he found a way to profit by the friendship. Gandil would give him tips on ball games. "How is the great Walter Johnson feeling today? . . . Is there any reason why he might not be effective this afternoon?" This sort of innocent-sounding information gradually led to a more advanced procedure. When the Washington Senators were not in Boston, a timely long-distance phone call might elicit a piece of news that would alter the balance of the odds . . . like an unexpected change in pitching plans. If Sullivan alone had such a tip, he could use it to great advantage. His office would immediately get busy on the several long-distance hook-ups to various gambling centers and place bets accordingly. His resulting success baffled others, gaining him a reputation as something of an expert on baseball. A number of prominent sporting people began to commission him to bet for them, granting him a profit of 20 per cent on the winnings.

While there was nothing actually illegal about such manipulations, their effectiveness was limited. This was the problem that Sullivan, like all gamblers, had to contend with. Baseball was a complicated game. It was extremely difficult to dope out the probabilities on any one afternoon. There were simply too many variables. While this might well present a challenge to the shrewder among them, its unpredictability often left them frustrated. Constantly seeking to minimize the margin of doubt, they kept their ears open and waited for an opportunity. Sullivan, however, did more than wait. Having found Gandil, he went to work on him. He quickly saw that the big, tough, unschooled rube, literally from the Wild West, glowed in the company of successful men in big cities. Gandil liked the slick, prominent urban types. To be welcomed among them was, he felt, a mark of his own rising status in the world. Sullivan the Bookmaker could boast of an intimate acquaintance with V.I.P.'s like millionaire Harry Sinclair and George M. Cohan, and he made sure that Gandil met them. Gandil was thrilled. They were all pleasant, friendly guys.

Today Gandil was in his hotel room alone. Sullivan greeted him with his usual friendliness. In less than three minutes of small talk the dour ballplayer got down to business, remarking to the gambler that he had a proposition for him.

Sullivan kept his normally big mouth shut. When Gandil started to talk about the coming World Series, Sullivan sensed what was in the air.

Gandil was saying, "I think we can put it in the bag!"

His proposition was simple enough. He would guarantee to involve a sufficient number of ballplayers to insure the defeat of the highly favored White Sox. He wanted $80,000 cash as payment for their implication. He had come to Sullivan because he knew no one else who could raise that kind of money.

Sullivan listening, maintaining a cool façade. He acknowledged that such a scheme had possibilities, and told Gandil he would think it over. But when he left that hotel room, he knew only one thing: the biggest gambling bonanza in the history of baseball was being dropped magnificently into his lap like manna from heaven. Here was the big pay-off for all his efforts, the return for all those beers, the pool games, the fifty-cent cigars. He was the persistent salesman who'd finally made a big sale, bigger by far than he'd ever dreamed.

The fact that this was a shatteringly dishonest venture did not escape him. Curiously enough, he found the immorality of the scheme momentarily more troublesome than any fear of its consequences. It barely occurred to him that he was in any way vulnerable to the law, even assuming that something should happen to expose the fix. He could take this position not out of ignorance, but out of precedent. He knew of no case in which a gambler had gotten into serious difficulty for this kind of manipulation. Sullivan had always laughed at the workings of law and politics, for he had all the connections he needed to stay out of trouble.

Yet he had to admit that fixing a World Series was something else again. It was a very special American event. To tamper with it seemed treacherous, almost like sacrilege. On the other hand, this very circumstance could also make the deal fantastically rewarding—which, of course, was the determining factor.

But Sullivan was worried. For all his blustering, he never really considered himself either powerful or adept enough to assume control over a project as mighty as this one. It was not the kind of thing he would initiate. However, it had been brought to him; the problem was to whom he, himself, could take it.

In the last analysis, Sullivan would make peace with the fix readily enough. He would go with it wherever it led him and play it strictly by ear. He would keep the escape channels open in case he found himself in over his head.

There was always the chance that he could pull it off.

Claude "Lefty" Williams walked out to the mound to a sustained ovation. It was a statement of their respect for him as much as a rousing plea for another victory. With his usual solemn mien, he did not seem to hear. He neither tipped his cap nor stopped to respond. With typical deliberateness, he toed the rubber and took his warm-up pitches as if every one of them had to be perfect.

The last practice pitch he threw was a curve ball. He snapped it off like the whole World Series was riding on it. It broke sharply, down and away, thrown so viciously that Schalk had trouble hanging on to it. It cut the outside corner just a bit over the knees of the unseen hitter. It was a beautiful, perfect pitch.

It was the last perfect pitch Lefty Williams threw that day.

Behind him, Weaver, Risberg, Collins, and Gandil were tossing the ball around the horn, a final circuit of throws before the game began. Williams turned to watch them. Behind them, Jackson, Nemo Liebold, and Felsch were fanning out over the vast outfield grass. And all around him, the fans of Chicago. This had been his home for four exciting years. He had pitched for this ball club in 144 games. He was twenty-six years old and he thought of himself as a decent man, very good at his job, well liked by those who knew him and worked with him. But Lefty Williams was in trouble. In all his life, he never dreamed that anything like this could happen to him. It seemed so fantastic that even the fact that it was all very logical meant little to him. It would, however, be indelibly recorded in his brain for all time:

Around 7:30 last evening, Williams and his wife were returning from dinner. He had eaten carefully, knowing he was going to pitch the next day. He had seen him then—a man in a bowler hat, standing at the entrance to his building, smoking a cigar. The man recognized him and immediately got ready to greet him. The man was stiff but polite. He wanted to have a word with him, in private, and a nod indicated to Lefty's wife that she should excuse herself.

The man went right to the point. He bluntly told Williams he was to lose the next game. Lefty had shaken his head violently and started to turn away. But the man stopped him, restraining him with a vice-like grip on his arm. No, it wasn't a question of money any more. Williams was not going to get paid another dime! He was going to lose that game or something was going to happen to him. Maybe something might happen to his wife, too.

Williams had choked up at the thought of it. His fists had clenched with a sudden desire to tear into the man. But fear had stopped him. He merely stood there, unable to speak or act.

There was more to the threat. It all had to be done in the first inning. The man eyed him, seeking confirmation of this in Williams's eyes. That's right, the man repeated: Williams was not to last even one inning!

"Play ball!" The umpire was yelling it a third time, louder this time, and more demandingly.

Williams stalled a moment more, toeing the dirt in front of the mound. He had, of course, said nothing to his wife, who, as usual, was sitting in a box behind third base. Schalk was barking at him and he turned to go to work.

Maurice Rath stepped up to the plate to lead off for the Reds. The crowd roared approval as Williams threw the first pitch over for a strike. They roared again as Rath cut at the second and fouled it off. Then he popped feebly to Risberg at short and the first man was out. It took less than a minute.

Jake Daubert moved in and took the first pitch for strike one. On the second, he hit a soft liner to short center field. Nemo Liebold raced in for it, desperately trying for a catch off his shoe-tops. He never made it and it fell for a base hit. (Gleason had shifted Felsch to right after his feeble playing in previous games.) Williams got two strikes over on Heinie Groh, then Groh singled sharply to right. The crowd roared a steady stream of encouragement to Williams. The game was less than three minutes old, but the tension made every pitch a crisis. Schalk walked out to the mound and talked with Williams. In the press box, Christy Mathewson commented to Fullerton that Williams had been throwing only fast balls. He guessed that Schalk was trying to straighten him out. As Schalk walked back to his position, he stared fiercely at the bench, seeking out Gleason. Gleason nodded, signaled the bull pen for Bill James and Roy Wilkinson to get warm.

Big Edd Roush stood in the batter's box, calmly waiting to hit. The infield lay deep, hoping for the ground ball they could convert into a double play. Roush measured the first pitch—another fast ball—and smashed it savagely to right. Daubert scored easily from second, Groh settled on third, and Roush pulled into second standing up. Lefty Williams seemed in a hurry to pitch. Schalk was bellowing at him, shaking his fist. Williams stood tight-lipped on the mound. Behind him, the infield was drawn in, ready to hold Groh on third. Pat Duncan stepped in to hit, laid into the first pitch and sent a screaming liner into the left field seats, foul. Williams seemed flustered. He reared back and threw again. It went high and wide of the plate. Schalk had to leap for it, preventing a wild pitch with a desperate effort. He called for time-out, hollered at Williams again. Williams nodded, demanded the ball. Then Duncan lashed a single to left, right through the drawn-in infielders. Groh and Duncan scored easily. It was already 3–0.

Gleason moved up the dugout steps, scowling murderously. He stared at his bull pen where James was throwing hurriedly, trying to get warmed up. He shouted at Williams. Williams seemed to ignore him, and got set to pitch to Larry Kopf. He threw hard, and Kopf took it for strike one. It the press box, Matty shook his head. Another fast ball. Nothing but fast balls. No wonder Gleason was sore. Gleason was roaring at Williams again as he moved out of the dugout this time. He called to his bull pen for Bill James. That was going to be all for Williams. Fifteen pitches. Four hits. Three runs. Only one out.

Fullerton sat in a nervous sweat, remembering the last words of the Chicago gambler: "It'll be the biggest first inning you ever saw!"

The crowd was stunned. They watched Williams leave the field unable to believe what they saw. They despaired as Bill James gave up another run before the inning ended. In the second, the Reds scored again, making it 5–0.

But to Chicago baseball fans, baseball was a nine-inning game, and this was still their ball club battling to stay alive. They would battle along with them. When, in the third, Joe Jackson sent a tremendous blast into the right field stands for the first home run of the Series, they stood up and cheered him as if it was the crucial run of the game. And though the Reds proceeded to hammer James, then Wilkinson, for 5 more runs, these 33,000 stalwarts never lost heart. They stuck with them, inning after inning, roaring with every Chicago base hit like it was the opening gun for that one big rally that would win even this one for them. Then, in the eighth, with the score 10–1 against them, they rose to one final, magnificent splash of power.

Liebold opened with a fly to Neale in right. One out. Eddie Collins singled to center on the first pitch. Buck Weaver followed with a double over first base. Jackson stepped in, waving his big black bat, and crashed a roaring double to right center, scoring Collins and Weaver. The crowd was on its feet, yelling for more. This was the real White Sox club!

In Times Square, New York, there were 5,000 people watching the game on the simulated diamond. Most of them were losing interest, but suddenly they, too, came alive, sensing the possibility of a last ditch Chicago rampage. Others paused to watch. Suddenly, the word was out, passing through the area like a gust of wind. As the little dummy figure labeled FELSCH stepped to the plate, the 5,000 watchers had almost doubled!

At Comiskey Park, Felsch took a terrific cut at the first pitch, but popped it up to Daubert. Gandil followed with a long fly to right, but Neale lost it in the sun and it fell for a triple, scoring Jackson. Risberg followed with a short fly to center, just eluding Roush's glove. Gandil scored the fourth run of the inning. The crowd roared at Schalk to keep it going. But Schalk grounded to Rath, ending the inning.

It was over. All over. They were beaten. Twenty-four White Sox players and 33,000 White Sox fans.

In the locker room, Gleason was shouting at the reporters: "I tell you those Reds haven't any business beating us! We played worse baseball in all but a couple of games than we played all year. I don't know yet what was the matter. Something was wrong. I didn't like the betting odds. I wish no one had ever bet a dollar on the team!"

"Don't bring up Buck Weaver
Or how he looked that last time you saw
him
Begging a reporter six months out of
high school
To clear his name so he could play again.
'I'll play for nothing, tell 'em. Just
one season, tell 'em!'"

NELSON ALGREN

Early in December, five months after his acquittal, Buck Weaver walked into the offices of Commissioner Landis. "Sit down, sit down!" The Judge was warm and friendly. He offered Weaver a chew of his special cut tobacco. Weaver smiled: at least they had that in common. It relieved his nervousness and relaxed him. This was going to be a crucial hour for him.

To Buck Weaver, there was only one reality: he had played eight games in the 1919 World Series to the best of his great ability. He had not taken one dime of dirty money. He had stood trial and was acquitted of any crime. He was thirty-one years old and reputed to be the best third baseman in the game.

He was, above all, ready to play ball.

He proceeded to tell Landis how he'd been approached by Gandil back in 1919, how he was offered $10,000 to get in the fix. He'd just opened a drugstore with his brother and he needed cash, but he couldn't go through with a thing like that. Landis listened, told him that since he had knowledge of the fix, he should have done something to stop it. Weaver cringed. Talk? He couldn't have talked. It was not in him to talk. He'd thought about doing it, to protect himself, but those men were his friends. Besides, he explained, he never really knew which of them got any money from it. He never really knew if they actually went through with it. Nobody ever said anything. He hadn't known enough to talk, even if he'd wanted to!

Landis nodded with apparent sympathy, but would not give him an answer. He would review the case and write Weaver a letter with his decision.

There was no letter. Just a blunt statement to the press:

"Birds of a feather flock together. Men associating with gamblers and crooks could expect no leniency."

This was Landis's reply. Weaver choked on it and bided his time.

Like Jackson, Weaver had signed a three-year contract in 1920, calling for $7,500 a year. Having received no money in 1921, he sued for the balance of his contract. The case dragged on for four years, until in Federal Court, it was dismissed when it came to trial: Weaver's lawyers had failed to appear. To add substance to the defeat, he was ordered to pay court costs. Nevertheless, he continued to pursue the matter relentlessly. And finally, in 1924, he forced Comiskey into a settlement out of court. To Buck, it was more than a few thousand dollars he so sorely needed: it was a statement of Comiskey's admission of guilt.

Again, Weaver appealed for reinstatement. Landis's reply this time was another frustrating distortion of reality: " . . . On the trial of this case, Burns gave a detailed account of his meeting with the indicted men and arranging with them for the throwing of the World Series games. Weaver was present in the Court during the testimony of this witness who most specifically stated that Weaver was present at the conference, and yet the case went to the jury without any denial from Weaver from the witness stand. . . . If the incriminating evidence was false, the public had a right to Weaver's denial under oath."

The Commissioner made argument impossible. How could Weaver have denied anything if he was denied the right to take the stand? How could he have testified if the best defense for the group was a united silence? Did he not ask for a separate trial? Was it not denied him? Was he not told by Judge Friend himself that on the basis of the evidence presented there was no chance for his conviction? Must he be punished for all that, too?

Weaver spent the years running his drugstore. He could be found there jerking sodas or passing out cosmetics over the counter. He also spent a lot of time at the race track, playing the horses. By 1927, he realized that his desire to play ball could no longer be repressed. He announced he would play semipro ball with a local club. More than three hundred local owners, managers, and players voted unanimously to let him play. It was the first opportunity for Southside fans to see him in action after seven years. They turned out in the numbers. It was a moment of joy for Weaver—but it was not enough, nor was it the real thing. He lived constantly with a sense of his guilty status in the eyes of others, the stigma of banishment that marked him lousy. He avoided social events where prominent sporting people gathered because he did not wish to be the subject of either their sympathy or their contempt. He would pass his time with a group of friends playing pinochle in the back room of a saloon. He never drank or caroused. His wife was devoted to him and he to her. They had no children of their own, but raised two children of relatives.

As time passed, Weaver grew too old to play. Ray Schalk, another Southsider whom he saw around town over the years, became manager of the Sox. Red Faber, also of Weaver's neighborhood, ran a tavern and bowling alley outside of Chicago. Faber was the last of the 1919 aggregation, and retired in 1933. Weaver worked at the pari-mutuel windows of the race track. Later, he organized and managed a girl's softball team. But he wanted to get back into organized ball. He could coach rookies, as Gleason had done. He could coach at some college, as Schalk would do at Purdue University. If only Landis would reinstate him, he would again feel like an honorable man.

He appealed repeatedly, maybe a half-dozen times, always with the same result. When Landis was replaced by Happy Chandler in 1946, Weaver appealed to Chandler. He went to visit Judge Hugo Friend, who was convinced of his innocence. The Judge was sympathetic and wrote the Commissioner of his knowledge and opinion, reviewing the 1921 trial, recommending a special leniency in Weaver's case. But Chandler and his successor, Ford Frick, turned it down.

Thirty-five years passed and they were all the same. When James T. Farrell met Weaver he found, " . . . a thin, pale, gray man in his sixties. He dressed on the sporty side, and there were many small red blotches on his face. He smiled easily and readily." The single, dominating thought on his mind was still to clear his name. More than anything else, he wanted that. He wanted to bring that to his now-ailing wife whom he took care of, and to his cronies with whom he played pinochle. . . .

Then, one cold, grim morning in January, 1956, Buck was walking down 71st Street on Chicago's Southside, on his way to an income-tax consultant. Suddenly, he writhed in pain and began to fall. He clutched at a picket fence to hold himself up. A man named John Spengler, a heating contractor, was driving by and saw him. He stopped to help, but before he could get to him, Weaver toppled over. Spengler called a policeman while passersby gathered around. But it was too late. At the hospital, it was simply reported that Weaver had died, at sixty-six, of natural causes.

At the funeral, a man shook his head sadly and said, "I was just a kid in 1922, sitting in the stands at the White City Park where the Black Sox were playing a gang called the Southside All-Stars. Weaver sat down next to me. Risberg and Felsch came up and asked Buck to play. He waved them away. 'Nothing doing. I'll be back in the majors soon, and you guys will still be semipros.'"

He never made it.

1919

I'm Forever Blowing Ball Games*

RING LARDNER

I'm forever blowing ball games
Pretty ball games in the air.
I come from Chi.
I hardly try,
Just go to bat and fade and die.
Fortune's coming my way,
That's why I don't care,
I'm forever blowing ball games,
And the gamblers treat us fair.

* SUNG TO THE TUNE OF "I'M FOREVER BLOWING BUBBLES"

1919

Dispatches from the
World Serious

RING LARDNER

The incomparable Ring Lardner put his unique stamp on the 1919 World Series. Although his parody of "I'm Forever Blowing Bubbles" reveals his suspicions about the fix, in his reporting he disguised his thoughts a little more. Following are select reports.

GENTS: LARDNER SAYS THE UMPIRES

INTERFERE WITH HIS "DOPE" ON BIG SERIES

YOU NEVER CAN TELL WHAT THEY ARE GOING TO DO DECLARES EXPERT WHO COMPARES PLAYERS OF BOTH TEAMS AND A FEW WHO ARE NOT

Cincinnati, Sept. 28—Gents: In doping out a conflict like the threatened world serious, an expert like myself works under a heavy strain as they's no way of telling what those d—m umpires is going to do and in the case of a couple of even matched ball clubs like the White Sox and Reds neither 1 of which has ever lose a world serious why some finicky notion of some umpire is libel to raise havioc.

An expert's 1st duty then is to make a study of the umpires that has been chose to rule or ruin the comeing serious and comparison between the 4 of them in this case shows the advantage to be all in their favor. Suppose for inst. Heinie Groh was to hit a high fly and nobody catched it, but the umpires got it in their head to play a practical joke on the big Dane and call him out why they wouldn't be no recourses for Heinie only to walk off the field and join the New York Yanks. So as I say a man that is not in the umpires confidents and trys to make predictions may make a monkey of himself instead.

But wile it never settled a world serious 1 way or the other to figure out whether Limbo has it all over Bimbo as a bench warmer or vice versa why still and all it's a habit amidst the experts, and one that don't do it lays himself open to the abuse that is always heaped onto a reformer, so I may as well try and remember who is on the different clubs and set down the facts about them in Black and White and plain water.

REDS PITCHING STAFF SAVORS OF THE BIBLE

STARTING OFF with the catchers, Bill Rarideh was born in Bedford, Ind., and Ray Schalk was born in Litchfield, Ill., so neither one of them is libel to be dazzled by the big crowds. The edge, if any, belongs to Bill; as he has lived more different places than Ray. As for Ivy Wingo and Byrd Lynn, why Byrd has more ys in his 8 letters, but when it comes to slideing home they's very few people afraid of a Byrd wile the White Sox don't know but maybe Ivy is poison. Both clubs will miss Larry McLean.

Coming to the pitchers, I had to buy a paper to see who was the regulars on the Reds and the only name that pitched for them that day was Luque, but I suppose the others is Mathew, Mark and John. Mathew is probably Mathewson's old man and has got some of the family traits, which means he will have about as much luck in a world serious as the crown prince at Verdun. Mark, of course, has got a unfortunate name, but that don't seem to make no differents in a pitcher, as you take Ruth for inst. and you wouldn't never think it was a girl. I looked up John's record and about the only place where he mentions athaletics is where he outrun Peter and you can't judge nothing by that, as Peter may of triped over his beard or something.

IT'S AN EVEN BREAK BETWEEN HOBLITZEL AND ISBELL

NONE OF THE WHITE SOX pitchers has ever wrote a gospel and any way they's only 2 of them to hear some people tell it. The 2 is Wms. and Cicotte, of which Cicotte is 1 of the most baffling pitchers in baseball, as you can't never be sure 2 days in succession how he is going to be pronounced. Wms. was baptized Claude, but has growed up normal outside of being a left hander. Of the others in the list Dick Kerr throws left handed and hits the same way, while Grover Lowdermilk throws right handed and hits seldom.

It looks like a even break between Hoblitzell and Isbell on the initial sack, as I have nicknamed 1st base, and at second base the rivals appears to be peers on paper, though they tell me Morris Rath is going to get marred this fall, but on the other hand you take a bird like Collins and they's no telling what he will do under fire, as a man like he is liable to blow sky high in a pinch. For inst. in the last game vs. the Giants 2 yrs. ago he lose his head completely and run home backwards from 3d base though Heinie Zimmerman that was chasing him is 1 of the fastest men in the Natl. League and can beat his own throws.

MORAN AND GLEASON WIDELY DIFFERENT TYPES

THE SHORTSTOPS CAN be past over, as they seldom never cut any figure in a event of this kind, and that brings us to Weaver and Groh at 3d. base both of which is the greatest 3d. baseman in the game today. Comparisons is obvious but they tell me Heinie is libel to quit as for inst. when he was first born his old man said Heinie Groh and Heinie started but soon give it up.

The least said about the 2 outfields the better as they are about equally bad and the only chance for argument is who has got the cutest nickname Shoeless Joe Jackson or Greasy Neale.

The rival mgrs. is widely different types as Moran gets his results by rough houseing wile Gleason is the soft spoken effeminate kind that a person would think to hear him talk that he was secretary of war or something. In the off season Moran is a Deutscher Artz at Fitchburg, Mass., wile the big Greek runs a handkerchief store in Philly. Neither 1 of them is hardily out of their teens you might say.

As far as the utility men is conserned it looks to me like it was a exageration to call them that.

DAUBERT FOOLS LARDNER

REFUSES TO STAY DOWN; SOX LACK "STRATEGEM"

Cincinnati (O.), Oct. 1.—Gents: Up to the eighth innings this pm we was all setting there wondering what to write about and I happened to be looking at Jake Daubert's picture on the souvenir program and all of a sudden Jake fell over and I thought he was dead so I said to the boys:

"Here is your story. Jacob E. Daubert was born in Shamokin, Pa., on the 17 of April, 1886, and he lives in Schuykill Pa. and began playing with the Kane, Pa., Club in 1907. With Cleveland in 1908 and Toledo for two years. Joined the Brooklyn Club in 1910 and remained there until this season. Then joined the Cincinnati Reds and fell dead in the 8th inning of the 1st game of the World Serious."

So everybody got up and cheered me and said that was a very

funny story but all of a sudden again Jake stood up and looked at the different pts of the compass and walked to 1st base and wasn't dead at all and everybody turned around and hissed me for not giving them a good story.

Well Gents I am not to blame because when a man has got a fast ball like Grover Lowdermilk and hits a man like Jake in the temple, I generally always figure they are dead and the fact that Jake got up and walked to 1st base is certainly not my fault and I hope nobody will hold it vs me. ·

That was only 1 case where Mr. Gleason's strategy went amuck. His idear there was to kill the regular 1st baseman and then all Mr. Moran would have left to do would be to either stick Dutch Reuther on 1st base where he couldn't pitch or else stick Sherwood Magee over there where he couldn't coach at third base. But Jake gummed it all up by not dying.

Well another part of Mr. Gleason's strategy was dressing the White Sox in their home uniforms so as they would think they was playing on the home grounds in front of a friendly crowd but the trouble with that was that the Reds was all dressed in their home uniforms so as you couldn't tell which club was at home and which wasn't and it made both of them nervous. Then to cap off the climax Mr. Gleason goes and starts a pitcher that everybody thought he was going to start which took away the element of surprise and made a joker out of the ball game.

If he had of only started Erskine Mayer or Bill James or any of the other boys that I recommended why the Reds breath would have been took away and even if they had of hit they couldn't of ran out their hits.

The trouble with the White Sox today was that they was in there trying to back up a nervous young pitcher that never faced a big crowd in a crux before and when he got scared and blowed why it was natural for the rest of them to also blow up. But just give these young Chicago boys a chance to get use to playing before a big crowd with money depending on it and you will be surprised at how they get on their ft and come back at them.

Nobody should ought to find fault with Mr. Gleason, however, for what happened today. As soon as it was decided that they would have 9 games in this serious why the Kid set down and figured that the rules called for 9 men on a side and if 1 Red was killed per day and the serious run the full 9 games why they would only be 1 man left to play the final game and 1 man cant very well win a ball game even vs the White Sox the way they looked. But Daubert didn't die as expected and they will know better next time then to hit a left handed 1st baseman in the egg.

As for the game itself they has probably never been a thriller game in a big serious. The big thrill come in the 4th innings when everybody was wondering if the Sox would ever get the 3rd man out. They finally did and several occupants of the press box was overcome. The White Sox only chance at that pt was to keep the Reds in there hitting till darkness fell and made it a illegal game but Heinie Groh finely hit a ball that Felsch could not help from catching and gummed up another piece of strategem.

Before the game a band led by John Philip Sousa played a catchy air called the Stars and Stripes Forever and it looks to me like everybody would be whistling it before the serious runs a dozen more games.

It now looks like the present serious would be 1 big surprise after another and tomorrow's shock will occur when the batterys is announced which will be Rube Bressler for the Reds and Lefty Sullivan for the Sox. This will be the biggest up set of the entire fiasco.

I seen both managers right after today's holy cost and Moran said hello old pal, and Gleason said hello you big bum so I am picking the Reds from now on.

"BALLYHOO" FOILS GLEASON

SCORE BOARD BALKS; "HAPPY" FELSCH IS LUCKY

Cincinnati (O.), Oct. 2.—Gents, the biggest scandal of a big year of baseball scandals was perpetrated down here this afternoon when the American League turned against itself and beat the White Sox out of the second game of the present horror.

Whoever is running the serious went and hired Mr. Announcer at the Washington ball park to come and announce for this serious thinking he was a fair minded American Leaguer, and what does he do today but announce Mr. Ivy Wingo as the catcher for the Reds and fool a Mr. Gleason into thinking Mr. Ivy was going to catch and he hits left-handed, so Mr. Kid started a left-hand pitcher instead of going through with his original plan, which was to pitch Mr. Red Faber.

Before the mistake could be rectified Mr. Game started.

If I was running an event as big as this I would try and get a loyal Mr. Announcer who would announce the right Mr. Catcher and not cross up his own league, and as far as that is concerned I could of got down there and told the people the right Mr. Catcher who was going to catch, and maybe nobody could of heard me, but at least they wouldn't of had to go to the expense of getting a Mr. Man from Washington to announce the wrong catcher, as some other goof is paying my expenses down here.

That was the first break of the game, and the second was the trick Mr. Score Board, which could not register strikes. This was fatal.

For instance, in the fourth inning up come Mr. Morris Rath, and Mr. Williams kept pitching to him and pitching to Mr. Rath and had him struck out at least a dozen times, but Mr. Evans would look up at Mr. Score Board and no strikes was registered there, so Mr. Evans finally got sick of looking at the left side of Mr. Morris' profile and said, "You walk, Mr—" so Mr. Morris had no choice only to walk and say thank you. Mr. Umpire, as an umpire is a czar in a event of this kind.

The next bird up, who I have forgot his name, and anyway it don't make no differents, and besides that he got out. But a man named Mr. Groh and a man named Mr. Roush kept their bat on their shoulder and watched the score board, and next thing you know they was both misters on base, and then Mr. Larry Kopf popped one up between Messrs. Felsch and Jackson for three bases and Mr. Me took a long nap, and the next time I looked at Mr. Score Board some club had three runs, which I have nicknamed Mr. Tallies.

From a baseball standpoint, if there is any such thing, the thing that impressed me most was Mr. Felsch, who I have decided that the minute we get back to old Chi we will have his first name changed from Mr. Happy to Mr. Lucky.

The first three or four times Mr. Felsch came up Mr. Felsch sacrificed, and then all of a sudden Mr. Felsch popped up a fly to Mr. Roush while Mr. Weaver was loitering on Mr. Third Base, and Mr. Roush seems to have caught it while facing Kentucky, and if he hadn't of why Mr. Felsch could of scored three times, which would of tied up the game.

Later, in Mr. Eighth Inning, up come Mr. Lucky again with Mr. Jackson on the keystone sack and knocked down Mr. Groh, but when Mr. Groh finally got up Mr. H. Groh had the baseball in his hands and threw it over to this First Mr. Baseman, who I have forgot his name. But speaking of names, it will be Mr. Lucky Felsch hereafter far as Mr. Me is concerned.

In the seventh inning a effigy was threw out of a airship and landed on the middle of Mr. Diamond, and for a minute I hoped it was me, but it turned out different.

I don't know who was playing, but I think it was Columbus and Ohio. Anyway I think Mr. Ohio won. Pay your war tax as you pass out.

LARDNER AIDS CHISOX

KEEPS OFF 'EM; LITTLE "DICK" DOES REST

Chicago (Ill.), Oct. 3—Gents, credit, if any, for beating the Reds today belongs to Dick Kerr and I, Dick on account of his pitching and me for not betting on the White Sox.

The very instant I made up what is left of my mind not to lay a bet on Gleason's birds, I knowed they would win and if I had of went a step further and bet on the Reds the score would of been 6 to nothing instead of half that amount.

In the place of going up in the press coop where I would of had to set next to Bud Fisher or who knows what I set this time in a box right close to the White Sox bench and as soon as the boys come out to warm up I told them I was not wagering, which gave them the added confidents needed to win.

Another advantage of me setting down there is that I could keep my ears open and overhear a lot of witty remarks which certainly would never happened up in the press coop, even setting next to Mr. Fisher.

For instants, when Heinie Groh came out to practice, a bird in the next box hollered, "Hellow, you big egg," which is certainly a vivid description of Heinie, who is pretty near as big as Dick Kerr and looks more like a cucumber than an egg though he may resemble Mr. Egg in one respect, namely, being worth a whole lot of money.

On another occasion somebody hit a foul ball out in left field and Pat Duncan couldn't get to it a bird setting a couple of boxes away yelled "You couldn't catch nothing you big bum." Pat is bigger than Heinie all right but I have met him and never seen any evidents on him that he is a bum and when the man said he couldn't catch nothing he was telling a fib about him, as I seen him catch several baseballs down in Cincy.

Now, you take Charlie Risberg and Jimmie Smith and Heinie himself and if they had been calling each other eggs or bums, why it would have been just a laughing matter instead of them getting all het up and pretty near coming to blows but it must of been something else they was calling each other and I am sorry I wasn't in a position to hear all of their conversation so I could tell you birds what it was all about but the only remark I heard was when Heinie said to Charley "You will be setting on the bench next yr."

Well he shouldn't ought to say a thing like that if he don't know if its true or not and I don't believe that Mgr. Gleason has been confiding his plans for next summer to no Cincinnati ball player, even if Heinie is their captain.

From where I set I could see every decision Billy Evans made and I am pleased to state that he was right on every occasion and I wished I could say the same for the rest of the umpires but I wasn't close enough to watch them with the naked eye but will try and give a report on them later.

It looked at the start of the battle like the Reds was going to try and play a bunting game on Dickie and I guess maybe it was because perhaps they had heard that he was the best fielding pitcher in the American League and wanted to find out if it was true. Towards the finish they quit trying to bunt and some of them even went so far as to swing their bats all the way around and hit line drives to the catcher.

I suppose a great many of the other experts will criticise Ray Fisher for how he pitched, but I will say nothing about him as I expect to move down to Connecticut as soon as this holy cost is over and he teaches school down there in the winter and I might meet him some day when he had his switch on him or he might even stoop so low as to lick my kids if they happened to be wished onto his school.

So I will hafe to heap my verbal abuse on somebody else and I guess it better be Adolfo Luque, as I understand he don't read many words of English. Well then it Luques to me like he should of went to Fisher's relief earlier in the day and the score might of been 1 to 0 or 2 to 1 instead of disgraceful figures like 3 to 0.

The only unsportsmanlike thing I seen occur was in the third innings when Buck Weaver came up with Collins on first base and the Reds expected him to bunt but he hit a single over Kopf's kopf and I don't know what Cincinnati will think of Chicago's hospitality after that.

I know of no more fitting way to close than by giveing a report of the inning Luque pitched in pure Cubanola. El Lieboldo whiffoed. Si si senor Collins was outo Jake Dauberto to Adolfo. Bucko Weavero outo Ratho to Dauberto. No runos. No hittos, no bootos.

RINGS ARE MUCH ALIKE

JIM HAS MORE SPEED; NINE GAMES HIT MORAN

Chicago, Oct. 4.—Gents! There is a strong family resemblance between the Rings. Both of them is tall and handsome and has beautiful curves. Both of them is inclined to be a trifle wild. Jim has a bit more speed. Neither of them has much luck, at least they told me down in Cincy that Jim was the jinx bird of the National League all summer, as the Reds never batted much behind him.

As for me, the boys has been batting around me only a trifle. Jim pitches better than I write and I pitch better than he writes. Jim is a decided blonde wile I am kind of a dapple gray since the serious opened up.

On acct of Jim's complexion he don't look so bad when he don't have a chance to shave. Jim got a lot of praise today wile all I got was insults. For inst I was down in the hotel before the game and a Chicago man and a man from Cincy was trying to bet but they couldn't find no one to put it up with and finely the Chicago man spots me and introduces me to the Red bird and the latter said he wouldn't bet under such conditions.

As for today's game they was a scribe downtown this am that 2 men asked him who was going to pitch today and the scribe said Cicotte and 1 of the men said you are crazy as Cicotte has such a sore arm that he cant wash the back of his neck so when we come out to the park this scribe told me about it and I said they wasn't nothing in the rules of Monday's game that required Cicotte to wash the back of his neck or any of the newspaper men neither.

"Well," said the other expert, "the man was just speaking figurative and meant that Eddie had a sore arm."

"Well," I said, "if he has only got one sore arm he can still wash the back of his neck as I only use 1 even when I am going to a party."

"The back of your neck looks like it," said the other expert.

"Yes," I said, "but what is the differents or not about Cicotte only having 1 sore arm as he only pitches with 1 arm."

"Yes you bum but that is the arm that the man said was sore." That is the kind of clever repartee that goes on between the experts and no hard feelings on neither side.

No gents it wasn't no sore arm that bent Eddie today but just the other member of the Ring family finely getting some of the breaks and the way I seen the games you couldn't make me believe that either of the 2 birds had any impediment in the old souper as I have nicknamed it. Eddie had a sore heart when it was all over but theys other seasons comeing and may be another game in this serious which dont look like it would end for a month as I look for another 1 of them 40 day rains to begin early tomorrow am.

Gents do you remember when they decided to have the serious go 9 games instead of the conventional 7 and a whole lot of people said that was soup for the Reds as Mr. Gleason didn't have the pitchers to go 9 games.

Well now it looks like the disadvantage was vs. P.J. Moran as if the serious had of only been skedoodled to go 7 games why by now he would of only had 1 more to win by now where as on the other hand Mr. Gleason has still got the same pitchers he had to begin with. The only people therefore that gets the advantage is the athaletes themselfs as they get paid for 5 games instead of 4 and I beg to assure the public that the newspaper men wishes they had kept it 4 games as we don't even get the priviledge of talking back to the umpire.

Tomorrows game will be postponed till the 4th day of November and I hope before that time they will give me a rm with bath.

RING TELLS UMPS' SECRET

KERR AN OIL MAGNATE; SCHALK RIGHT WITH BAN

Cincinnati, Oct. 7.—Gents: Instead of going to the Latonie today I sent my Jack over by a messenger and told him to throw it through the gate and in the meanwhile I went to the so-called national pastime. My first experience was trying to get into the park without showing a ticket and the guy stopped me and says where is your ticket brother?

Well I never seen this bird before in all my born days but I have got 3 perfectly good brothers so I gave him a keen glance to see maybe he was 1 of them but if he was he had changed a whole lot so I said "Which of my brothers is you?" and he kind of fumbled and stalled and couldn't answer nothing back so I simply passed it up by showing him my ticket and going into the ball park.

Up on the runway I met a lady from Philadelphia who says "Well the series will be all over today" and I asked her how did she know and she said because Cincinnati is a one night stand as all they have got to see here is Fountain Square and the Ohio River and Garfield Statue so I quit talking to her as I have seen more than that and I know for a fact that theys a whole lot more to be seen here than is visible to the nude eye if you stick around here a while which it looks like we would do so now.

After leaving the lady from Philadelphia much to her regrets I went in the banquet hall and who should I run into but the presidents of the other league. "Well Ban" I said, "are you going to suspend Cracker Schalk for what he done yesterday?"

I call Schalk Cracker because he calls me biscuit.

"What did he do?" says Ban.

"Why," says I, "he hit an umpire and didn't kill him."

"I didn't see it," says Ban, and I asked him if he was out to the game and he said he was so that makes 2 people that can go to the game and not watch them not including the umpires.

A great many of you gents may wonder why I keep bragging the umpire like this. Well I don't really mean it and the real purpose is kind of subtle but I would just as leaf tell you birds what it is.

The other day I met Bill Evans and he said, "Keep putting my name in the paper," so I have to sort of pan them or how could I do it but at that I was kind of wondering around amidst the bugs in the 9th inning this pm and Bill called a strike on whoever was up to the bar and a lot of maudlins around me begin to pan Bill so i stepped up and said, "Do you know why they have the umpires down there on the field?" and one bird said "No," so I said "It's because they can see the plays much better than if they was up in the grandstand." That silenced them.

But to get back to Ban I said "If you arent going to suspend Cracker why dont you suspend Carl Mays as you ought to live up to your reputation as a suspender?" Its a wonder he didnt give me a belt in the jaw.

After banqueting on a special brand of ham recommended by

Garry Herrmann but I wont mention its name in pure reading matter why I went up in the press coop and looked down on the field and some birds from Texas was just presenting Dickie Kerr with a bunch of oil stock. The differents between a bunch of oil stock and a bunch of flowers which they usually wish on a pitcher is that a bunch of oil stock waits 2 days instead of one before it withers and dies.

Well in the 5th, they was a man on third and second and first and very few out and Cocky Collins hit one by his drives which dont never seem to go safe and somebody caught it and whoever was on third scored an waffles Schalk stuck on second base but Dickie was still thinking about this here oil stock yet and he run down to second and found that somebody else had a lease on that property and along come Sheriff Groh and tagged him and said you are it you cant expect a left hander with oil stock to respect other peoples leases on bases.

Between that inning and the subsequent inning Dickie took off his shoe to rest his dogs and it took him such a long while that I was going to walk out and leave the ball game flat as I though the serious was over any way and I got down on the next floor and first thing you know Dutch Reuther wasn't in there pitching no more as Happy Go Lucky Felsch had finely got one and Pat said to himself if a man is unlucky enough to let Felsch get a base hit he is better in the clubhouse than here anyway.

I looked out there to see who was pitching and it was the other member of the Ring family, so that is why I stayed through the ball game and pretty soon I was parked right beside Dutch Reuther himself and he said "Well it ought to be over by now but I lost my stuff."

So I said let us go to the races tomorrow and he said that was my intentions but now I have got to come back here again, he acted kind of disappointed over not winning but great heavens when he gets to be my age he will be glad to be alive let alone mournin over one ball game.

Well along come the tenth inning and the Sox got a couple birds on the bases and Dutch said goodbye as I dont want to see this whatever happens as I cant stand no more strain so he left me and I promised to tell him how the game come out and I will as soon as I see him.

They tell me that the Reds went out on 3 pitched balls in their half of the tenth and that is all I would pitch in any inning if I was doing it but any way I didn't see the Red part of the tenth as I was looking up at a sign on the fence which says "Vote your protest, Vote wet November 4th," so it looks like we would be here a long while and even then I will protest by voting dry.

LARDNER HAS SHINE BALL

PRESENT FROM UMP; KOPF COULDN'T HIT IT

Cincinnati, Oct. 8.—Gents: This is the most scandalous and death dealing story ever wrote about a world serious ball game. They have been a whole lot of talk in this serious about one thing and another and it finely remained for me to get at the facts.

Well, those of you who was out at todays game dont have to be explained to that in the fifth inning Eddie Cicotte pitched a baseball to Larry Kopf and Larry missed it and turned around to Mr. Quigley who was supposed to be umpiring behind the plate and asked this bird to let him (Kopf) see the ball.

Well, Mr. Quigley give Mr. Kopf the ball and he looked at it and Mr. Quigley said "Larry do you want the ball," and Larry said "No I dont want it." So Mr. Quigley said "All right throw the ball back to the pitcher. I cant stop this ball game all day to let an infielder look at a ball." Then I stepped in and said "Give me the ball" so they did.

Well, they give me the ball and here it is laying in front of me and I want to say to all infielders who of course never kep a ball long enough to look at it just what a baseball looks like and if I was an infielder I would catch a ball some time and hold on to it till after the game was lost and then I would study the ball.

Well, here is the ball right in front of me as I try to write. I will describe to you guys as I see it. Well this ball looks to me like a National League ball. That is what probably deceived them.

Well you see the reason that an infielder dont know what a baseball looks like is because the minute he gets it he has to throw it somewhere. Well as I said before here is what the baseball looks like. The National League baseball is nearly round.

This baseball which I am going to keep and give to my oldest child is a baseball that needs further description. It is the same baseball that Larry Kopf looked at and I only wished I was as nice looking as him and I wouldn't be writing this horrible stuff or working at baseball.

Well, then here is about that baseball. It is nearly round and looks nearly like an American League baseball except it has more seams and to be exact it has got 126 seams and if you take an American League ball why it has got 140 seams so why shouldnt you hit them.

But at that you take any ball and start counting seams on it and you can count all night and get innumerable seams. Well to distinguish this ball from its brothers it says John A. Heydler on it which makes it a cinch that it is a National Leage ball as it is a certainty that John wouldn't sign a ball that belonged to the other league.

Well as for the rest of the ball it looks soiled on the northwest side and I will worry my life away wondering who put a dirty finger on that ball which I have got and my children will still have it after me.

Now we have wrote almost a whole story about a ball. Now let us take a different angle about the game and start in on Morris Rath. At one stage of the game Morris hit a ball and broke his bat and the man setting next to me said that is the only time Morris ever broke a bat in a world's serious.

Another funny thing I heard was as follows.

A man named Wingo came up to the bat and the bird setting next to me said come on Wingo get a bingo.

1919

From *Blue Ruin*

BRENDAN BOYD

SOME WILL KNOW THE END of this story, others will guess it. Cicotte confessed; Jackson, Felsch, and Williams followed quickly.

On October 22, 1920, thirteen indictments were handed down: the eight players, Abe Attell, Bill Burns, Nat Evans, Hal Chase. And me.

The trial began on June 27, 1921, and lasted five weeks. Attell and I were tried *in absentia*. The jury deliberated two hours, finding each defendant innocent on every count. Attell and I could return if we wanted to. I didn't want to. I'd worried little about the outcome, assuming Rothstein would take care of it.

One week later, all the players were banned from baseball for life. None ever played another game. That's the one thing I hadn't known, what nobody could have known. The last fix had been put in by professionals.

After the first death there are sometimes others, it turns out.

Chick Gandil became a plumber in Calistoga, Eddie Cicotte a game warden in Michigan. Joe Jackson opened a package store in Greenville, Lefty Williams a pool hall in Chicago. Swede Riisberg and Happy Felsch fronted bars, in San Francisco and Milwaukee, respectively. Fred McMullin moved to Los Angeles, and disappeared.

Comiskey never finished in the first division again. Gleason managed three more years, then retired. Bill Burns moved to west Texas, for the climate. Abe Attell stayed on Broadway, for the company. All are gone now. Only one preceded them.

On November 4, 1928, Arnold Rothstein was shot between the left cheek and earlobe during a poker game in the Park Central Hotel on West 56th Street.

As for me, I stayed in Mexico.

It was the most foreign place I'd ever visited. I immediately felt at home there. The years slipped by almost imperceptibly. Whole decades have left no visible trace.

My life's second half has often seemed an appendix to the first. That's as it should be, I suppose. Perhaps it's what I was seeking all along, a great distance from which all events appear hypothetical.

Mexico wasn't as I'd envisioned it, of course, though its reality was often as vivid as my imaginings. My houses were more wood than adobe, the heat more oppressive than comforting, the endless intrigues so thick with repercussion that no real gambler would have had any complaint.

In any event I've long since forgotten my dreams of it. I've long since forgotten most of my dreams, actually, except the one dream the rest were meant to induce, the dream of my perfect scam.

It is the only dream no disappointment can ever tamper with. It has changed somewhat, but only as my life has changed, and then mainly in its nuances.

It no longer steals on me in the moments preceding sleep, but greets me now as I flee the night's entanglements, in those increasingly lengthy intervals before I summon the will to rise.

In the pure tropic silence I can almost swim in it, as the black turns deeper blue against the dawn.

I am alone. I am calm. I have prepared well. My path of flight awaits me. I have approached Gandil. I haven't allowed him to speak. I haven't contacted Burns. I go to Saratoga to await the

Series. I meet a beautiful woman, leave her, win the necessary capital at the races. I go to Chicago. I am even more alone. I bet, collect, flee—to the mountains perhaps, somewhere vast, foreign, someplace not unlike where I am today.

I do not go to Rothstein. I never even see Rothstein. And that is the real difference.

Perhaps it wouldn't have made any actual difference, but it might have, and that's all that matters now.

The end of the dream remains as it has always been, except for one significant detail.

I do none of these things, but only imagine them, keeping it all a dream.

Instead I take long walks, sketch, read voraciously, sitting in my lush, untended garden, staring up through the swaying jacarandas, picturing again all the loveliest scenes as they could have been, and as, no doubt, they someday will be, in some country, in some year, in this brief life whose realest parts are what we dream of it, in this best of dreams, which is, at last, my own.

1923

New York Giants 5, New York Yankees 4

DAMON RUNYON

THIS IS THE WAY OLD CASEY STENGEL ran yesterday after-noon, running his home run home.

This is the way old Casey Stengel ran running his home run home to a Giant victory by a score of 5 to 4 in the first game of the World Series of 1923.

This is the way old Casey Stengel ran, running his home run home, when two were out in the ninth inning and the score was tied and the ball was still bounding inside the Yankee yard.

This is the way—

His mouth wide open.

His warped old legs bending beneath him at every stride.

His arms flying back and forth like those of a man swimming with a crawl stroke.

His flanks heaving, his breath whistling, his head far back.

Yankee infielders, passed by old Casey Stengel as he was run-ning his home run home, say Casey was muttering to himself, adjuring himself to greater speed as a jockey mutters to his horse in a race, that he was saying: "Go on, Casey! Go on!"

People generally laugh when they see old Casey Stengel run, but they were not laughing while he was running his home run home yesterday afternoon. People—60,000 of 'em, men and women—were standing in the Yankee stands and bleachers up there in the Bronx roaring sympathetically, whether they were for or against the Giants.

"Come on, Casey!"

The warped old legs, twisted and bent by many a year of baseball campaigning, just barely held out under Casey Stengel until he reached the plate, running his home run home.

Then they collapsed.

They gave out just as old Casey slid over the plate in his awkward fashion as Wally Schang made futile efforts to capture the ball which eluded him and rolled toward the dugout. Billy Evans, the American League umpire, poised over him in a set pose, arms spread to indicate that old Casey was safe.

Half a dozen Giants rushed forward to help Casey to his feet, to hammer him on the back, to bawl congratulations in his ears as he limped unsteadily, still panting furiously, to the bench where John J. McGraw, chief of the Giants, relaxed his stern features in a smile for the man who had won the game.

Casey Stengel's warped old legs, one of them broken not so long ago, wouldn't carry him out for the last half of the inning, when the Yankees made a dying effort to undo the damage done by Casey. His place in center field was taken by young Bill Cunningham, whose legs are still unwarped, and Casey sat on the bench with John J. McGraw.

No one expected much of Casey Stengel when he appeared at the plate in the Giants' side of the ninth inning, the score a tie at 4 to 4.

Ross Young and Irish Meusel, stout, dependable hitters, had been quickly disposed of by the superb pitching of Bullet Joe Bush.

No one expected Stengel to accomplish anything where they had failed. Bush, pitching as only Bush can pitch in an emergency, soon had two strikes and three balls on Casey.

He was at the plate so long that many of the fans were fidgeting nervously, wondering why he didn't hurry up and get put out, so the game could go on. Casey Stengel is not an imposing figure at bat, not an imposing figure under any circumstances. Those warped old legs have something to do with it. A man with warped legs cannot look very imposing.

People like to laugh at Casey—Casey likes to make people laugh.

A wayfarer of the big leagues—Brooklyn, Pittsburgh, Philadelphia, and finally New York—he has always been regarded by the fans as a great comedian, a funny fellow, a sort of clown.

The baseball land teems with tales of the strange didoes cut by Casey Stengel, whose parents started him out as Charles, with his sayings.

Who knows but that "Bullet Joe" may have been thinking of Casey Stengel more as a comedian than as a dangerous hitter when he delivered that final pitch yesterday afternoon? Pitchers sometimes let their wits go wool-gathering.

"Bap"—Stengel's bat connected with the last pitch, connected surely, solidly. The ball sailed out over left field, moving high, moving far.

Long Bob Meusel and Whitey Witt, the Yankee outfielders, raced toward each other as they marked the probable point where the ball would alight, and in the meantime Casey Stengel was well advanced on his journey, running his home run home.

As the ball landed between Meusel and Witt it bounded as if possessed toward the left center-field fence. Everybody could see it would be a home run inside the yard, if Casey Stengel's warped old legs could carry him around the bases.

Witt got the ball about the time Stengel hit third, and about that time Stengel was laboring, "all out." Witt threw the ball in to Bob Meusel who had dropped back and let Witt go on. Meusel wheeled and fired for the plate, putting all his strength behind the throw. Few men have ever lived who can throw a baseball as well as Bob Meusel.

Stengel was almost home when Meusel's throw was launched, and sensing the throw Casey called on all that was left in those warped old legs, called no doubt on all the baseball gods to help him—and they helped.

It is something to win a World Series with a home run, and that home run inside the yard.

John J. McGraw perhaps feels that his judgment in taking Stengel on at a time when Casey was a general big-league outcast has been vindicated.

If you are curious to know the origin of the nickname "Casey," it might be explained that Stengel's home town is Kansas City.
The nickname comes from "K.C." One of these many little coincidences that are always popping out in baseball is the fact that Stengel and Bullet Joe Bush are great pals. They made the baseball four to Japan last winter as roommates.

Stengel is around thirty-three, if you are seeking more information about the first hero of the World Series of 1923. They call that old in baseball. He has been with the Giants since 1921, from the Philadelphia club. He is all right, Casey Stengel is, and you can prove it by John J. McGraw.

The expected struggle of Mind vs. Matter, or Intelligence against Brute Force, with John J. McGraw representing the one, and Babe Ruth the other, did not materialize.

Both sides began batting the ball so freely that thinking was not necessary.

Ruth got a three-bagger and was cheated out of another hit through an astonishing play by Long George Kelly, perhaps one of the most sensational plays ever seen in a World Series. Kelly got a hit from Ruth's bat with one hand at a seemingly impossible angle and threw a man out at the plate.

Quite as sensational was a play by Frankie Frisch, who backed out into short right field, caught a short fly from Bob Meusel's bat, turned and threw Ruth out at the plate. This was immediately after Ruth's three-bagger. Perhaps if Casey Stengel had not run his home run, Frisch's play would be picked as the feature of the whole afternoon.

The Yanks were three runs ahead of the Giants when McGraw's men caught and passed them, hammering Waite Hoyt for all their runs except Stengel's home run. It was the first real bad inning the one-time Brooklyn schoolboy ever had in a World Series, so say the experts.

Bush took Hoyt's place and pitched marvelous ball. Poor Bush, as usual, suffered from "the breaks," from the bad luck of the game. He has been in a number of World Series, and was always what baseball calls a "tough luck pitcher" in them. He won one game for the Athletics in his first year in the big leagues. Since then he has been a consistent loser.

The Yanks drove John Watson, of Louisiana, from the game early. Then Wilfred Ryan did the pitching for McGraw's men— and did it well. The Yanks outhit the Giants, however, twelve to eight.

It seemed to this writer that the Yanks were very stupid in some of their base running. At least one example probably cost them a run.

However, it was a great game for the spectators. A thrill a minute, finally topped off by the real big thrill of Casey Stengel, running his home run home.

The umpires, four solemn-looking gentlemen in dark, funeral blue uniforms with little blue caps, held a meeting at the home plate just before game time. They were Billy Evans of the American League, who can wear an umpire's uniform in such fashion that he looks trim and neat, Dick Nallin, of the same league, and Bill Hart, and Hank O'Day, a dour-looking man of the National League.

After the umpires conferred, the Yanks posed in a group at the plate, and Benny Bengough, the Yankee catcher, a young man from Buffalo, was presented with a traveling bag, presumably by his admirers.

Meanwhile, in front of the stand, Waite Hoyt and John Watson were warming up with deliberate motions, to the great surprise of some of the experts who had expected Arthur Nehf and Herb Pennock, left-handers, to start the series.

The breeze died away and the flags were hanging limply on their staffs when Miller Huggins, the little short-legged manager of the Yankees, and Davy Bancroft, captain of the Giants, held their last conference with the umpires and presented their line-ups.

Babe Ruth got the honor of making the first put-out of the game. He easily caught a fly from Beauty Bancroft. Hoyt's first pitch to Bancroft was right over the plate. Bancroft let it go by and Evans called it a strike. The next pitch was a ball, then Bancroft hit the fly to Ruth.

The bandy-legged Groh, waving his bottle-shaped bat, was at the plate but a short time. He hit the first ball thrown by Hoyt for a sharp single across second. The crowd babbled as Groh rushed to first.

Frankie Frisch, slim, graceful—called the "Fordham Flash"—was next to face Hoyt. The first pitch was called a ball, then Hoyt put over a strike. Frisch hit a bounder to Scott, who threw the ball to Ward at second, forcing out Groh.

With Ross Young, the Texan, at bat, Frisch, fastest of the National League base runners, tried to steal second. Schang whipped the ball to Aaron Ward at second, and Ward slapped the ball on Frisch's head as the "Fordham Flash" went sliding in, head foremost, as he always slides, and as few other players slide. That ended the inning.

McGraw was starting his old line of attack early. McGraw is a great believer in speed. He always sends his fast men out to run on the opposing pitcher when they have the opportunity. McGraw argues that a man may as well be thrown out stealing as to have a put-out in some other fashion.

The Yankees quickly set the stage for Babe Ruth in their side of the first inning. That was what perhaps two-thirds of the crowd was waiting for—the appearance of Ruth.

Babe came with Joe Dugan on first base, after Whitey Witt had hit a liner to Bancroft. Whitey was first of the Yankees at bat. Dugan got a base on balls from John Watson. Then "Along came Ruth."

The crowd buzzed as Ruth stood his stalwart frame alongside the plate, his legs slightly spraddled, his long bat waving menacingly at Watson. The first pitch was inside, but over the plate, and Evans motioned a strike. Babe set his feet more firmly. He swung at the next pitch and missed the ball by several inches. The crowd, always buzzing at Ruth's slightest move at bat, now murmured loudly.

The next pitch was a ball far outside the plate. On the following pitch Ruth swung. He drove the ball solidly toward third, directly at Heine Groh. The ball took one fierce bound before reaching Heine. It was going with such force that it bounced off Heine's glove. Then Groh recovered the ball and threw it to Frisch at second for a force play on Dugan.

Now came Long Bob Meusel, brother of the Giants' "Irish," batting one notch ahead of his usual place in the Yankee line-up.

The tall Californian hit the ball a solid smack. As it sailed to center Casey Stengel raced for the spot in which he saw it would land. He got one hand on the ball as it struck the ground, then it twisted away from him elusively.

Meantime, Ruth was thundering around the bases. Stengel threw the ball in the general direction of third, but Ruth was home by that time. Meusel was at second, and the crowd was roaring.

It went as a two-base hit for Meusel. Pipp, the next man up, a tall, raw-boned Michigander, once called "the Pickler," because of his slugging ability, raised a fly to Irish Meusel, leaving brother Bob on second.

Events now began moving with great rapidity. One thrill after another swept the slopes of Islanders.

The Giants were retired without incident in their side of the second. Ward, first of the Yankees up in the last half of the inning, singled to left. Schang followed with a single. Scott bunted to

Kelly who tagged him out, but necessarily permitted Ward and Schang to advance.

Hoyt struck out, but Witt banged a single past Frisch and Ward and Schang scored. The Yankees were three runs ahead, as Dugan ended the inning by grounding out to Watson.

It seemed a terrific load to the supporters of the Giants. The fans asked each other why McGraw had not taken Watson out when it was evident that the North Carolina farmer "had nothing."

They were still murmuring their discontent when George Kelly, towering first baseman of the Giants, opened the Giants' third with a single. The murmuring stopped momentarily as Lank Hank Gowdy drew a base on balls. Gowdy, lean backstop of the McGraw club, and once the greatest of heroes of a World Series, was taken out of the game immediately and Maguire, a fleet young Giant recruit, put on first base to run for him. The "Master Mind" on the Giant bench seemed to be working.

Now Watson—John Watson the Third, of North Carolina—also was out of the game. Big Jack Bentley, the left-handed pitcher from Baltimore, who looks something like Babe Ruth, was advancing to the plate to bat in place of Watson. Bentley was accounted a tremendous hitter when he was the star of Jack Dunn's Baltimore Orioles.

Hoyt worked on him with great care, knowing Bentley's reputation, having seen him hit in exhibition games between the Yankees and the Orioles. He soon had two strikes on Bentley, one of them a vicious foul bounder across first which barely missed being safe.

Bentley dropped a looping fly in center field, just outside the clutches of Whitey Witt. It was not far enough out for anyone to score, but it filled the bases.

McGraw, from the Giant bench, called Bentley in and Danny Gearin, a midget recruit pitcher, went to first to run in place of Bentley.

The bases full and no outs. Small wonder the Giant sympathizers were roaring with excitement. Beauty Bancroft drove a slow roller at Everett Scott, and the Yankee shortstop threw the ball to Ward at second, forcing out Gearin. Meantime, Kelly scored and Maguire reached third.

Now the bandy-legged Groh and his bottle-shaped bat were before Hoyt, and the Yankee rooters were squawking nervously "Take him out."

Bancroft suddenly quit first on a pitch to Groh, stealing second well ahead of Schang's throw—so far ahead, in fact, some of the Giant fans laughed derisively.

Now Groh clipped the ball across first, the drive hitting in fair territory, bouncing away past Pipp to right field. Ruth was lumbering in to meet the ball when it struck the screen in right field, and bounded away at a wicked angle. Ruth got his hands on the ball, but the carom deceived him. He could not hold it, and away it went across the grass.

While Ruth was chasing it, two Giants were scoring, the crowd was in a spasm of excitement, and Huggins was raging on the Yankee bench and motioning at Hoyt. Groh reached third before Ruth got the ball. Then Hoyt dejectedly left the field, and out of the flurry of players in front of the Yankee bench came Joe Bush another one-time hero of other World Series.

Bush pitched to Frisch, who singled past Pipp, scoring Groh. Young forced Frisch at second on an infield bounder, and Young himself was an easy out when he tried to steal second.

The Giant rooters fell back limply in their seats, completely exhausted from their vocal efforts during the inning.

Four runs—and the Giants now one run ahead. The Giant rooters felt they had earned their right to demonstration.

Wilfred Ryan—nicknamed "Rosey," for no apparent reason—went in to pitch for the Giants. Nearly all ballplayers have nicknames. Some of them mean much. Some of them mean little, if anything. "Rosey" is one of those names.

Ryan is a Holy Cross man, and a good right-handed pitcher when he is "right," that is to say, when the ball is obeying his muscles as it should.

In the Yankee half of the fifth inning, Ruth, in his fourth trip to the plate, took a shorter grip on his bat than is his habit— "choked up," the ballplayers call it—and swatting a short, sharp smash at the first ball pitched by Ryan drove the ball to deep left. It struck the low concrete in front of the left field pavillion, and bounded away from Irish Meusel.

Ruth was rambling into third when Meusel got the ball and let fly to Groh. The big slugger of the Yankees fairly threw himself at the bag, his long feet reaching for the base as Groh got the ball and plunged at him. It was a close play. Groh thought he had the Babe. He raged for a fleeting instant when Bill Hart waved the runner safe. The scorers called it a three-base hit.

Dugan had gone out just before Ruth went to bat, and now Long Bob Meusel lifted a little fly that rose slowly over the infield and floated on back over short right field, well back of the base line between first and second.

It was a dangerous looking little fly, one of the kind called "Texas Leaguers." Young came racing up from right field and Frisch went running backward, his eye on the ball, his hands waving Young away.

Frisch was twisting and turning with the descending ball; his back was turned from the infield when he caught it. Ruth instantly left third and tore for home. Frisch turned and threw blindly in the direction of the plate, and it happened to be an accurate throw.

The ball bounded in straight and true to huge Frank Snyder, who had taken Gowdy's place behind the plate. As Snyder clasped the ball Ruth came lunging in. The big men collided with terrific force, but Snyder clung to the ball, tagged Ruth with it, and Ruth was out. It was a great play—it was a thrilling play.

Casey Stengel got the first hit off Bush since he relieved Hoyt in the seventh. It was a single. Kelly hit into a double play immediately afterwards.

Bush was given a round of applause when he went to the plate in the Yankees' seventh and Joe, as if by way of acknowledgment, singled to center, his second hit. Witt lifted an easy fly to Meusel in short left field. The Yankee rooters, briefly stirred by hope, sighed dismally and sank back in their seats only to come up shrilling an instant later when Jumping Joe Dugan, third baseman of the Yanks, smashed the ball to the right-field bleacher barrier.

It was a clean, hard drive, well out of reach of Young. Bush raced around the bases, and on across the plate, with Dugan not far behind him. Kelly's throw was right to the mark, and Snyder tagged Dugan a yard from the plate. Bob Meusel ended the inning with a fly to Young, after Ruth had almost been caught napping off first.

"The Giants are getting all the breaks," moaned Yankee sympathizers.

However, it seemed to the ordinary observer that the Yankees made some of the breaks against themselves.

From *Damon Runyon*

JIMMY BRESLIN

ANOTHER RUNYON SPORTS STORY lasted by word of mouth as long as if it had been issued on a bronze plaque. This occurred on a Sunday in October of 1926, when the seventh game of the World Series between the St. Louis Cardinals and the Yankees was played at Yankee Stadium. The thirty-nine-year-old Grover Cleveland Alexander had won two games for the Cardinals and, with an arm numb from all that pitching at his age, expected that he wouldn't be needed in the seventh game except to sit in a jacket on the bench. He prepared for this by spending most of Saturday night at the bar in Billy LaHiff's Tavern on West 48th Street. On Sunday morning, he returned to LaHiff's and told the porter that he wanted coffee, and when the porter produced coffee, Alexander threw it at him. He caused such a commotion that Billy LaHiff had to run down.

Alexander made LaHiff sit with him and he began drinking. Was he going to attend the game? "What am I, some fan?" Alexander said. "I've done my job. Let them take it from here." He said he was going to spend the day as he should. Right after serving one great big good drink, LaHiff excused himself and went to the phone and called Runyon at home, which he did out of loyalty but also because he understood that Runyon was the only writer in the city who would think that Alexander sitting in the bar was a fine story, perhaps as good as the game itself. Runyon rushed down to the tavern by cab, paid his respects to Alexander and took a cab up to the stadium. He had the scene of Alexander in his pocket and intended to use it in his story. At the time the first pitch was thrown, Alexander was sitting on a stool, barside, LaHiff's Tavern, West 48th Street, New York City. This was a considerable distance away from Yankee Stadium, which was up the length of Manhattan and across a river to East 161st Street in the Bronx.

At this point, both Runyon and Alexander had great luck.

In an early inning, Jesse Haines, pitching for the Cardinals, came back to the dugout and began inspecting the index finger on his throwing hand. There was a red lump on it. "It's nothing," O'Farrell, the catcher, said. Haines shrugged. Manager Rogers Hornsby walked over and looked at it. Then he looked up and down the bench. "Where is Grover?" Hornsby asked. Somebody knew and a call was made to LaHiff's.

"They want you," LaHiff said to Alexander.

"For what?"

"Hornsby says he might need you."

"They're crazy."

Alexander took the phone, listened and decided he would have to go to the ballpark. "I'll sit in the effin' bullpen and have to watch the whole game from there," he muttered.

By the seventh inning, the Cardinals were ahead, 3–2, and Alexander was in the left field bullpen. The Yankees were up with two out when Haines, the St. Louis pitcher, felt the finger split on a waste pitch, which was a fourth ball to Lou Gehrig. This loaded the bases. The next Yankee hitter was Poosh 'Em Up Tony Lazzeri. While the nickname once had been a slur, it now was a threat. In all the years of the sport there were only one or two second basemen who could hit the ball as frequently and as far as Lazzeri. He batted sixth in a lineup that included Babe Ruth, hitting third, and Lou Gehrig, fourth. While Haines shook his finger, the Cardinals' manager, Hornsby, walked out of the dugout, looked at the open split on Haines's finger and then turned to left field and held his right arm high in the air. A right hander. Alexander. It was the start of a great American sports story, and was told with an anecdote by Runyon:

Old Grover Cleveland Alexander, with his cap perched high above his ear, shambled in out of a fog into the seventh game of the World Series of 1926 up at the Yankee Stadium yesterday just in time to fan Poosh 'Em Up Tony Lazzeri with the bases full, and to hold a one-run lead that made the St. Louis Cardinals champions of all the baseball world.

It was fortunate for the Cardinals that they located old Grover Cleveland Alexander at the moment Haines' finger began to pain him. Some say Grover had been heating himself up under the bleachers.

Others claim that he was found in his favorite chair down at the Tavern, discoursing over his two previous victories in the series with Mine Host Will LaHiff and that the Cardinals chipped in towards a taxi to send for Grover.

They sent word by the taxi jockey that his presence was urgently requested at the baseball orchard and that it might be worth $2,000 to him to make the trip. Old Grover sighed and accompanied the taxi back to the Yankee Stadium, but it is said he insisted that Mr. LaHiff go with him.

He did not care to take such a long ride without somebody to talk to. I do not vouch for this report, you understand. All I know is that Old Grover Cleveland Alexander may usually be found at the Tavern when he is in New York and that he appeared out of the fog that hung over the Yankee yard in the seventh inning.

Mr. LaHiff waited for him in the taxicab outside. He knew Grover would not be long. Meanwhile, poor Lazzeri was waiting at the plate, mind filled with foreboding as he watched Grover Cleveland Alexander shambling in out of the fog, walking first on one foot and then on the other.

He then looked down at catcher O'Farrell and pitched what the umpire called a ball to Tony Lazzeri. The next Mr. Hildbrand, umpire, said was a strike. Then Tony fouled one into the stand that caused the clients to jump. It was the second strike.

On the next pitch Poosh 'Em Up Tony shattered the air with the force of his blow and everybody got right up and yelled for the Grover.

It all came together here. Here was a story naming the very bar stool on which Alexander sat while he got drunk, and of course LaHiff's Tavern never was closed for an hour of a day of a week throughout the entire Prohibition. And Alexander filled the need for stories that could keep men talking on stoops and bar stools for the entire winter.

1923

New York Yankees 4, New York Giants 2

HEYWOOD BROUN

THE RUTH IS MIGHTY AND SHALL PREVAIL. He did yesterday. Babe made two home runs and the Yankees won from the Giants at the Polo Grounds by a score of 4 to 2. This evens up the World Series with one game for each contender.

It was the first game the Yankees won from the Giants since October 10, 1921, and it ended a string of eight successive victories for the latter, with one tie thrown in.

Victory came to the American League champions through a change of tactics. Miller Huggins could hardly fail to have observed Wednesday that terrible things were almost certain to happen to his men if they paused any place along the line from first to home.

In order to prevent blunders in base running he wisely decided to eliminate it. The batter who hits a ball into the stands cannot possibly be caught napping off any base.

The Yankees prevented Kelly, Frisch and the rest from performing tricks in black magic by consistently hammering the ball out of the park or into sections of the stand where only amateurs were seated.

Through simplicity itself, the system worked like a charm.

Three of the Yankees' four runs were the product of homers, and this was enough for the winning total. Aaron Ward was Ruth's assistant, Irish Meusel of the Giants also made a home run, but yesterday's show belonged to Ruth.

For the first time since coming to New York, Babe achieved his full brilliance in a World Series game. Before this he has varied between pretty good and simply awful, but yesterday he was magnificent.

Just before the game John McGraw remarked:

"Why shouldn't we pitch to Ruth? I've said before and I'll say again, we pitch to better hitters than Ruth in the National League."

Ere the sun had set on McGraw's rash and presumptuous words, the Babe had flashed across the sky fiery portents which should have been sufficient to strike terror and conviction into the hearts of all infidels. But John McGraw clung to his heresy with a courage worthy of a better cause.

In the fourth inning Ruth drove the ball completely out of the premises. McQuillan was pitching at the time, and the count was two balls and one strike. The strike was a fast ball shoulder-high, at which Ruth had lunged with almost comic ferocity and ineptitude.

Snyder peeked at the bench to get a signal from McGraw. Catching for the Giants must be a terrific strain on the neck muscles, for apparently it is etiquette to take the signals from the bench manager furtively. The catcher is supposed to pretend he is merely glancing around to see if the girl in the red hat is anywhere in the grandstand, although all the time his eyes are intent on McGraw.

Of course the nature of the code is secret, but this time McGraw scratched his nose to indicate: "Try another of those shoulder-high fast ones on the Big Bum and let's see if we can't make him break his back again."

But Babe didn't break his back, for he had something solid to check his terrific swing. The ball started climbing from the moment it left the plate. It was a pop fly with a brand new gland and, although it flew high, it also flew far.

When last seen the ball was crossing the roof of the stand in deep right field at an altitude of 315 feet. We wonder whether new baseballs conversing in the original package ever remark: "Join Ruth and see the world."

In the fifth Ruth was up again and by this time McQuillan had left the park utterly and Jack Bentley was pitching. The count crept up to two strikes and two balls. Snyder sneaked a look at the little logician deep in the dugout. McGraw blinked twice, pulled up his trousers and thrust the forefinger of his right hand into his left eye. Snyder knew that he meant: "Try the Big Bozo on a slow curve around his knees and don't forget to throw to first if you happen to drop the third strike."

Snyder called for the delivery as directed and Ruth half-topped a line drive over the wall of the lower stand in right field. With that drive the Babe tied a record. Benny Kauff and Duffy Lewis are the only other players who ever made two home runs in a single World Series game.

But was McGraw convinced and did he rush out of the dugout and kneel before Ruth with a cry of "Maestro" as the Babe crossed the plate? He did not. He nibbled at not a single word he has ever uttered in disparagement of the prowess of the Yankee slugger. In the ninth Ruth came to bat with two out and a runner on second base. By every consideration of prudent tactics an intentional pass seemed indicated.

Snyder jerked his head around and observed that McGraw was blowing his nose. The Giant catcher was puzzled, for that was a signal he had never learned. By a process of pure reasoning he attempted to figure out just what it was that his chief was trying to convey to him.

"Maybe he means if we pitch to Ruth we'll blow the game," thought Snyder, but he looked toward the bench again just to make sure.

Now McGraw intended no signal at all when he blew his nose. That was not tactics, but only a head cold. On the second glance, Snyder observed that the little Napoleon gritted his teeth. Then he proceeded to spell out with the first three fingers of his right hand: "The Old Guard dies, but never surrenders." That was a signal Snyder recognized, although it never had passed between him and his manager before.

McGraw was saying: "Pitch to the Big Bum if he hammers every ball in the park into the North River."

And so, at Snyder's request, Bentley did pitch to Ruth and the Babe drove the ball deep into right center; so deep that Casey Stengel could feel the hot breath of the bleacherites on his back as the ball came down and he caught it. If that drive had been just a shade to the right it would have been a third home run for Ruth. As it was, the Babe had a great day, with two home runs, a terrific long fly and two bases on balls.

Neither pass was intentional. For that McGraw should receive due credit. His game deserves to be recorded along with the man who said, "Lay on, Macduff," "Sink the ship, Master Ginner, split her in twain," and "I'll fight it out on this line if it takes all summer." For John McGraw also went down eyes front and his thumb on his nose.

Some of the sportsmanship of the afternoon was not so admirable. In the sixth inning Pep Young prevented a Yankee double play by diving at the legs of Ward, who was just about to throw to first after a force-out. Tack Hardwick never took out an opposing back more neatly. Half the spectators booed Young and the other half applauded him.

It did not seem to us that there was any very good reason for booing Young, since the tradition of professional baseball always has been agreeably free of chivalry. The rule is, "Do anything you can get away with."

But Young never should have been permitted to get away with interference. The runner on first ought to have been declared out. In coming down to second Young had complete rights to the baseline and the bag, but those rights should not have permitted him the privilege of diving all the way across the bag to tackle Ward around the ankles.

It was a most palpably incompetent decision by Hart, the National League umpire on second base. Fortunately the blunder had no effect on the game, since the next Giant batter hit into a double play in which the Giant rushline was unable to reach Ward in time to do anything about it.

Ruth crushed to earth shall rise again. Herb Pennock, the assistant hero of the afternoon, did the same thing. In the fourth inning, Jack Bentley toppled the slim Yankee left-hander into a crumpled heap by hitting him in the back with a fast ball. Pennock went down with a groan which could be heard even in the dollar seats. All the players gathered around him as he writhed, and what with sympathy and some judicious massage, he was up again within three or four minutes, and his pitching efficiency seemed to be in no wise impaired. It was, of course, wholly an accident, as the kidney punch is barred in baseball.

Entirely aside from his injury, Pennock looked none too stalwart. He is a meager athlete who winds up with great deliberation, as if fearful about what the opposing batter will do with the ball. And it was mostly slow curves that he fed to the Giants, but they did nothing much in crucial moments. Every now and then Pennock switched to a fast one, and the change of pace had McGraw's men baffled throughout.

Just once Pennock was in grave danger. It looked as if his three-run lead might be swept away in the sixth inning. Groh, Frisch and Young, the three Giants to face him at that point, all singled solidly. It seemed the part of wisdom to remove Pennock immediately after Young's single had scored Groh. Here Huggins was shrewd. He guessed wisely and stuck to Pennock.

Irish Meusel forced Young, and it would have been a double play but for Young's interference with Ward's throw. Cunningham, who followed, did hit into a double play, Scott to Ward to Pipp. The Giants' rally thus was limited to one run.

Their other score came in the second inning, when Irish Meusel drove a home run into the upper tier of the left field stands. It was a long wallop and served to tie the score at that stage of the game, as Aaron Ward had made a home run for the Yankees in the first half of the inning. Ward's homer was less lusty, but went in the same general direction.

In the fourth the Yankees broke the tie. Ruth began it with his over-the-fence smash, and another run came across on a single by Pipp, Schang's hit to right—which Young fumbled long enough to let Pipp reach third—and Scott's clean line hit to center. This is said to be Scott's last year as a regular and he seems intent on making a good exit, for, in addition to fielding spryly, he made two singles.

The defensive star of the afternoon was Joe Dugan, third baseman of the Yankees. He specialized on bunts. McQuillan caught him flat-footed with an unexpected tap, but he threw it on the dead run in time to get his man at first.

Again he made a great play against Kelly, first batter up in the last half of the ninth. Kelly just nicked the ball with a vicious swing and the result was a treacherous spinning grounder that rolled only halfway down to third. Dugan had to run and throw in conjunction this time, too, but he got his man.

For the Giants, Frisch, Young and Meusel batted hard, and Jack Bentley pitched well after relieving McQuillan in the fourth. He was hit fairly hard and he was a trifle wild, but the only run scored against him was Ruth's homer in the fifth.

As for the local color, the only bit we saw was around the neck of a spectator in a large white hat. The big handkerchief, which was spread completely over the gentleman's chest, was green and yellow, with purple spots. The rooter said his name was Tom Mix, but offered no other explanation.

1924

Washington Senators 4, New York Giants 3

BILL CORUM

DREAMS CAME TRUE IN THE TWELFTH—Washington's dream and Walter Johnson's—and when the red September sun dropped down behind the dome of the Capitol the Senators were the baseball champions of the world.

Washington waited twenty-five years for a World Series, but when it came it was the greatest one in history, and the king of pitchers waited eighteen years for the sweetest victory of his career.

For just long enough to beat the Giants, 4 to 3, in the seventh and deciding game the Old Master was the Johnson of old, the Kansas Cyclone, sweeping the proud champions of the National League down to their bitterest defeat.

"The team that won't be beaten, can't be beaten." Today that team was Washington. But the Giants did not deserve to lose. Chance and fate turned against the gray-clad team from the banks of the Hudson, but they went down fighting in the only way they knew and New York may still be proud of them.

Fate made a mark after the name of John McGraw in the eighth and closed the book. It was in that inning the Little Napoleon of the Diamond met his Waterloo. With the dogged, never-say-die Senators an all but beaten team and victory hovering over the

a

Giants' bench, Bucky Harris hit a lucky bounding single over the head of young Lindstrom which scored two runs, tied the count and stemmed the tide that a moment before had been sweeping his team to defeat. It was not a hard hit, nor a clean one, but it counted and the Giants never quite recovered from it.

When the Senators took the field it was behind the broad shoulders of Walter Johnson, and this time their hero did not fail them. In danger in every one of the four innings that he worked, he rose superbly to every emergency. In each succeeding crisis he became a little more the master, a little more the terrible blond Swede of baseball fable. Twice he struck out Long George Kelly when the game hung by a thread so fine that thousands in the tense, silent throng turned their heads away with every pitch.

Somewhere, perhaps, in that little patch of sunlight that was filtering through the shadowy stands and down in front of the pitcher's mound the once mightiest arm of all was finding the strength to do the thing that twice before had balked it. In those four innings the grand old man struck out five batters, and when his need was direst he was best. Twice he turned McGraw's team back with two runners waiting to score and two other times with one.

In the very first inning that Johnson pitched, Frisch, the second batter to face him, tripled and then stayed on third to fret and fume while the calm Kansan passed Young intentionally, struck out Kelly and then made Meusel roll to the third baseman for the final out.

Again in the tenth, Wilson, first to face him, drew a pass, stayed on first while Jackson fanned and then died in a double play, Johnson to Bluege to Judge.

But it was in the eleventh that Johnson reached his greatest heights. Here it was that McGraw made his most desperate bid for victory. He sent the crippled Heinie Groh up with his bottle bat to hit for McQuillan when the inning began, and Heinie delivered a difficult single to right. Southworth scurried down to first to run for Groh, and no sooner was he there than Lindstrom moved him on to second with a perfect sacrifice bunt. The winning run was on second, there was only one out and Frankie Frisch was at bat.

Here was a situation to make any pitcher quail. That is, any pitcher but Walter Johnson. Frisch was captain of his team, but not of his fate, as it turned out; that was in the big, broad palm of the man he was facing. Up and down went that right arm. There was a prayer on every pitch, but there was something else on them, too. Frisch will tell you that. He swung three times, missed three times and sat down.

But the danger was not over yet. Young and Kelly were still to come. Young came, and went to first on four pitched balls. Kelly came, and went to first on three strikes, but the rest of the Giants went with him, and the Senators came in to bat. Long George had paid dearly for that home run he hit off Johnson last Saturday. He knows now why they call Walter the Old Master.

Once more in the twelfth the Giants put the Big Train in the hole at the start when Irish Meusel singled to right, but this time the lower end of the batting order was up and Wilson fanned, Jackson grounded to Bluege and Gowdy flied to Goslin.

Johnson not only saved the game with his arm, he also helped to win it with his bat. In the tenth he nearly turned the trick all alone. He drove a mighty fly to deep left center, but it lacked a few feet of being long enough for a home run, which would have turned a great game into an epic.

Wilson was under the ball and Sir Walter was out, but not down. He came back in that fierce and final rally in the twelfth. With Miller out on a grounder to Frisch, Gowdy made a $50,000 muff of a foul pop off Muddy Ruel's bat when he stumbled over his mask and let the ball get away from him. It was baseball history repeating itself. McGraw and Christy Mathewson lost the 1912 championship when Fred Snodgrass dropped a fly ball in the tenth.

Granted this reprieve, little Muddy from the Big Muddy hammered a double over third base and Washington's first baseball championship was in the making. Johnson jabbed a hard grounder at Jackson and Travis made the second error of a bad afternoon. Ruel wisely clung to second while Jackson scrambled for the ball.

With first and second occupied, Earl McNeely hit another hopper over Lindstrom that was a twin brother to Harris' hit of the eighth except that it was a little harder and, therefore, a more legitimate hit. As the ball rolled into left Ruel, running as he had never run before, rounded third and charged toward the plate. Meusel, galloping from deep left, picked up the ball, but didn't even throw it. It would have been the proper gesture, but neither one of the Meusel boys are given to gestures.

Irish knew, as did the joy-mad crowd, that the game was over. He kept running on in toward the plate with the ball in his hands. The rest of the Giants stood motionless and stunned and in the next instant the crowd swirled over the field and blotted out the quiet men in gray and leaping ones in white.

Many in the roaring throng that came piling on the field like college boys after the victory of their football team thought that it was Pep Young who carried off the ball that beat the Giants. With two out and two on, in the Senators' half of the eleventh, and Bluege, a dead left-field hitter at bat, McGraw had shifted Young and Meusel to get the faster man into left, but they went back to their regular positions in the twelfth.

This jockeying about of players was typical of the entire game, for it was a battle of wits as well as bats and balls. Manager Harris tried to cross his veteran rival on the New York bench even before the game started. He announced that he would pitch Curley Ogden, a right-hander, and actually sent him to the mound, although he planned to have him pitch to only one batter. The idea was to induce McGraw to name the line-up he had been using against right-handers and then to send Mogridge, a southpaw, to the mound.

The New York manager could, of course, shift his team to meet the change, but if he did he could not change back again if

Mogridge was knocked out and Marberry, another right-hander, sent in. In other words, Terry's being named in the line-up actually put him in the game and he could not be withdrawn and then sent back.

Ogden struck out Lindstrom and then started walking toward the Washington bench, but Harris showed himself to be a shrewd leader by calling him back and having him pitch to Frisch also. If Ogden was going to have a great day—and that would have been wholly possible in the face of his record—Bucky wanted to take advantage of it. He worked the same trick in Detroit near the end of the American League race, and successfully, but against the canny McGraw he derived no great benefit from it.

McGraw allowed Terry to stay in until the pinch in the sixth, when he substituted Meusel. Harris met the change by waving in Marberry to replace Morgridge, but Meusel hit the Texas right-hander for a fly that traveled long and far to right and Young scored with the tying run. So while there was no very decisive and far-reaching effect from the strategy one way or the other, what little there was came to McGraw.

Just prior to this, and in the same inning, McGraw had introduced a bit of strategy on his own part which had far more effect on the game. With Young on first, Kelly at bat and Mogridge patently nervous, McGraw called for the hit and run, with the count three balls and one strike on Kelly. The obvious play, of course, would have been to let Kelly take the next one in the hope that it would be a fourth ball. But McGraw seldom does the obvious thing. He figured that Mogridge would try for the heart of the plate, and that was just what Mogridge did. Kelly singled over second and Young easily reached third. It was from that point that he counted on Meusel's fly, and it was smart baseball that had put him there.

From the eighth on both teams were threatening each time they came to bat and any one of a hundred things might have changed the result completely.

"It might have been" were sure to be the saddest words, no matter which team lost. Many a Washington fan who had more gray hairs in his head tonight than he had this morning could testify to the chances that the Giants had and missed. Time after time any kind of a hit or any kind of a play but the one which was forthcoming would have settled the issue for good and all. When the break came finally, it came to Washington. Washington had waited for it, watched for it, and deserved it, but all the heroes did not wear spotless white.

There was Virgil Barnes of Centerville, Kan., for instance. Virgil proved that while all the great pitchers may come from his state they do not all come to Washington. For seven and two-thirds innings Barnes was a master pitcher. Until Harris hit a long fly, which just did drop over the temporary bleachers wall for a home run in the fourth, the Senators had not got a single ball past the Giant infield. Only three batters faced Barnes in each of the first three innings, four in the fourth, three in the fifth and three in the sixth, and four in the seventh again, making only twenty-three batters to face him in seven innings.

In those seven frames he yielded only three hits, a homer and fluky single by Harris and a single by Goslin. Even in the eighth, when he was taken out, he did not break completely, but he faltered, and that was enough to let the Senators break through and cause his downfall. That blow of Harris', which a high bound and the sun in Lindstrom's eyes helped to make a hit, was the one that ruined him. Until then he had furnished the most brilliant bit of pitching seen in the series. Besides Barnes, there were Frisch, Kelly and Wilson, all three of whom made sparkling plays in the field and timely hits at bat.

But to the victor belong the spoils. When future generations are told about this game they will not hear about Barnes, or Frisch, or Kelly, or even about Harris or McNeely. But the boy with his first glove and ball crowding up to his father's knee, will beg:

"Tell me about Walter Johnson."

1926

Boy Regains Health as Ruth Hits Homers

NEW YORK TIMES

BOY REGAINS HEALTH AS RUTH HITS HOMERS

JOHN D. SYLVESTER, SON OF NATIONAL CITY BANK EXECUTIVE, NOW ON ROAD TO RECOVERY.

SPECIAL TO THE NEW YORK TIMES.

Essex Falls, N. J., OCT. 7—John Dale Sylvester, 11 years old, to whom physicians allotted thirty minutes of life when he was stricken with blood poisoning last week, was pronounced well on the road to recovery this afternoon, after he had contentedly listened to the radio returns of the Yankees' defeat of the Cardinals. His father, Horace Sylvester Jr., Vice President of the National City Bank, and the physicians, are convinced that John owes his life to messages of encouragement which the boy received Wednesday from Babe Ruth and other world series players. They had learned of his plight and of his request for autographed baseballs from his father.

The physicians say that the boy's return to health began when he learned the news of Ruth's three homers in the fourth game of the series. His fever began to abate at once, and the favorable course was hastened today after he had listened to the radio returns, clutching the autographed baseballs which he received by air mail on Wednesday night.

John's intense interest in the world series and in home runs especially, were explained to his family today when his chums told of the boy's ability on the sand lots. He had modestly refrained from mentioning the fact that he has a reputation as a home run hitter and a skillful third baseman.

His recovery had reached the point tonight where he was already making plans for a return to the diamond, and he promised one caller that he would soon bring his team to a neighboring town for a game.

The boy's father sent letters to the managers of both teams today thanking them for their assistance in helping his boy to recover.

1932

Chicago Isn't Like New York

MARSHALL SMELSER

The fans ride Tiny pretty hard all over the circuit and they may shout things at him that will make you feel uncomfortable. Chicago isn't like New York. They're not cosmopolitan like us. They haven't got any manners.
—*Heywood Broun,* The Sun Field

THE WORLD SERIES OF 1932 was more of a grudge fight than most. The Cubs had let Joe McCarthy go; now he was coming back to attack them as manager of the American League champions. The Yankees didn't fear the Cubs. When Ruth, with the help of his panel of literary shades (whose advice he didn't always follow), picked his 1932 all-star team for the Christy Walsh syndicate, he included only one Cub, pitcher Lon Warneke.* But he had three Yankees—Dickey, Lazzeri, and Gomez.

Before every World Series each team votes on the division of the expected loot. In 1932 the Yankees were generous. They voted three-quarter shares each to their trainer and their traveling secretary, half a share to Charlie Devens, a rookie who came late in

*Lonnie Warneke (1909–   ), pitcher, fifteen seasons, 1930–1945, Cubs, Cardinals. Won 193, lost 121, earned-run average 3.18.

June after school let out at Harvard and pitched only nine innings that year, and half-shares each to a man who left for the Reds in June and to another who quit baseball.

The Cubs surprised everybody by their stinginess. The front office had fired manager Hornsby in August. The Cubs voted him nothing, on the ground that he got the whole of his forty-thousand-dollar salary. They voted their traveling secretary and trainer half-shares each, and quarter-shares to some late arrivals. What particularly drew the eyes of the Yankees and the world was that Mark Koenig, the former Yankee, joined the Cubs in August, played the last thirty-one games at shortstop, batted .353, won praises from manager Charlie Grimm* for having made the pennant possible, and was awarded half a share. To the Yankee bench jockeys this was a red flag. Koenig told the author the Cubs could have voted him a full share at a cost of about fifty dollars apiece.

Newspaper speculation on the likely winner of the Series went through the usual exercises of weighing the season's earned-run averages and batting averages, but John Kieran spoke for the *volk* when he wrote, ". . . The Babe has managed to work his way into a record number of World's Series. There must have been some connection between the presence of G. Herman Ruth on a team and the presence of that team in a World's Series." The book-makers made the Yankees favorites at 9 to 5.

The first game was played in the Stadium on Wednesday, September 28. Even before the game Ruth took off the new man, Xaverian Brother George, and put on the old, the Baltimore waterfront slob. For the rest of the Series he had a coarse and glorious time. There was more vituperation, invective, and abuse in this Series than in most, and Ruth was the prime mover. Usually he was a dugout-taunter only in self-defense or when trying out

---

*Charles John Grimm (1898–), first basemen, twenty seasons, 1916–1936, Athletics, Cardinals, Pirates, Cubs, batting average .290.

his heavy boyish humor, but this time he stung the foe. To get to their own dugout the Cubs had to go through the Yankee dugout. Ruth greeted Koenig with, "Hi ya, Mark, who are those cheap-skate nickel-nursing sonsabitches you're with?" (or words much like that). Other Yankees joined their cantor and didn't let up on the Cubs until the Series ended. Bell-like shouts of "nickel-squeezers," "penny-pinchers," and "tightwads" stirred the Cubs to scoff at Ruth's ambition to be a manager, to question "grand-pop's" legs and his ability to touch his toes, and to twist his origin from rebel-against-compulsory-schooling to bastard foundling. The tone of the New York contests was faithfully reported in Chicago before the Yankees arrived for the third game. Chicago was prepared. Westbrook Pegler, a man very easily vexed, took sides with the Cubs in print, using more elegant language.

As for the game, the Yankees made light work of it. After the Cubs scored twice in the first, Guy Bush* gave the Yankees neither a hit nor a walk for three innings, but the Yankees got three runs in the fourth and five runs in the fifth. They ended with a 12–6 win for Red Ruffing, though making only eight hits. The too care-ful Cub pitchers walked twelve batters.

In the second game the Cubs again started with a lead (a run in the first), but the Yankees immediately scored two, and the Cubs didn't get the lead again. Gomez won it 5–2, beating Warneke.

> **They were too careful. The way to pitch to the Yankees is not to be over-awed by their reputations but to throw caution to the winds.**
>
> *—Charlie Root's** ghost writer,*
> Chicago American, *September 30, 1932*

*Guy Terrill Bush (1901–), pitcher, seventeen seasons, 1923–1945, Cubs, Pirates, Braves, Cardinals, Reds. Won 176, lost 136, earned-run average 3.86.

**Charles Henry Root (1899–1970), pitcher, seventeen seasons, 1923–1941, Cardinals, Cubs. Won 201, lost 160, earned-run average 3.58.

The Yankees had an acid reception in Chicago. By introducing Ladies' Days that summer the Cubs had created a new breed of fans. When Claire and Babe reached the Edgewater Beach Hotel there was a narrow lane to the door, lined with "hysterical, angry" ladies who were fluent in strong language and had every intention of spitting on Babe and Claire, especially Claire.

On the day of the game, October 1, there was a strong wind blowing toward the outfield. Gomez came into the hotel and reported, "It's blowing sixty miles an hour. . . . Babe and Lou ought to hit a dozen." In batting practice Babe hit nine into the bleachers and Lou seven. When Ruth went out to left field to catch flies, customers threw an occasional lemon at him. He cheerfully tossed it back each time.

By game time the crowd, which included Franklin D. Roosevelt, neared fifty thousand. When Ruth came to bat in the first inning with two runners on base, more lemons. But he put the Yankees three runs ahead with a home run, his fourteenth World Series home run. When he went out to left field in the bottom of the first the bleacher people booed and waved him away. Ruth theatrically flung his arm out to point to the place where the home-run ball landed. When he came to bat in the second inning he was accompanied by rolling lemons. He flied-out to the satisfaction of the customers.

Babe Silences Jeering Cubs
—The Times, *October 2, 1932*

Ruth's next turn at bat came in the fifth inning with the bases empty and the score tied 4–4. Both starters, Pennock and Root, were still in the game. Sewell had just grounded out.

A single lemon rolled to the plate as Ruth stepped into the batter's box from the first-base side. In reply he looked around and then waved his right hand toward the outfielders. As the crowd booed, he took his place at the plate, pointed his shoulder at Root, Joe Jackson style, cocked his bat, and waited.

The first pitch was a called strike. Ruth held up a finger. Only the umpire and Gabby Hartnett* could hear him murmur the famous axiom, "It only takes one to hit it." The next two pitches were balls. The fourth pitch was a called strike. Ruth extended two fingers on his right hand as he swung his arm straight up. The Cubs were crowded on their dugout steps shouting slanders. Trainer Andy Lotshaw and pitcher Pat Malone** were the loudest. Ruth pointed his bat into the Cub dugout and told the Cubs he was spotting them two strikes. Privately he hoped he might foul a pitch into their dugout. Then he turned to Root and pointed a finger at him: "You still need one more, kid. I'm going to put the next pitch right down your throat!" Ruder words were scattered in this statement but haven't been preserved.

As the crowd booed angrily, Root collected himself and threw a slow curve into the strike zone, high and inside. Pock! Johnny Moore,† the center fielder started back, then stood to watch the ball fall. A home run.

Ruth trotted mincingly and mirthfully around the bases with a happy insult for every infielder. As he rounded second he repeatedly thrust the palms of his hands at the men in the Cub dugout in triumphant mockery, shouting "Squeeze the Eagle Club!" and, to Malone, "Meathead!" Ah, this was even better than life on Baltimore's wharfs and piers. Combs said the Cubs took cover "as if they were being machine-gunned."

When Ruth reached the Yankee dugout Chapman quickly asked him what he had been saying out there in the batter's box. "I called Charlie Root everything in the book," which is close enough for a happy man who was briefly short of breath.

*Charles Leo Hartnett (1900–1972), catcher, twenty seasons, 1922–1941, Cubs, Giants, batting average .297. Hall of Fame.

**Pierce Leigh Malone (1902–1943), pitcher, ten seasons, 1928–1937, Cubs, Yankees. Won 134, lost 92, earned-run average 3.74.

†John Francis Moore (1902–), outfielder, ten seasons, 1928–1945, Cubs, Reds, Phillies, batting average .307.

It was the last of his record-making fifteen World Series home runs.* Over the years the ball was picked up by many people at many points outside the park behind center field. Actually it landed in the center-field bleacher ticket-sales booth at the far corner of the field, 436 feet from home plate. (The park has been remodeled, so the scene is not now the same.)

Hartnett grieved. "We tried every kind of pitch on Ruth in that series. It didn't make any difference." Root later said, "I should have wasted that pitch."

Legend has Ruth predicting a home run when he pointed to young Root. Only one witness, of the many who immediately wrote down what they saw, said Ruth had called the shot. When he first came to the plate he did wave in the direction of the outfield as a way of defying the unfriendly fans who greeted him with a lemon. Any hit, a screaming single, would have made good the gesture. The legend first appeared in print early in 1933. Babe, some weeks later, first told it at Claire's parties during spring training that year. By 1948 Babe believed there was a man on base when he hit it! Several writers who reported the game exhaustively on the day it was played didn't report the near miracle, but years later they were confident believers. Faith, we are taught, is a gift, and those writers should be grateful. The legend is harmless and is even comforting to some who need a Hercules.

The run put the Yankees ahead. Gehrig, lost in the glare of Ruth's sparkle, came up next and on the first pitch hit a forgotten home run which completed the two-run margin of the final score, 7–5.

After the game, in the clubhouse, Ruth explained the physics of the thing: "The wind was with us, that's all. Any time they let us hit it into the air, zowie, the wind did the rest."

With the Yankees leading three games to none, McCarthy decided there wouldn't be a fifth game. With the kind of cocki-

---

*The record is now eighteen, held by Mickey Mantle.

ness Greek tragedy warns against, he passed the word to the traveling secretary who posted a notice that the train would leave for New York after the fourth game.

McCarthy (or Zeus) pulled it off. The Yankees closed down the World Series in four games by winning on October 2 before a sullen crowd of fifty-one thousand which saw the Yankees trail for awhile after the first inning, 1–4, and rebound to win 13–6. Ruth was hit in the right forearm by a pitched ball and probably couldn't have played in a fifth game the next day. When he came into the clubhouse after the game "he cut loose with a piercing yell. . . ." Art Fletcher started the team song, and they all joined in "The Sidewalks of New York." Landis and League President Will Harridge came in to shake hands all around. The team dressed hurriedly because their special train had steam up.

With Claire and McCarthy on board the return to New York was a joyous journey, but not a violent one as in 1928. A crowd jammed Grand Central Station, but Claire and Babe had left the train earlier at Hyde Bridge. Xaverian Brother George was in charge again.

It was the tamest series since 1927, and even less entertaining.
—Spalding Baseball Guide, *1933*

The Yankees handled the Cubs so roughly that reviews of the series as a work of art were cool. The Cub pitchers were afraid of the Yankee batters. They pitched so timidly they walked twenty-three men. It was a landscape with too many figures, and a few hits would bring in runs in bunches like grapes. The Yankees made eight errors, which dimmed *their* brilliance. The accumulated score of the thirty-six innings reads:

	R	H	E
New York	37	45	8
Chicago	19	37	6

We may say it was a mismatch. The erratic Cubs couldn't stand up to a steady team which had been in first place since the middle of May. What the Yankees could be proudest of was winning twelve straight World Series games (1927, 1928, 1932).

Joe McCarthy had the inner glow any man would feel who left off managing the Cubs, because, as Cub owner William Wrigley, Jr., put it, "I want a man who can bring me a world's championship."

The only stirring aspect of the Series as a whole was the size and fury of the crowds in Chicago. There were thousands of empty seats in New York; there was standing room only in Chicago. Attendance at the four games was slightly more than attendance at the five-game series of 1929, in which the Cubs lost to the Athletics. But the games at Yankee Stadium in 1932 drew even fewer than the first two games of the 1931 Series, which were played in the small St. Louis park. The Depression was getting tougher. As an editorial writer said of the New York attendance, "Even that is a better showing than our steel production figures or our car-loadings."

Ruth is now remembered as the hero of the 1932 Series. The part played by poor bland Gehrig, who did most to win it, is forgotten. To put Ruth's share in proportion we need some more baseball numerals:

	RUTH	GEHRIG
at bat	15	17
hits	5	9
home runs	2	3
runs	6	9
runs batted in	6	8
average	.333	.529

Gehrig, like Uriah, was in the van of the battle.

This was Ruth's last series. In forty-one World Series games he had collected a barely believable set of World Series records, as they stood in 1932, leading all men in World Series home runs, total bases, extra bases, bases on balls, runs, strikeouts, runs batted in, most times batted .300 or more, and many more single-Series and single-Series-game records. The records aren't the man, any more than the collar size is the man, but they help to take his measure.

As mentioned before, Westbrook Pegler, a good builder of sentences who later graduated from writing knowledgeably about boxing to writing ignorantly of public affairs, joined the lemon-tossers and booers of Chicago. A malicious example: "One of their outfielders is a fat, elderly party who must wear corsets to avoid immodest jiggling, and cannot waddle for fly balls, nor stoop for grounders." Anyone who knows about athletic equipment can tell from photographs taken in 1931 and 1932 that Ruth wore an athletic supporter with a wide waistband, say six inches. Such a support can be had in any sporting-goods store. When Ruth wore it, it pushed his late-summer paunch up a bit. And a well-etched picture like Pegler's doesn't fade. The Pulitzer Prize–winning historian William E. Leuchtenburg picked it up and imprisoned it in the amber of his book *The Perils of Prosperity, 1914–1932,* describing Ruth as "a pathetic waddling figure, tightly corseted, a cruel lampoon of his former greatness. . . ." (We might add that Ruth also wore an elastic bandage on one thigh during the 1932 Series.) Ruth in 1932 had what a Wilkie Collins character called "an autumnal exuberance of figure."

He was also on base that season, by hits and walks (not counting errors), 286 times in 587 trips to the plate, or 48.7 percent—still impressive at bat. Of the twenty-four regular American League outfielders, however, only three made fewer putouts and only eight made more errors. The mighty Ruth had fallen to the rank of a journeyman major-league outfielder.

A good deal of what has been written about Ruth—like the

called-shot home run in the 1932 World Series—is something like creative art. The artists have a purpose other than to inform. Most often they wish to entertain, sometimes to shock. To try to learn about Ruth from such sources is possible, but it is something like trying to learn the public morals of a foreign nation by visiting its graveyards, temples, and civic monuments. It is a hard way to get the inside story.

Babe Ruth was no longer the greatest. Lou Gehrig surpassed him. It was an open question whether Ruth would ever again be so honored in his generation, such a glory of his time.

1934

St. Louis Cardinals 11, Detroit Tigers 0

JOHN DREBINGER

AMID THE MOST RIOTOUS SCENES in the history of modern World Series play, Frankie Frisch's ripsnorting band of Cardinals today brought an amazing and crushing finish to the seven-game struggle for the world's baseball championship.

The intervention of Commissioner K. M. Landis was made necessary before the Cardinals, who already had achieved unprecedented deeds this year by coming from nowhere to gain a pennant in the final leap to the tape, won the crown.

With their inimitable Dizzy Dean back on the firing line once more to give a final display of his matchless pitching skill, the National League champions fairly annihilated the Tigers, led by their wounded but doughty Mickey Cochrane. The score of the seventh and deciding game was 11 to 0.

Figuratively and literally this most astonishing ball club of modern times tore the game apart. In a whirlwind sweep they blasted seven runs across the plate in the third inning, the first three riding home on a two-bagger by the indomitable Frisch himself. They routed Elden Auker, Schoolboy Rowe, only a short time ago the pride of all Detroit, and two other pitchers.

For a finish, one of their cast, Jersey Joe Medwick, touched off the spark that sent part of the crowd into a raging demonstration that interrupted the game for twenty minutes and for a time threatened to end the battle without further play. Commissioner Landis then took a hand and quelled the disturbance by ordering the Cardinal outfielder from the field.

The uproar had its inception during the upper half of the sixth inning. Medwick bounced a triple off the right-field bleachers and finished his dash around the bases with a slide into third while the disconsolate gathering looked sullenly on.

Just what provoked Medwick could not be seen as he crashed into the bag in a cloud of dust, with Marvin Owen, the Tiger third baseman, standing over him. Suddenly the St. Louis player was seen to lift his left foot and strike out with his spikes toward Owen's chest.

Medwick missed his mark, but the flare-up was sufficient to arouse the hostile feeling between the rival teams that had been brewing for several days, and players of both sides rushed to the spot. However, the four umpires quickly stepped in between the irate players. When Bill Klem, dean of the National League staff and the arbiter at that base, decided to take no action, the uproar subsided.

It looked like the end of the disturbance, but it proved to be only the beginning.

With the end of the Cardinal inning, Medwick started out for left field and was greeted by rounds of boos from the 17,000 fans packed solidly in the huge wooden bleachers. Pop bottles, oranges, apples and anything else that came ready to hand were hurled out on the field and the Cardinal player beat a retreat toward the infield while the umpires called time.

Attendants rushed out to clear away the debris and Medwick returned to his post. The din now increased twofold, more bottles and fruit were showered on the field, and once more the umpire had to call time. Four times the performance was repeated and each time the anger of the fans increased in its intensity. In vain an announcer implored the fans to desist and allow the game to continue. These Detroit fans were boiling mad and doubtless would have continued the demonstration until the end of time.

Finally, after another deluge of refuse on the playing field, Commissioner Landis rose in his box and waved the umpires to come to him. He ordered Umpire Klem, the two players, Owen and Medwick, and the rival managers, Frisch and Cochrane, to stand before him, and there, out in full view, he held an open court.

The hearing lasted not more than a minute and the upshot of it was that Landis ordered Medwick to remove himself quickly and quietly from the field. The fiery Frisch attempted to protest, but Landis, with an angry gesture, motioned the St. Louis leader to get out on the field and resume play without further delay. Chick Fullis, utility outfielder, took Medwick's place in left and the crowd, very much appeased, actually cheered this unassuming St. Louis player as he came trotting out.

Later Commissioner Landis, in explaining his action, stated he primarily ordered Medwick off the field as the only means of continuing the game in the face of the crowd's hostile demonstration.

"Before the series," said baseball's czar, "the umpires are instructed not to put any player off the field unless the provocation is very extreme. I saw as well as everybody what Medwick did, but when Umpire Klem took no action and the players quieted down I hoped the matter was ended. But when it became apparent that the demonstration of the crowd would never terminate I decided to take action.

"I asked Owen whether he knew of any reason why Medwick should have made such an attack on him. He said he did not, and with that I ordered Medwick off the field. I do not intend to take any further action."

The uproar, of course, quite overshadowed all else that happened on the field, even taking the play away from the marvelous Dizzy Dean, who was out to revenge himself for the beating he had taken in the fifth game in St. Louis last Sunday. Although he had only one day of rest, the elder Dean was in marvelous form as he shut out the Tigers on six hits, to round out the fourth and final victory of the celebrated Dean family. Paul, his twenty-year-old brother, had won the third and sixth game of the series. He himself had won the first game.

Now Dizzy was back to display his complete mastery with the only shutout of the entire series. With his brother he had pitched the Cardinals into a pennant when the entire nation deemed the feat impossible. Together the pair had brought to St. Louis its third world championship since 1926.

The paid attendance was 40,902 and the receipts were $138,063, bringing the total for the seven games up to $1,031,341. The total attendance was 281,510.

Against the sort of pitching the older and greater Dean turned on, the Tigers simply had nothing to offer. They strove valiantly, however, to rally around their leader, the stout-hearted Cochrane. Despite the fact that he had spent the night in a hospital nursing a spike wound in his left leg received yesterday, Mickey insisted on playing behind the bat.

When in that torrid third inning the Tiger pitchers crumbled before the fury of the aroused St. Louis host the entire bottom fell out of the game. In all, Cochrane tossed six hurlers into the fray.

All the Detroit pitchers who had appeared previously in the series passed in review. But there was no restraining this remarkable St. Louis team. Shortly after Labor Day these same Cardinals had trailed the New York Giants by eight games in the National League pennant race, only to rout last year's world champions out of the picture on the final two days.

The crowd was still coming through the gates as the rival forces squared off. Auker, after pitching three straight balls to Martin, fanned the overanxious Pepper. Jack Rothrock rammed a double in deep left center, but Auker retired Frisch on a pop fly to Rogell and Medwick on a foul to Owen.

In the second the Cards clipped Auker for two more hits but wound up the inning without a run or a man left on base. After

Collins singled, De Lancey grounded into a double play, snappily executed by Owen, Gehringer and Greenberg. Orsatti, after sending a hit into right, was thrown out on an attempted steal.

The Tigers themselves were able to make no headway whatsoever against Dean in those first two innings, only one of their cast reaching first base. He got on only because Collins dropped a low throw by Durocher after Leo had made quite a dashing pickup of Rogell's awkward bounder in the infield.

Then the first explosion came. It came without warning after Durocher opened the third inning by lifting a high fly to White in center. Still nothing threatened as Dizzy strode to the plate.

Dean hit a high foul behind the plate and right there, had the usually alert Cochrane been himself, a lot of subsequent disaster might have been avoided. The ball dropped just inside the front row of boxes. Cochrane, had he made a try for it, doubtless could have easily caught it.

The next moment the singular Dean person shot a double to left. Martin outsprinted an infield hit to Greenberg, Dean going to third. A moment later Martin stole second. Then the charge was on.

Auker passed Rothrock, filling the bases, and Frisch came up. He ran the count to two and two. Then he hammered a double down the right-field foul line, and all the three Cardinals on the bases crossed the plate.

Frisch's blow finished Auker, and Rowe was called to the mound but didn't stay there long. Schoolboy pitched to three batters and his day's work was done. He got Medwick on a grounder, but then Collins' sharp single to left chased Frisch across the plate. De Lancey connected for a long two-bagger to right, Collins was in with the fifth run, and Rowe was out.

Elon Hogsett was Cochrane's next selection and the left-hander, too, had a short stay in the box. Orsatti, the first man to face him, walked. Durocher, making his second appearance at the plate during the inning, singled to right and again the bases were filled. Dean scratched a hit along the third-base line and De Lancey came in, leaving the bags still filled.

Martin drew a walk on four straight balls, forcing Orsatti over the plate for the seventh St. Louis run. Now Tommy Bridges, victor over Dizzy Dean in last Sunday's game, relieved Hogsett and managed to bring the inning to a close, Rothrock grounding to Gehringer to force Martin at second for the third out.

Bridges stopped the scoring until the sixth. Martin opened that frame with a drive to left and raced to second when Goslin handled the ball poorly. Pepper was held at second while Goslin gathered in Rothrock's fly. Frisch then flied to center, bringing Medwick up, and Jersey Joe walloped the triple which brought on his entanglement with Owen after he slid into the base, Martin scoring. Collins lashed a single to center, where White fumbled the ball. Medwick came home with the second run of the inning and the ninth of the battle.

There followed the twenty-minute uproar that preceded Medwick's final retirement from the game under orders from Landis. Dizzy Dean, wearing a bright Cardinal windbreaker, stood around the infield while the demonstration was going on in full blast, utterly unmindful of what was happening. When play was finally resumed for the last of the sixth the wonder pitcher of the day returned to his task of mowing down the Tigers.

Whenever the Tigers threatened, Dizzy merely turned on the heat and poured his blazing fast ball and sharp-breaking curve right down the middle. One could scarcely imagine that this man in the final week of the National League pennant race had pitched his team to victory in three successive starts, that he was making his third appearance in the series and with only forty-eight hours intervening since his last game.

It was superhuman. Three days before he had entered a game as a pinch runner and had received a belt on the head with a thrown ball that might have slain most any other man. But nothing perturbs Dizzy, except when he is in a fit of anger. Then he may tear up uniforms and do all sorts of things. But nothing disturbed his equanimity today. He smiled and joked through it all.

In the seventh the Cards scored two more. Leo Durocher tripled. Gehringer fumbled Martin's grounder and Leo counted. Martin stole his second base of the day. Then came a long double to left center by Rothrock and the Wild Horse of the Osage thundered over the plate.

Fred Marberry pitched the eighth and fell for a hit, but escaped without a score against him. Alvin Crowder, who had started that ill-fated first game when the Tiger infield exploded five errors all around him, pitched the ninth and retired three Cards in a row.

The Tigers had only two scoring chances in the entire battle. They had runners on second and third with only one out in the fifth. They also had runners on first and second with one out in the ninth. Whereupon Dizzy fanned Greenberg for the third time, turning around even before the third strike reached the plate, and Owen ended the battle with a grounder to Durocher.

And so Detroit, faithful to its Tigers to the last, is still seeking its first world championship. It won three pennants in a row in the days of Ty Cobb and the immortal Hughie Jennings from 1907 to 1909, but lost all three World Series clashes. It waited twenty-five years for another chance. But an amazing ball club, with two of the most remarkable pitchers baseball ever has seen grow up in one family, blocked the path.

Less than a month ago these Cardinals did not appear to have one chance in a thousand of reaching their present goal. But they edged Bill Terry and his Giants right off the baseball map and today they crushed the Tigers.

1941

WINNING BY
STRIKING OUT

RED SMITH

BROOKLYN, 1941

IT COULD HAPPEN ONLY IN BROOKLYN. Nowhere else in
this broad, untidy universe, not in Bedlam nor in Babel nor in the
remotest psychopathic ward nor the sleaziest padded cell could
The Thing be.

Only in the ancestral home of the Dodgers which knew the
goofy glories of Babe Herman could a man win a World Series
game by striking out.

Only on the banks of the chuckling Gowanus, where the dizzy-
days of Uncle Wilbert Robinson still are fresh and dear in memory, could a team fling away its chance for the championship of
the world by making four outs in the last inning.

It shouldn't happen to a MacPhail!

As Robert W. Service certainly did not say it:

> *Oh, them Brooklyn Wights have seen strange sights.*
> *But the strangest they ever did see,*
> *Today was revealed in Ebbets Field*
> *When Owen fumbled strike three!*

Among all the Yankee fans in the gathering of 33,813 who
watched the fourth game of the World Series, only one was smil-

119

ing when Tommy Henrich faced Hugh Casey in the ninth inning with two out, nobody on base, the Dodgers in front by one run, and a count of three balls and two strikes on the hitter.

That one gay New Yorker was Jim Farley, whose pink bald head gleamed in a box behind the Dodger dugout. He sat there just laughing and laughing—because he hadn't bought the Yankees, after all.

Then The Thing happened.

Henrich swung at a waist-high pitch over the inside corner. He missed. So did Catcher Mickey Owen. Henrich ran to first. Owen ran after the ball but stopped at the grandstand screen.

That was Mickey's biggest mistake. He should have kept right on running all the way back home to Springfield, Missouri.

That way he wouldn't have been around to see and suffer when Joe DiMaggio singled, Charley Keller doubled, Bill Dickey walked, Joe Gordon doubled, and the Dodgers went down in horrendous defeat, 7 to 4.

Out of the rooftop press box in that awful instant came one long, agonized groan. It was the death cry of hundreds of thousands of unwritten words, the expiring moan of countless stories which were to have been composed in tribute to Casey.

For just as Owen has taken his place among the Merkles and Snodgrasses and Zimmermans and all the other famous goats of baseball, so now Casey belongs with the immortal suckers of all time.

The all-American fall guy of this series—round, earnest Casey—was only one pitch short of complete redemption for his sins of yesterday.

Remember that it was he whom the Yankees battered for the winning hits in the third game of the series. It was he whom Larry MacPhail castigated for failing, in MacPhail's judgment, to warm up properly before relieving Fred Fitzsimmons yesterday.

Now he was making all his critics eat their words. He was making a holy show of the experts who snorted last night that he was a chump and a fathead to dream that he could throw his fast stuff past the Yankees.

He was throwing it past them, one pitch after another, making a hollow mockery of the vaunted Yankee power as each superb inning telescoped into the one before.

No one ever stepped more cheerfully onto a hotter spot than did Casey when he walked in to relieve Johnny Allen in the fifth inning.

The Yankees were leading, 3 to 2, had the bases filled with two out, and the hitting star of the series, Joe Gordon, was at bat.

Casey made Gordon fly to Jim Wasdell for the final putout, and from there on he fought down the Yankees at every turn.

He made Red Rolfe pop up after Johnny Sturm singled with two out in the sixth. He breezed through the seventh despite a disheartening break when DiMaggio got a single on a puny ground ball that the Dodgers swore was foul.

Leo Durocher said enough short, indelicate words to Umpire Lary Goetz on that decision to unnerve completely anyone within earshot. But Casey, determined to hear no evil and pitch no evil, shut his ears and shut out the Yanks.

In the clutch, the great Keller popped up. The ever-dangerous Dickey could get nothing better than a puerile tap to the mound.

So it went, and as Casey drew ever closer to victory the curious creatures that are indigenous to Flatbush came crawling out of the woodwork. They did weird little dances in the aisles and shouted and stamped and rattled cowbells aloft and quacked derisively on little reedy horns.

Their mouths were open, their breath was indrawn for the last, exultant yell—and then The Thing happened.

Far into this night of horror, historians pored over the records, coming up at last with a World Series precedent for "The Thing."

It happened in the first game of the 1907 series between the Cubs and Detroit, when the Tigers went into the ninth inning leading, 3 to 1. With two out and two strikes against pinch-hitter Del Howard, Detroit's Wild Bill Donovan called catcher Charley Schmidt to the mound for a conference.

"Hold your glove over the corner," Donovan said, "and I'll curve a strike into it."

He did, but Schmidt dropped the strike, Howard reached base, and the Cubs went on to tie the score. The game ended in darkness, still tied after twelve innings, and the Cubs took the next four contests in a row.

That's about all, except that it should be said the experts certainly knew their onions when they raved about the Yankee power. It was the most powerful strikeout of all time.

1942

From *Catching Dreams*

FRAZIER "SLOW" ROBINSON WITH PAUL BAUER

S INCE THE MONARCHS WERE THE Negro American League champions in 1942, we got to play the Homestead Grays, who had dominated the Negro National League, in the Negro World Series. Joe Greene's hand had gotten better, and since he had been with the club all season and was the first-string catcher, he came back to do the catching for us in the Series. We had that great infield of Souell, Williams, Serrell, and O'Neil. And our pitching staff was the best in baseball and one of the best ever with Satchel, Hilton Smith, Connie Johnson, Jack Matchett, Booker McDaniels, and Lefty LaMarque. The Grays, on the other hand, were one of the greatest hitting teams of all time and had beaten up just about everybody that season. They were a solid team built around the power of Buck Leonard at first and Josh Gibson behind the plate.

Buck Leonard had learned baseball from a couple of the masters—Ben and Candy Jim Taylor—who had played with the great Indianapolis ABCs teams of the teens. He was the best fastball hitter in the league. Buck Leonard was. He would take the ball out of the park. And you couldn't throw him a curveball too fast because if you did, he'd get wood on it. You had to go to school on him. You had to slow the ball up on him, or he'd kill you. He could hit any fastball pitches you threw, but if you just walked it up there, changed up on it, you could get him out. He'd slap it up or something like that. But you couldn't let him know when that change-up was coming so you had to throw him fastballs too and that's where you could go wrong. If you were lucky, he'd pull it foul. Otherwise, he'd just pull it over the fence. But if you could walk it up there without him looking for it, you could get him out. Easier said than done. Buck was always a quiet man. He'd talk with you if you talked to him. Cool Papa Bell was the same way. You'd talk with them and know right away that they were churchmen.

What you couldn't do to Buck Leonard was pitch around him because after Buck you'd get Josh, and the greatest hitter I ever saw was Josh Gibson. Josh was powerful to look at it with big arms. If you threw anything across that plate, he could reach it. And when he hit the ball, it would go. They taped a lot of his home runs. He didn't have a weakness. You might throw him a pitch, and he'd swing at it and miss and look bad on it. But you'd throw it again, and he'd hit it out of the ballpark. The only way you could get him out was to watch the way he moved at the plate. You'd see whether he crouched or stood straight up; then you could try to keep him from getting the big end of the bat on the ball. Sure as he gets the big end of the bat on it, it's going out of the park. Now if he leaned over too far, you could pitch high and tight on him. Most times that's a brushback pitch. Move him off the plate. But he didn't care where you pitched him. If he's crouched or leanin' over the plate like, you try to pitch him up. By the time he straightens up, he can't get all that bat on the ball. And if he kind of stands straight up, you can break the ball down and away. Let him go down and away. That was about all you could do with Josh was to pitch to spots—inside, outside, high, and low—and hope the umpire was in a generous mood. Just keep him guessing and hope you can make a strike out of that pitch. That's the only way you could try to get Josh out.

Since Josh and Buck Leonard were both power hitters and both played for the Grays, and since you could get Buck Leonard out with off-speed pitches, some pitchers figured they could get Josh the same way. It didn't work because Josh was strong enough to just manhandle the ball, whether you let up off it or not. Didn't matter to Josh. And he didn't take no vicious cut either. A lot of times he'd just stand back in the box, wait until that ball was almost in the catcher's mitt and had done whatever it was going to do, and then he'd hit that ball nine miles. He had such quick wrists that he could just wait on the ball. That's why Josh, I believe, had a chance to hit all those home runs. He could wait. A whole lot of times you'd have to tell the umpire to draw a line back there for Josh's rear foot. Otherwise he'd back it right up in your lap. He could wait and he'd break his wrists. That was the secret to Josh's success.

The only other guys I saw that had wrists like that were Marvin Williams of the Philadelphia Stars, Ernie Banks who would play for the Cubs, and a guy I would eventually play with named Lester Lockett.

Marvin, Ernie, and Lester all had quick wrists, but Josh was more powerful. Of course, there is one other guy whose quick wrists were legendary. Fellow named Hank Aaron. And just about everybody can remember what he did to baseballs. If you want to picture Josh, don't think of Ruth, Mantle, or McCovey. They had longer swings. Think of Hank Aaron, short and sweet.

Josh used a 40-ounce bat, and he had different models. His bat had a big head on it and a solid handle where he could grip it good. I'm quite sure they made a bat for him with his name on it. When you'd see Josh coming to the plate, he'd have four or five bats in his hands, swinging them to get loose. It was a sight you'd never forget.

Josh could run for his size, but he wasn't much of a threat to steal. But then Josh hit very few singles. When he hit the ball, it was either up against the fence for a double or out of the ballpark. He didn't hit too many singles. He did get a lot of intentional walks—*a lot* of them. He'd hit 55 home runs and be walked 75 or 80 times. They'd walk him because they knew this was one way to keep him from hurting your ballclub. And when Josh did hit one out of the park, the fans would go wild. That's what they come to see was those home runs.

Norman told me about one day in Baltimore when he was playing third base and they went to pitching Josh low so he couldn't get the ball up to get it out of the ballpark. That was fine except that he started hitting line drives and ground balls so hard that it made a couple of the infielders sick! It made them sick! Remember that those infields weren't very good, so you could expect a ground ball to take a bad hop and with Josh that could cost you your front teeth. Norman told me that these guys got in front of the ball and it shook them up some kind of way. Pee Wee Buck was playing shortstop, and Roy Campanella was catching. The second baseman was a utility man. Norman said he caught a ball off of Josh that he *had* to catch. If he doesn't catch it, it's going to hit him. He said it kind of shook him up. Any time Josh hit the ball on the ground, it was on you so fast. Of course I found out later that Norman had ulcers. I don't know whether Josh gave him ulcers, but he could certainly upset your stomach. Josh was hitting the ball so hard that it made Norman and Pee Wee sick in the stomach. I don't think they were afraid of getting hit by the ball as much as it was what you'd call a nervous stomach. At least that's what they told me.

I think Josh could have had a whole lot of infielders drinking milk if he'd have been a groundball hitter. But he very seldom hit balls on the ground, and I played against him quite often—sometimes two and three times a week. Most balls he hit were in the air. He hit the ball so hard that if he hit it on the ground and you weren't standing right in front of the ball, you couldn't knock it down noways. It was just like when Ted Williams hit the ball. If he hit it on the ground towards you and you didn't get down real fast, you ain't gonna touch it. He was just that strong.

Josh and Buck weren't the only Grays who could hurt you. They had another boy called Howard Easterling and he could hit something like Buck. Easterling was a great, great ballplayer. He was a good defensive third baseman and he could really hit. Easterling was one you didn't want up late in a close game. He had a little drinking problem and that's what finally ruined him. Easterling was a line drive hitter, and he could hit so hard it'd look like it'd bend when it left the bat. Where Josh would hit it over the fence, Easterling and Buck Leonard looked like they wanted to hit it *through* the fence.

Sam Bankhead, who played outfield and shortstop, was another one of the Grays that could hit. He was one of three brothers that played. Sam was one that you would underestimate. Guys would say, "He ain't gonna hit nothing too much." But you'd look up and he'd mess your ballgame up. You'd underestimate what he could do. You make a mistake on him and Sam could cost you a ballgame.

The Grays also had Vic Harris in left. Jerry Benjamin, who had been with the Grays for a long time, was in center. Lick Carlisle was playing second base. Pitching, they had Raymond Brown with his great curveball and the two Roys—Welmaker and Partlow. Both lefties. Both with excellent control. They also had a fine right-hander by the name of Wilmer Fields. Fields was such a fine athlete that when he wasn't pitching, you'd find him in the field.

So this was what we were up against when we opened the 1942 Series against the Grays at old Griffith Stadium in Washington. We were confident but knew that things could quickly blow up in our faces if we weren't careful. It was a Tuesday evening in September. The night before the Boston Red Sox had played the Senators before a crowd of about 12,000. Despite cold weather and a light mist falling, our game doubled that number and filled the stands with several thousand more standing in the aisles. They had to turn away people because they didn't have seats or standing room for them. That packed house in bad weather shows that people would turn out for good baseball no matter what color the players were. Even though we couldn't play the major league players on the field, we could compete at the box office. It goes to show you that our teams were drawing, and our owners were making money.

When we arrived at the park that evening, the Red Sox and Senators had just finished their day game. As we went past the Grays' part of the clubhouse to get to our dressing area, Cool Papa Bell was wrapping his legs up. Cool hadn't been with the Grays very long. He always seemed to have a contract that let him move as he pleased, and it seemed like he was always popping up where a catcher least wanted to see him—in the other team's locker room taping his legs up. This was in his later years—he must have been about 39—and he'd tape both legs. He'd want you to think that he was slowing down. And if you asked him how he was feeling, he'd say, "Feel pretty bad tonight." And then he'd steal you regular as soon as he got out there. He wasn't fooling nobody by telling you that he was hurting. He could run and you'd better be careful.

Josh's locker was next to Cool's, and Josh was sitting there pulling at his pants when Satchel walked up, dropped his bag in front of Josh, and said, "Well Josh, the time has come. I told you about this a long time ago. We're on different teams now. You're trying to beat me, and I'm *going* to beat you. Your batting average is going to be .000 when this Series is finished." And Josh just looked at him and smiled. He didn't say nothing. Satchel always tried to use psychology on people.

The Grays were putting their ace lefty, Roy Partlow, up against Satchel. In that first game Josh faced Satch three times. He struck out once and then he hit the ball to the outfield, but he didn't have much bat on it. He just hit it out there kind of soft and they caught it. Just popped it up, that's what he did. They had gone to pitching him in, out, high, and low. If he stood up straight, they'd pitch him low. If he crouched, they'd pitch him high. High and tight, they called it. All of our pitchers had gone to school on him. Satchel had worked with the pitchers and told them how to pitch to him. Josh went 0–3. Satchel went the distance and shut them out 8–0. Willard Brown's home run and Bill Simms's triple off Roy Partlow down the right field line were all we needed. Didn't too many Grays get on that night.

After the game we got our first real clue that we were getting beat out of a lot of money. It turned out that somehow J. L. Wilkinson couldn't take anymore gate money. If he did, he had to turn it over to the government. So in the locker room he said, "You boys, cut this money among the different players." We couldn't believe how much money there was. We knew that we had played to crowds like this before, and we knew that our salaries were low. They just didn't pay that much. So that was when we first started to suspect that we weren't getting our fair share. Nobody complained though. We always said, "Beats pickin' cotton." And that's what we went by.

Game #2 was the following Thursday night at Forbes Field in Pittsburgh. Only a few thousand turned out for this game, but people still talk about it. The legend has it that Satchel was pitching, gave up a single, and then intentionally walked the next two Grays just so he could pitch to Josh with the bases loaded. Then, as the story goes, Satchel slipped a curveball by Josh for a called strike three. It's a great story and Satchel loved to talk about it, but I'm sorry to say it didn't happen—at least not in that Series, and I saw every game from the dugout. Satchel never even appeared in that game. Our starter was Hilton Smith who pitched a complete game, and we won 8–4. Look, if it happened the way the story goes, wouldn't it have made headlines in the Negro papers? No such story was written in September 1942 because no such a thing happened. And besides, Satchel wouldn't pull a stunt like that in a World Series game. But that story gets told all the time because he *was* noted for doing things like that—just not in a big game. *Never* in a big game. I'm not saying that something like that between Satchel and Josh never happened, just that it definitely did not happen in the '42 Series.

We moved to Yankee Stadium for Game #3 on Sunday before a large and noisy crowd that included Joe Louis and his wife Marva and the actor James Edwards. We won again, 9–5, behind Jack Matchett. This game was the first of a doubleheader with an exhibition game following. In the exhibition game we had Lefty McKinnis pitching, and he shut the Grays out. The game didn't count but that didn't stop the Grays' Sam Bankhead from chasing a ball from his shortstop position into the stands and banging up his ribs in the process. The next game in the Series would be back in Kansas City on that following Sunday, and we looked forward to playing in front of our hometown fans. After sending Jack Matchett, our Game #4 starter, on ahead to Kansas City to rest up, we played several games against the Cincinnati Clowns.

Meanwhile, Cum Posey, the Grays owner, was granted permission to replace Bankhead and went shopping for another shortstop. Things would have been fine if he had stopped with the pickup of Bus Clarkson, Newark's shortstop. But Posey's team was down three games to none and the temptation to slip in Lennie Pearson, Ed Stone, and Leon Day with Clarkson proved too much. Or maybe Posey just figured that Clarkson would be lonely without some familiar faces. These guys from Newark weren't just throw-ins. They were some of Newark's best players. Pearson was the Eagles first baseman and had excellent power. Ed Stone was an outfielder who'd make you pay if you tried to take an extra base. And Leon Day was a right-handed pitcher with a fastball that helped him set strikeout records in just about every league he played in. Day was only about 5'7" or something like that, but he was such a great all-around athlete that when he wasn't pitching, you could expect to find him pinch-hitting or playing the field. Leon was simply one of the greatest ever, and in 1942 he was in his prime.

While Cum Posey was wheeling and dealing with Mrs. Manley, the lady who ran the Eagles, we barnstormed our way home—the whole time believing Jack Matchett was resting and waiting in Kansas City. It turned out that instead of Jack staying in condition, he was out there drinking and would have gotten more rest pitching in our barnstorming game with the Clowns. So when the

Series resumed on Sunday, the Grays were surprised to see Satchel Paige warming up. But they weren't as surprised as we were when Leon Day started getting loose for the Grays. Frank Duncan, our manager, who was catching this game was very upset. And while J. L. Wilkinson wasn't happy that we had to face Leon, a good crowd had turned out and he liked the idea of refunds even less. So we played. Satchel was kind of tired and Day beat Satchel 4–2, but Wilkinson's protest about the "Gray Eagles" was upheld and the game was thrown out. So it was on to Chicago to replay Game #4.

It was now October and we ran into sleet and snow in Chicago so we got back in the bus and headed for Philadelphia. Shibe Park was drier but almost as cold. There is a story told about this game and Satchel that I also remember differently. The story is that Satchel was scheduled to pitch the game but was slow in leaving the company of a pretty young lady in Pittsburgh. In his rush to get from one end of Pennsylvania to the other he was stopped for speeding and held up at a Lancaster, Pennsylvania, traffic court while the judge got a haircut. He finally arrived in the fourth inning, so the story goes, just in the nick of time to bail out Matchett who was getting it hard on the mound. It's a popular story because rushing from a girl to the mound with a speeding ticket in between sounds like Satchel, sounds *just* like Satchel. Like the showdown with Josh, it may have happened some time but not in the 1942 Series. And none of our pitchers got hit hard in any game of that Series.

What did happen in that final game at Shibe Park is this. Satchel pitched five innings and Hilton Smith pitched four. The Grays went with Roy Partlow. Josh, who was hitless in the Series, finally got a bloop hit over the shortstop off of Hilton, but it was too little and too late as we beat 'em 9 to 5 to sweep the Series.

Josh never did get a hit off Satchel in that Series, and Satchel's boast to Josh at the opener in Washington that they'd gone to school on him and his batting average would be .000 came very close to the truth. Not to take anything away from Satchel and our other pitchers, but something was wrong with Josh. You could tell by looking at him. He *looked* different. The reason I noticed something was wrong was because Josh was always jolly, laughing, kidding, and full of fun. Always saying, "Come over here man. Come here and tell me something funny." Always mingling with the ballplayers and a happy-go-lucky guy. Whenever I saw him, whether we were getting ready to play or sitting around at the hotel, we'd talk about different things and have a laugh. He made people feel good, and they loved to be around him. He even got along with umpires. But when I saw him in this particular Series, he wouldn't say nothing to nobody. Not even to his teammates. He was quiet and kind of segregated himself. He'd just sit there, quiet like. He would just catch and when his time would come to bat, he'd come to bat. Something changed inside of him. No, he wasn't at hisself in that 1942 Series.

Josh was mixed up in several different things. They said that his wife, in a lawsuit, had taken both of their homes. Then he went down to Mexico and Puerto Rico and played down there, and something drove him to use that reefer. Eventually, he got so bad that we heard he got drugged up while playing winter ball in San Juan, Puerto Rico, took off all his clothes, and it took half of the police force to try to put him up because he was so strong and powerful. They said that they put him in a straightjacket, and he broke out of it. The police said they knew who he was and didn't want to hurt him, but they had a problem trying to take him to where he could get a little help. They said he had been smokin' some kind of dope, but I never heard of marijuana changing you like that.

Following winter baseball he'd been with the Grays all of that 1942 season but something was wrong. He wouldn't have nothing to do with you. He'd just sit. He wouldn't talk much, wouldn't joke around, he'd just lost that spark. I think he knew that we'd heard about his troubles. After he come back to the States, he'd just changed his personality altogether. Josh was jolly all the time, but starting in 1942 he didn't say nothing to nobody and he never was quite the same after playing winter ball south of the border. Never was.

Despite winning that final Series game at Shibe Park, I wasn't in a mood to celebrate. That's because right during the game a girl brought me a letter from the draft board saying I must come or they'd be coming after me. That was the last baseball I saw for a long time.

1945

Tiger Triumph

JIMMY POWERS

CHICAGO, OCTOBER 10—

WELL, KIDDIES, NOW YOU CAN ALL GO and join the nearest rattlesnake cult for rest and relaxation. This madcap 1945 World Series, involving sundry screwball characters who at times did not appear to be major-league players or reasonable facsimiles thereof, came to a halt this sun-kissed afternoon with that priceless collection of athletic antiques from Detroit defeating Chicago's heirlooms, four victories to three.

The deciding contest, a comparatively sane affair, was won for Detroit by Hal Newhouser, a left-handed bowler with the general contour of a mop handle. This skinny stand-in for a Japanese prisoner of war pitched a 9–3 victory, his second of the Series, that was worth exactly $62,000, the difference between the winners' and the losers' pool in the players' jackpot. The Series set a record for total attendance and total receipts.

Hank Borowy, who had previously been credited with two Series victories, was the losing pitcher. He lasted exactly four and a half (nine pitches), and was practically slugged silly before he rose from his stool after the first bell rang.

The Tigers socked Borowy and his relief, Paul Derringer, for five runs on four hits and two bases on balls in the opening chukker. They kept hammering away at a sorry parade of ineffectual flingers comprising Hy Vandenberg, Paul Erickson, Claude

Passeau and Hank Wyse until they had, as the dugout patois goes, the old ball game in the old burlap.

Newhouser was in command all the way and, as in the past six games, the box score again comes close to being a fraud and a deceit. Two of the Cub runs were the results of fly balls that fell as hits. Newhouser coasted smoothly behind his fat five-run lead and bore down only when necessary, wisely pacing himself to go the route. He struck out 10 Cubs and most of those strikeouts hurt.

Newhouser's total of 22 Series strikeouts set a modern record, eclipsing George Mullen, George Earnshaw, Walter Johnson and Chief Bender, all of whom had 20 strikeouts.

His curve ball was hooking so sharply that four of the strikeouts were called by umpire Art Passarella much to the chagrin of the befuddled batters, who stared hypnotized with their sticks reposing on their shoulders.

Webb, Mayo and Cramer singled in succession off Borowy at the start. Cramer's hit was a juicy blooper that scored Webb.

Derringer came in with little or no warmup. Greenberg sacrificed. Cullenbine was purposely walked, filling the bases. York popped to the third sacker. Outlaw walked, forcing in Mayo. With the bases still jammed, catcher Paul Richards rammed a double so hard and so deep into left that it caromed off two brick walls and eluded Peanuts Lowrey, who was stabbing desperately at it like a man trying to snatch a rabbit by the ears. This double scored the three runs that made it 5-love.

Johnson's double and Cavarretta's single gave the Cubs a run in their half of the first, but the Tigers matched it with a run in the second when Cramer singled to right and Greenberg, Cullenbine and York walked in succession. This caused Derringer to go away and Vandenberg to come in, but the damage was done.

The Cubs picked up a run in the fourth when, after Cavarretta singled, Cramer let Pafko's fly fall on the grass by his side for a fluke triple. The teams rolled along with the Tigers leading, 6–2, until the seventh. They touched up Erickson for a run on

Cullenbine's walk and Richards' double, his second of the afternoon. He banked this one against the center field wall to demonstrate his impartiality, no doubt.

Passeau, who had turned in an elegant one-hitter in Detroit, appeared at the start of the eighth as a succession of proxy-hitters were being fanned each time they came to bat for a Chicago pitcher. Passeau walked Webb. Mayo doubled to left, scoring Webb. When Cramer grounded out, Mayo went to third, from which spot he scored on Greenberg's fly to left.

Big Hank had no sooner returned to his position in left field with the score 9–2 than Lowrey sent up a fly that Hank was unable to reach in time and the ball fell in front of him for a gift single. Cavarretta rolled a single through the box, putting Lowrey on third. Lowrey scored on Nicholson's double to center.

That was the last of the Cubs' three runs and the last of the scoring for the day. Newhouser finished strong. Hughes dribbled a single through the box. Pinch-hitter McCullough fanned. Hack flied to center and Johnson forced Hughes.

All the lads came out of the Detroit dugout except Richards, who had retired in the eighth when he split his little finger on Nicholson's foul tip. They unashamedly embraced Newhouser, kissing him, patting his back and wringing his hands as he shuffled off, his black peanut cap perched jauntily on the back of his head and a wide sweat-stained grin baring his white teeth.

The literary artists who labor in the pressbox covering the World Series for their beloved readers from coast to coast are only human, which may or may not be the subject of debate. At any rate, they do have moments when they discard the judicial air they assume while dictating play-by-play to their operators. The operators, of course, are entranced by the activities below and occasionally neglect to "read" copy on the dictation. Frank (Buck) O'Neill, president of the Baseball Writers' Association, was anxious to get an early start from the Cincinnati ball park some years back. The Giants had piled up an early lead and Buck wrote his story leaving only a blank to be filled in with the final score. He assumed the Giants would win easily. The Reds, however, spoiled everything by putting in a ninth-inning rally. Buck was dictating play-by-play to his operator when Edd Roush poked out the game-winning hit. The following line appeared in Buck's paper that night, exactly as Buck's literal-minded operator dispatched: "Edd Roush, the contemptible cad, tripled to left-center, scoring three runs and winning this accursed game."

It was the same park in which a fan reached over the bleacher wall and interfered with a ground ball that, at best, would have been a two-baser. Instead, the hit was ruled an automatic home run. Bill Phelon was dictating the play-by-play and a message came clicking back from his makeup man, a green hand, who wanted Bill to suggest a headline. Bell sent a sarcastic headline, never dreaming it would be used. Imagine his consternation to find the latest edition of his evening paper bearing this flaming message: "Insufferable Ass Loses for Reds!"

There are always a great many sinister characters and camp followers of both sexes hanging around a World Series. Leo Durocher has been the target of much criticism in this regard, and now Happy Chandler and Larry MacPhail are in for the same harpooning. In every instance it is not their fault. Various shady personages, bookies, gamblers, hot shots and angle-guys all have plenty of brass and thrust themselves practically into the laps of headliners seeking an edge or some scrap of inside information so that they can pull off a betting coup. You will see this lunatic fringe in the newsreels or in photographs taken in hotel lobbies and dressing rooms surrounding the winning World Series heroes. It reminds us of a former colleague of ours, George Phair, who saw Jack Dempsey make a grandiose entry into a big hotel shortly after he had defeated Jess Willard. George opened his story with this couplet: "Hail, the conquering hero comes, surrounded by a bunch of bums!"

* * *

There is such tremendous pressure to be first on the street with the result of a ball game that typographical errors inevitably get by. One of the most famous occurred in Cleveland. The Indians were going haywire in mid-season and several of the boys were paying more attention to their girl friends than their base hits. In fact, the wild parties of several of his headline athletes caused the manager to call his bleary charges together in a pre-game meeting in the clubhouse. . . . He gave his lads Hell and ended by saying, "So, I don't want to hear anything more about wimmen interfering with your work." That night on his way home, the manager read the following in the play-by-play: "Three wild pitches spoiled the ninth inning." Only it didn't come out "pitches."

Well, the Series is over and it will be a long time, we hope, before we will see another like it. It will take another World War to do it. The Tigers, officially, are the best baseball team in the continental limits of the United States, but everyone concedes that there are teams in the Pacific comprised of younger and better players who could beat the Tigers easily. It was a silly Series and a historic one. The caliber of play was probably the poorest in history, yet more people paid more money to see it than any other collection of fans since the first World Series was held in 1903.

The games were exciting and sometimes the errors were so startling that players and umpires alike stared open-mouthed in amazement. The Tigers were the better hitters all the way, despite what the composite boxscore may say. Most of their hits were well-tagged hits. The Cubs were very lucky to take it to seven games. Under the circumstances, it would be grossly unfair to term anyone the goat. Manager Steve O'Neill rates a bow for his skillful manipulation of pitchers, but then he is an old big-league catcher and should know how to handle pitchers. The Cubs were full of fight and manager Cholly Grimm instilled them with a spirit that carried them much farther than they might have gone under a perfectionist of another temperament. The fans received their money's worth in thrills and spills, and so much happened that many a gin mill will be filled with violent debates through the coming winter.

1947

Brooklyn Dodgers 3, New York Yankees 2

DICK YOUNG

O UT OF THE MOCKERY AND ridicule of "the worst World Series in history," the greatest baseball game ever played was born yesterday. They'll talk about it forever, those 33,443 fans who saw it. They'll say: "I was there. I saw Bill Bevens come within one out of the only series no-hitter; I saw the winning run purposely put on base by the Yankees; I saw Cookie Lavagetto send that winning run across a moment later with a pinch-hit double off the right-field wall—the only hit, but big enough to give the Brooks the 3–2 victory that put them even-up at two games apiece."

And maybe they'll talk about the mad minute that followed—the most frenzied scene ever erupted in this legendary spot called Ebbets Field: How some of the Faithful hugged each other in the stands; how others ran out to the center of the diamond and buried Lavagetto in their caresses; how Cookie's mates pushed the public off because they themselves wanted the right to swarm all over him; how Cookie, the man who had to plead for his job this spring, finally fought his way down the dugout steps—laughing and crying at the same time in the first stages of joyous hysteria.

Elsewhere in the park, another man was so emotionally shaken he sought solitude. That was Branch Rickey, the supposedly cold, calloused businessman, the man who has seen thousands and thousands of ball games and should therefore be expected to take anything in stride. But Rickey had to be alone. He left his family, sat down in a quiet little room just off the press box, and posted a guard outside the door.

After ten minutes of nerve-soothing ceiling-staring, Rickey was asked if he'd see a writer. He would. Now he was calm and wanted to talk. He wanted to talk about the ninth-inning finish—but he started a little earlier than that.

He flashed back to the top half of the frame, when Hughie Casey had come in with the bases loaded and one out, and got Tommy Henrich to hit a DP ball right back at him on the first serve. "Just one pitch, and he's the winning pitcher of a World Series game," Branch chuckled. "That's wonderful."

Rickey then turned to his favorite subject. "It was speed that won it," he said. This tickled Rickey because it had been the speed of Al Gionfriddo which saved the game. They had laughed at Gionfriddo when he came to the Brooks back in June in that $300,000 deal with the Pirates. They had said: "What did Rickey get that little squirt for; to carry the money in a satchel from Pittsburgh?" And they had added, "He'll be in Montreal in a couple of weeks."

But, here it was World Series time, and "little Gi" was still around. Suddenly he was useful. Furillo was on first with two out. Carl had got there just as eight Brooks before him had—by walking. For a prospective no-hit pitcher, Bevens had been under constant pressure because of control trouble. A couple of these passes had led to the Brooks' run in the fifth, and had cut New York's lead down to 2–1.

That's the way it still was when Gionfriddo went in to run for Furillo, and Pete Reiser was sent up to swing for Casey. Only now Bevens was just one out away from having his bronze image placed among the all-time greats in Cooperstown. Already, at the conclusion of the eighth frame, the chubby Yank righty had pitched the longest string of no-hit ball in series history—topping Red Ruffing's 7⅔ innings against the Cards in '42.

Now Bill was out for the jackpot. He got the first out in the ninth on a gasp provoker, a long drive by Edwards which forced Lindell up against the left wall for the stretching grab. Furillo walked and Jorgensen fouled meekly to McQuinn, who was white as a sheet as he made the catch.

One out to go—and then came the first of several switches that were destined to make a genius of Burt Shotton and an eternal second-guess target of Bucky Harris.

"Reiser batting for Casey," boomed the loudspeaker, "and Gionfriddo running for Furillo."

Soon the count was 2–1 on Pete. Down came the next pitch—and up went a feverish screech. Gionfriddo had broken for second. Berra's peg flew down to second—high, just high enough to enable Gi to slide head first under Rizzuto's descending tag. For the briefest moment, all mouths snapped shut and all eyes stared at umpire Babe Pinelli. Down went the umpire's palms, signaling that the Brooks had stolen base No. 7 on the weak-winged Yankee backstop corps.

The pitch on which Gionfriddo went down had been high, making the count on Reiser 3-and-1. Then came the maneuver that makes Bucky Harris the most second-guessed man in baseball. The Yankee pilot signaled Berra to step out and take an intentional fourth ball from Bevens.

The cardinal principle of baseball had been disdained by Harris. The "winning run" had been put on—and Miksis replaced the sore-ankled Reiser on first.

It was possible for Reiser to hurt more than Stanky in such a situation—and the Brooks had run out of lefty pinch hitters. But a good right-side swinger, a clutch money player like Lavagetto, who batted for Muggsy, didn't get to be a fourteen-year man by being able to hit only one kind of chucking.

On the first pitch, Harris' guess still looked like a good one.

Cookie swung at a fast ball and missed. Then another fast one, slightly high and toward the outside. Again Lavagetto swung. The ball soared toward the right corner—a territory seldom patronized by Cookie.

Because of that, Tommy Henrich had been swung over toward right-center. Frantically, Tommy took off after the drive, racing toward the line. He got there and leaped, but it was a hopeless leap. The ball flew some six feet over his glove and banged against the wooden wall. Gionfriddo was tearing around third and over with the tying run.

The ball caromed under Henrich's legs as Tommy struggled to put the brakes on his dash. On the second grab, Henrich clutched it and, still off balance, hurried a peg to McQuinn at the edge of the infield. The first-sacker whirled desperately and heaved home—but even as he loosed the ball, speedy young Miksis was plowing over the plate with a sitting slide. A big grin on his puss, Eddie, just turned 21 last week, sat right on home plate like an elated kid. He was home with the winning run, and he didn't want to get up. For what seemed like much more than the actual three or four seconds, Miksis just sat there, looked up at his mates gathered around the plate and laughed insanely.

That's when God's Little Green Acre became a bedlam. The clock read 3:51, Brooklyn Standard Time—the most emotional minute in the lives of thousands of Faithful. There was Lavagetto being mobbed—and off to the side, there was Bevens, head bowed low, walking dejectedly through the swarming crowd, and completely ignored by it. Just a few seconds earlier, he was the one everybody was planning to pat on the back. He was the one who would have been carried off the field—the only pitcher ever to toss a no-hitter in a series.

Now he was just another loser. It didn't matter that his one-hitter had matched the other classic performances of two Cub pitchers—Ed Reulbach against the Chisox in '06 and Passeau against Detroit in '45. The third one-hitter in series annals—but Bevens was still nothing more than a loser.

Bev felt bluer than Harry Taylor had at the start of this memorable struggle. In the first five minutes, Taylor had been a momentous failure. Unable to get his sore-elbowed arm to do what his mind demanded of it, the rookie righty had thrown his team into a seemingly hopeless hole before a Yankee had been retired.

Stirnweiss had singled. So had Henrich. And then Reese had dropped Robinson's peg of Berra's bouncer, loading the bases. Then Harry walked DiMaggio on four straight serves, forcing in a run. Still nobody out, still bases full. Taylor was through; he had been a losing gamble. In one inning, the Yanks were about to blow the game wide open and clamp a 3–1 lock on the series.

But, just as has happened so often this year, the shabby Brook pitching staff delivered a clutch performer. This time it was Hal Gregg, who had looked so mediocre in relief against the Yanks two days before. Gregg got McQuinn to pop up and then made Johnson bang a DP ball right at Reese.

Only one run out of all that mess. The Faithful regained hope. This optimism grew as DiMag was cut down at the plate attempting to score from first when Edwards threw McQuinn's dumpy third-frame single into short right. But, in the next stanza, as the Yanks did their only real teeing off on Gregg, the Brook hopes drooped. Johnson poled a tremendous triple to the center-field gate and Lindell followed with a booming two-bagger high off the scoreboard in right.

There was some hope, based on Bevens' own wildness. The Brooks couldn't buy a hit, but they had men aboard in almost every inning, sometimes two. Altogether, Bev was to go on to issue ten passes, just topping the undesirable series record set by Jack Coombs of the A's in the 1910 grapple with the Cubs.

Finally, in the fifth, Bill's wildness cost him a run. He walked Jorgensen and Gregg to open the stanza. Stanky bunted them along, and Jorgy scored while Gregg was being nailed at third on Reese's grounder to Rizzuto. Pee Wee then stole second for his third swipe of the series, and continued on to third as Berra's peg flew into center. But Robinson left him there with a whiff.

Thus, before they had a hit, the Brooks had a run. And right about now, the crowd was starting to grow no-hit conscious. A fine catch by DiMaggio, on which Joe twisted his left ankle slightly, had deprived Hermanski of a long hit in the fourth, and Henrich's leaping stab of another Hermanski clout in front of the scoreboard for the final out in the eighth again saved Bill's blossoming epic.

Then the Yanks threatened to sew up the decision in the ninth. Behrman had taken over the chucking an inning earlier as a result of Gregg's being lifted for a pinch swinger and Hank got into a bases-bulging jam that wasn't exactly his responsibility. Lindell's lead-off hit through the left side was legit enough, but after Rizzuto forced Johnny, Bevens' bunt was heaved tardily to second by Bruce Edwards. Stirnweiss then looped a fist-hit into right center. Hugh Casey was rushed in.

Hugh threw one pitch, his million-dollar serve which had forced DiMag to hit into a key DP the day before. This time the low-and-away curve was jammed into the dirt by Henrich. Casey's glove flew out for a quick stab . . . the throw home . . . the relay to first . . . and Hughie was set up to become the first pitcher credited with World Series victories on successive days.

Tough luck cost Hughie two series defeats against these same Yanks in '41. Things are evened up a bit now.

1948

From *Maybe I'll Pitch Forever*

SATCHEL PAIGE

LOTS OF PEOPLE HAVE TO WAIT a long time to get their life's ambitions. I wasn't any different. Oh, that big money'd come early, but getting into the major leagues took a long time.

And that same season I finally made the majors, I stood a chance of satisfying another ambition—playing in a World Series.

That was up to Mr. Lou, but the way I'd thrown for him I was sure he'd use me.

Even though I knew I was with a World Series team, it still kind of surprised me. You can't help being surprised when so many things happen in only three months. I'd made it to the top. I'd proved what I could do, to guys like Gene Bearden and Bob Lemon, who'd expected to see an old man with a handle bar mustache after Mr. Veeck signed me.

I did have a mustache, but not an old man's mustache, when they first saw me, but I'd clipped that off after I'd asked Mr. Veeck if he thought I should shave it.

"You can keep it if you want to," he told me, "but nobody else on my team has one."

I didn't either after that.

Without that mustache and with my trouble ball still causing troubles, I was just another kid on the team when the World Series against Boston started.

I almost didn't even get into the ball park for that first game. The gatekeeper wouldn't let me through. He didn't recognize me.

"I'm a ballplayer," I told him.

He just didn't listen.

Finally, one of my teammates came along and got me in.

The way that first game turned out, I could have stayed outside. Bobby Feller started and he didn't need help from me or anybody, even though he lost to Johnny Sain, one to nothing.

In the second game, Bob Lemon started for us and I just relaxed out there in the bullpen. I was doing my best not to wear myself out with any extra exercise like moving, just in case Mr. Lou did want me.

The fans sure wanted me, even those Boston fans. They were yelling, "We want Satchel."

I didn't let that excite me, as bad as I wanted to get in the World Series. I just relaxed in a chair out there in the bullpen, talking to the fans. One of them leaned over the rail and handed me a hot dog. I took it and broke off a piece of meat and picked off the skin. I had to watch my diet. I couldn't eat skin. It's bad for you. I just kept peeling and chewing.

A man had to do something when he wasn't pitching.

Then Lemon started having some troubles.

"Satch," somebody called, "Lou wants you to warm up."

"I can see him," I said, "and he can see me if he wants to look around. When he wants me to warm up he'll let me know."

I finished off that last piece of hot dog and threw the roll away and kicked those pieces of skin away from me.

Lemon was really staggering now, even if he was ahead.

"Maybe you'd better start throwing," somebody else said.

I finally started getting excited. Maybe it was my chance. But Mr. Lou still hadn't signaled for me so I tried to play it cool.

I dug a package of cigarettes out of my jacket, lit one, and blew smoke.

"Now I'm all warmed up," I told those guys sitting around me.

I still felt that excitement and I almost jumped out of my uniform when Mr. Lou turned around and signaled me to start warming up.

But I held myself down. No man likes for the whole world to see how he's churning inside.

I got up real slow and started lobbing the ball in there.

Maybe it's my chance, I kept thinking.

But Lemon got ahold of himself and I sat down, trying to act like it didn't matter.

I couldn't keep that sad look off my face, though. I'd wanted in there awfully bad.

I didn't get another chance in that second game. Lemon finished up strong and had him an eight-hit, four to one victory. That evened the World Series at one game apiece.

We only had a little bit of a party after getting that first World Series win. That's because we had to catch a train right off to get back to Cleveland, where we were going to play the third game.

On the train Mr. Lou told the reporters that Gene Bearden was going to pitch the third game. He didn't say who'd pitch the fourth game, but I kind of thought it would be me, so I was real loose on the train. I got into a kidding match with Spud Goldstein, the club's traveling secretary.

"How about a lower, Spud?" I asked him.

"We have nothing but roomettes on our train," Spud said. He sounded about as proud as a man with his first boy child. "Remember, Mr. Paige, you are with a big league club now."

I looked at him real serious. "If you boys ain't all careful, you all are gonna give me a swelled head."

Mr. Lou came along then and slapped me friendly-like.

"If Lemon hadn't settled down, Satch, you'd of probably been in your first World Series," he told me.

I figured for sure I'd make that fourth game then.

It just shows you how you can't always figure on things.

In the third game, Gene Bearden made it look like we never were going to need a relief pitcher. He shut out Boston, two to nothing, on five hits and gave us a two to one edge in the Series.

I was getting itchy. That fourth game had to be mine. I was sure of that.

Then Mr. Lou announced that Steve Gromek was going to pitch.

I felt sick.

When Steve beat Boston, two to one, and gave us a three to one lead, I started pressing. One more win for us and the World Series'd be all over.

"How 'bout startin' me next game?" I asked Mr. Lou.

A lot of sports writers were asking that now, too. So were the fans.

But Mr. Lou didn't say anything.

Then he announced that Bobby Feller was going to pitch and I was really troubled. Bobby was a mighty good hand and if he didn't need any relief help, that meant I'd miss pitching in the World Series.

Knowing Bobby, I figured he probably wouldn't need any help, even with him having only three days' rest.

I felt low as anybody ever felt.

The papers were on my side. They kept asking why Mr. Lou was pitching Bobby instead of me.

"Satchel deserves to pitch," one reporter wrote. "Not only is he rested, but he earned the right with his tremendous pitching during the 1948 season. His six victories were the key factor in getting the Indians into the American League play-off. Without those victories, there would not have been a play-off and Cleveland would not have been in the World Series."

But Mr. Lou didn't change his mind. He went ahead and started Feller on October 10 in Municipal Stadium.

I didn't want Bobby to get hit, but I guess deep down I was pulling against my own team. I wanted in that World Series awfully bad. I didn't show it. I didn't want anybody saying I was against my own team.

Before the game, I just talked free and easy with the reporters.

"Man, it took me a long time to get here, but it was worth it," I told them. "This is one of the biggest thrills I ever had, and you better believe it. If I get a chance to pitch, believe me, I'm gonna show the Braves some stuff they never saw before."

"You sure take things good, Satch," one of them told me.

"Ain't any other way to take it," I said.

"Aren't you nervous?"

"I've been in these things before. Not in these leagues. In the Negro leagues. I've been with the Kansas City Monarchs when they played in the World Series. Some of these other boys may be nervous, but I'm used to it."

They all started leaving. It was about game time.

"Good luck," one of them yelled.

"Luck? Luck is my middle name."

I only hoped it was. It looked like it was going to take luck to get me in the World Series.

Bobby wasn't sharp like he should have been. The Braves clipped him for three runs in the first inning, but Mr. Lou left him in there.

I just sat in the bullpen hoping and hoping.

We got back a run in the last of the first, but Boston got to Bobby for another run in the third. That gave them a four to one lead. Bobby seemed to settle down then and when we got four runs in the last of the fourth to go ahead, five to four, I thought it was all over for me.

I didn't even have hope left.

In the sixth Boston tied the score, five and five, by scoring one. But I still was a long way from getting in the game.

Why? All I could do was ask myself, "Why?" It was the same why

I used to ask myself when I couldn't get into the major leagues. There never was an answer.

Then came the top of the seventh.

Tommy Holmes of Boston led off against Bobby with a single. Mr. Lou signaled the bullpen and Ed Klieman, Russ Christopher, and me got up and started warming up.

Alvin Dark sacrificed Holmes to second and then Earl Torgeson singled, driving home Holmes to break the five-all tie.

Mr. Lou went stomping to the mound.

This was it, I thought. I threw harder and harder.

Mr. Lou waved to the bullpen. I jerked around. Then I sunk all inside me. He was waving in Ed Klieman.

I kept throwing. But I didn't want to. For about the first time in my life I didn't feel like throwing.

Ed Klieman must not have either. He walked two and gave up a single. Mr. Lou went to the mound again. I had a chance again. I lost it again.

Mr. Lou waved in Russ Christopher.

Why?

The fans wondered too. They kept chanting, "We want Satchel."

I was the only one left out in the bullpen throwing. I guess that's why Mr. Lou called on me when Russ gave up two singles in a row and Boston had six runs in for the inning and an eleven to five lead.

Maybe that's why he called me in. Or maybe it was because we already were so far behind.

When I walked out there the fans started cheering. There were better than eighty-six thousand out there watching and they yelled louder than they had any other time in the World Series up to then.

"I just hope Mr. Lou is hearing them," I muttered.

Then I forgot about Mr. Lou and the fans and everything. I had me a pitching job to do.

There was a man on first and only one out.

I guess everybody figured the game was over, but I wasn't going to let up. I was mighty serious out there, but I still gave them some fun. I didn't mean to, but the umpires thought I was trying to trick those Boston boys.

I spit on my fingers, just to get the dryness out, and then wiped my hand off on my uniform. But George Barr, the umpire behind the plate, must have been worried by that. He called for the ball to make sure I wasn't going to try to throw a spitter.

Ol' Satch threw a lot of things, but my natural stuff was always good enough. I didn't need any spit to help out.

Warren Spahn was up and I threw. It was ball one.

Then I stretched and held my arms still for a minute about halfway through my delivery, but before I could throw, out came George Barr.

He had a little talk for me on how you're supposed to throw in one continuous motion. Mr. Lou came running over to help me out. Then Bill Summers, another umpire, came over, I guess to even up the sides.

They finally left and let me pitch. I got Warren Spahn out of there. There were two outs with a man on first.

Tommy Holmes came up again, for the second time in the inning. I started my delivery to Tommy and reached way up high, then brought my hands down against my chest and rested a moment. That was all legal, but Billy Grieve, another umpire, came running over.

"Balk, balk," he yelled. "You wiggled the fingers of your glove. It's a balk."

They moved Eddie Stanky, who was that runner on first, down to second. I didn't have anything to say, but it made me so mad I gave Tommy Holmes my real trouble ball and got him out quick, ending the inning.

That finished my show. Mr. Lou took me out after that. We lost, by that same eleven to five score, but that didn't bother me any. I'd been in a World Series.

Sure, I'd pitched only two-thirds of an inning, but it was the first a colored boy'd ever pitched in a World Series. I didn't even feel mad at Mr. Lou any more because of that.

We won the World Series in the sixth game, beating the Boston Braves, four to three.

After it was over, there were parties and press meetings and everything like I'd never seen before. All the reporters had the same thing to ask me, "Will you be back with the Indians in 1949?"

"That's up to the boss," I told them. "As far as I'm concerned, Ol' Satch'll be back. The way I'm feeling, I figure I got at least three more years of baseball left, anyway, and there ain't much left for me to do but pitch."

I was telling those writers I thought I had me only three or four years left, but I wasn't believing it anymore. I was feeling like I could go on forever. And I kept living it up like those baseball paychecks'd be coming in forever. I didn't save a penny of that 1948 money for my old age. I put me three new cars in my garage, bought me a new boat and motor, and a couple more shotguns and some more hunting dogs.

Lahoma tried to keep me from doing it, but she couldn't hold me down altogether. I was smelling that major league money and it was filling up my head so I couldn't even hear her. But she kept after me and finally she did get me to buy another house, a real fine one on East Twenty-eighth Street in Kansas City.

Those two houses would have been mighty good investments if I could of kept both of them. But I just couldn't slow down that spending and when the money got a little short again, I had to sell that first house on Twelfth Street.

Socking away money for when you get old was something I still hadn't learned. It just seemed like I never was going to get too old to pitch.

1954

From *Willie's Time*

CHARLES EINSTEIN

T HE ODDS ON THAT 1954 World Series would favor the Cleveland Indians over the Giants by anything from 8 to 5 to 2 to 1. The record of the Cleveland club was awesome. It had won a record 111 games, lost only 43, for a percentage of .721. Its pitching staff had an earned-run average of 2.78, the only team ERA under 3.00 in the majors that season. Two of the pitchers, Early Wynn and Bob Lemon, tied for the American League lead in victories with 23 apiece; a third, Mike Garcia, had the best ERA. One of the hitters, Bob Avila, was the A.L. batting champion; another, Larry Doby, led the league in homers and runs batted in.

The only flaw in the Cleveland potential was one the odds makers completely overlooked. A clue to it lies in Roger Kahn's account of the Giants' trip to Las Vegas for an exhibition game with the Indians during spring training six months earlier. *Bob Feller pitched for the Indians. Sal Maglie opposed him. My scorebook is lost, but I believe the Giants won by one run.*

"We *always* beat the Indians in spring training that year," Alvin Dark said afterward. "Sure, you're getting into shape and trying things and looking at new players. That's what spring training's for. But any time we were leveling, any time it was our regulars against their regulars, they just couldn't beat us."

In the World Series, they would be leveling, regulars against regulars. And it was no contest. The Giants swept the Indians in four straight, and each verdict was more pronounced than the last. They had to go ten innings to win the first game, and from that moment the Indians never again in the Series had a lead on the scoreboard, not even for a single inning. Mays put the Giants ahead to stay with a two-out single in the first inning of the third game. By the time the fourth game was halfway through, the Giants were in front in that one, 7 to 0. They even wound up in the bizarre state of taking the pitcher out because he was too good! (That happened in the eighth inning, when Giant knuckle-baller Hoyt Wilhelm struck out Avila swinging. The pitch was right there when Avila swung, but by the time it reached catcher Westrum, a foot or so farther back, it was over Westrum's head, and the reprieved Avila scampered safely to first. A few dancing knucklers later, the Indians had two men on base, and Westrum called time and summoned Durocher from the dugout. "What's the matter?" Durocher asked. "You want a new pitcher?" Westrum shook his head. "No," he said. "I want a new catcher. If some-body's going to set a record for passed balls in the World Series, I don't want it to be me." Westrum may have had a point. Durocher turned and waved to the bullpen for his ace, Antonelli, who came on and put the Indians out of their misery.)

The Giants had a total of eleven innings in which they scored, over the four Series games, and Mays figured in eight of them. The one thing he had lacked as a rookie—true confidence at the plate—was lacking no longer. Here is a case where the figures are most descriptive. Counting his two partial years of 1951 and 1952 as one full season, which is what they add up to, then comparing them to his totals for 1954, one observes a striking contrast between the pre- and post-army Willie. Included here is his slug-ging average, which is computed like a batting average except that for slugging, a double counts as two hits, a triple as three, a home run as four.

	G	AB	R	H	2B	3B	HR	RBI	B.A.	SL.A.
1951–52:	155	591	76	157	24	9	24	91	.266	.459
1954:	151	565	119	195	33	13	41	110	.345	.667

Hitting honors for the 1954 World Series itself, however, would go to Dusty Rhodes, who had the only two Giant home runs of the Series, one of them a pinch homer that won the first game, and two other pinch hits besides; and Durocher dusted off the hoariest of General Grant jokes—that Al Lopez, the Cleveland manager, had asked him what Rhodes was drinking so he could distribute a case to his own men. But even with Dusty's derring-do, the one moment in the 1954 Series that electrified the fans, the moment that lives forever in scratchy kinescope replay, was a play known simply to this day as The Catch.

It came in the top of the eighth inning of the first game, with nobody out, Larry Doby on second for the Indians, Al Rosen at first, and Vic Wertz at bat. Wertz had had a perfect day so far against Giant starter Maglie, with a triple in the first, a single in the fourth, another single in the sixth. Durocher went and got Maglie and replaced him with Don Liddle. Wertz swung at Liddle's first pitch, and there it went, on a rising, soaring line toward deepest center field, just to the right of dead center. To be seated in the press section back of home plate, in the imperceptible flash of time it took to focus from the swing to the horizon beyond, was to encounter a sight: the number 24 on the back of Willie Mays's uniform, already in full flight toward the wall.

But an even more arresting view was recorded not by any writer in the press box but by a writer in the bleachers named Arnold Hano, who subsequently built an entire book around that game and that moment, a book called *A Day in the Bleachers*. Hano too watched Wertz as he swung, but

This ball did not alarm me because it was hit to dead center field—Mays' territory—and not between the fielders, into

those dread alleys in left-center and right-center which lead to the bull pens.

And this was not a terribly high drive. It was a long low fly or a high liner, whichever you wish. This ball was hit not nearly so high as the triple Wertz struck earlier in the day, so I may have assumed that it would soon start to break and dip and come down to Mays, not too far from his normal position.

Then I looked at Willie, and alarm raced through me, peril flaring against my heart. To my utter astonishment, the young Giant center fielder—the inimitable Mays, most skilled of outfielders, unique for his ability to scent the length and direction of any drive and then turn and move to the final destination of the ball—Mays was turned full around, head down, running as hard as he could, straight toward the runway between the two bleacher sections.

I knew then that I had underestimated—badly underestimated—the length of Wertz's blow.

I wrenched my eyes from Mays and took another look at the ball, winging its way along, undipping, unbreaking, forty feet higher than Mays' head, rushing along like a locomotive, nearing Mays, and I thought then: it will beat him to the wall.

. . . For the briefest piece of time—I cannot shatter and compute fractions of seconds like some atom gun—Mays started to raise his head and turn it to his left, as though he were about to look behind him.

Then he thought better of it, and continued the swift race with the ball that hovered quite close to him now, thirty feet high and coming down (yes, finally coming down) and again— for the second time—I knew Mays would make the catch.

. . . He simply slowed down to avoid running into the wall, put his hands up in cuplike fashion over his left shoulder, and caught the ball much like a football player catching leading passes in the end zone.

He had turned so quickly, and run so fast and truly, that he made this impossible catch look—to us in the bleachers—

quite ordinary. To those reporters in the press box, nearly six hundred feet from the bleacher wall, it must have appeared far more astonishing, watching Mays run and run until he had become the size of a pigmy and then he had to run some more, while the ball diminished to a mote of white dust and finally disappeared in the dark blob that was Mays' mitt.

One might argue whether any other outfielder could combine Mays's instinctive jump on the batted ball and his speed afoot, which is to argue whether any other outfielder could have made that catch. Many people, Hano included, seem to think not. For Mays himself, however, it was not the greatest catch he ever made. The ball had stayed up for him and he still had running room when it came down. ("For Willie," as Barney Kremenko had said, "that's nothing.") But it was a money catch, a World Series catch, the high point indeed of an otherwise dull event, as any Series must most likely be when somebody wins it in four straight games. And quite forgotten by now, here resurrected from Hano's book, is what happened next:

Mays caught the ball, and then whirled and threw, like some olden statue of a Greek javelin hurler, his head twisted away to the left as his right arm swept out and around. But Mays is no classic study for the simple reason that at the peak of his activity, his baseball cap flies off. And as he turned, or as he threw—I could not tell which, the two motions were welded into one—off came the cap, and then Mays himself continued to spin around after the gigantic effort of returning the ball whence it came, and he went down flat on his belly, and out of sight.

But the throw! What an astonishing throw, to make all other throws ever before it, even those four Mays himself had made during fielding practice, appear the flings of teen-age girls. This was the throw of a giant, the throw of a howitzer made human, arriving at second base . . . just as Doby was pulling into third, and as Rosen was scampering back to first.

The containing effect of the throw on the Cleveland runner enabled pitcher Liddle to get out of the inning unscored upon and two innings later Rhodes hit his game-winning homer which actually was an unremarkable pop fly along the right field line which met the grandstand just to the fair side of the foul pole. Along the lines, the park was as short as it was deep to center, and the phrase "That would've been a home run at the Polo Grounds" was heard repeatedly in other parks to deride routine fly balls such as Dusty's.

Many years later, following a tour the Giants had made of Japan, I served as master of ceremonies at a Giants Booster Club luncheon, and in introducing Mays to the audience, described a play he was said to have made in a game at Tokyo. It seems that with bases loaded, the batsman put up a fly ball to center field. The ball was caught up in one of the winds that are sacred to the Japanese, and Mays saw it was going to carry out of the park. But he also noticed that the exit gate in center field was open. So he raced through the gate and found himself on a tree-shaded avenue running away from the ball park. Going in the same direction was a fire engine in the process of answering an alarm, so Mays jumped aboard. Three blocks farther, he put up his glove and made the catch. One fireman at the back of the truck turned to another and said, "Home run at the Polo Grounds."

The tale having been told, I presented Mays and sat down while he fielded questions from the audience. Toward the end one rather unexpected query came up. "About that time you caught the ball while you were riding on the fire engine in Japan," the questioner said, "did the guy on third score after the catch, or was your throw in time to get him?"

That got a bigger laugh than the story itself. Mays, however, handled it straight-faced. "I didn't make any throw," he said. "Didn't have to. There was two out at the time."

1955

Paradise at Last

JOE TRIMBLE

THEY WON'T MAKE OCT. 4 a red-letter day in Brooklyn. They'll print it in letters of gold from now on because it's only the greatest date in the history of the batty borough—the day those darling Dodgers finally won the World Series. At exactly 3:45 yesterday afternoon in the Stadium, the Brooks got the third out of a 2–0 victory over the Yankees in the seventh and deciding game.

And when they print calendars over there, they won't bother with Marilyn Monroe's picture. Not good enough. They'll have pucker-faced Johnny Podres, the most heroic pitcher in Dodgertown since Dazzy Vance and the only Brooklyn thrower ever to win two games in a Series. It was Podres' brilliant, crushing pitching which ruined the AL champions, sending them down to their fifth Series loss in 21.

And who do you suppose knocked in both Brook runs? No one else but Gil Hodges, the batting flop of the '52 Series.

There were many memorable events bright and tragic on this earth on past fourths of October, but the hallowed pages of history must display yesterday's momentous triumph above them all.

What kind of a date has it been? Well, on Oct. 4, 1861, the Union forces massed to form the Army of the Potomac; in 1864, the Erie Railroad opened (probably not on time); in 1940, Hitler and Mussolini met at the Brenner Pass and, in 1944, the U.S.

160

Army broke through the German West Wall. Al Smith, the beloved Governor of New York and Presidential candidate, also died on the latter date.

As far as Brooklyn is concerned, nothing ever could match the events of yesterday, when all the years of frustration and defeat were wiped out in one blazing afternoon. It was the 49th Dodger Series game in eight appearances, and the tightest, most tense and thrilling of them all.

At the finish, when Pee Wee Reese sure-handedly threw out Elston Howard, the big park in the Bronx exploded with human emotion as the entire Dodger team raced out on the field and danced and drooled in delight around Podres.

While the 62,465 customers were cheering the new champs, the proud Yankees were filing slowly into the losing dressing room; a unique experience for them. Of all, only coaches Frank Crosetti and Bill Dickey and shortstop Phil Rizzuto had ever experienced a loss before. They had it but once, when the Cardinals smeared the Yankees four in a row after losing the 1942 opener.

The Dodgers are in paradise, finally succeeding after numerous Brooklyn teams had tried for four decades. The 1916 Flatbushers were knocked off by the Red Sox and the 1920 crew by Cleveland. Then the drought set in and it wasn't until 1941 that a pennant waved alongside the tree that grew in Brooklyn. But that year they had to play the Yankees, and Mickey Owen muffed a third strike and everything went black in the borough.

Four times since then, they won the NL flag only to find those merciless Yankees on the other side of the field—and the Brooks on the losing end of the payoff. They went down in 1947 in seven games, in 1949 it was five, in '52 seven again and six in '53.

So the Brooks also went home with their heads hanging and the taunt of "Wait 'til next year!" shattering their eardrums. Now that's over. Next year came on Oct. 4 this time.

This not alone was the greatest day in Brooklyn's history. It also brought to a wondrous climax the richest World Series ever. Due to increased admission prices and the maximum number of games, the $2,337,515.34 taken in at the box office is an all-time high.

Numerous records were set, but the one the Brooklyn players will remember most was their achievement in winning four of the last five games after dropping the first two. This kind of comeback had never happened in a seven-game Series before.

To do it, they had to get a second superior pitching job from the 23-year-old Podres, their little lefthander, and also they had to whip the Yankee pitcher who had given them the most trouble, 35-year-old Tommy Byrne. Although they got the three hits off the graying southpaw before an error helped cause his removal in the sixth, they put them in exactly the right places.

Roy Campanella, who had gone hitless in 12 times up in the Stadium this Series and had a lifetime average of .070 in the big park, crashed a double to left after one out in the fourth. Duke Snider, who went all the way on his bad knee, fanned just before Campy's hit. Carl Furillo followed with a slow grounder, Rizzuto making a fine play to get him at first as Campy reached third. Gil Hodges, with a count of one ball and two strikes, swung at an inside curve. He didn't get much wood on the ball but it went safely to left field and the Brooks were ahead.

The other safety was a lead-off single in the sixth by Reese, the veteran whose victory appetite was greatest because he had been on the losing side against the Yankees five times.

The shortstop lined a hit to left-center and was deprived of a double when Bob Cerv made a fine retrieve. Reese eventually scored the insurance run after Bob Grim had taken the mound.

But before the Brooks opened the thin gap, they nearly gave the Yankees a run. Yogi Berra opened the bottom of the fourth with a lazy fly to center, a bit to Snider's right. Junior Gilliam came over from left, invaded the Duke's realm, and then they went into an Alphonse-Gaston act. The ball tipped off Snider's glove as he made a last-second grab after realizing Gilliam was letting him take it. That fluke double gave Berra the distinction of being the ninth man ever to hit safely in every game of a full length Series. The catcher made 10 hits, topping the batters on both sides.

The Yankee fans screamed for blood after the break. It's an old axiom that you can't make a mistake against the Bombers. They break through the opening and kill you. But Podres wouldn't buckle. He got the next three batters, all strong righty sluggers. Hank Bauer hit a fly to Furillo, Bill Skowron grounded to Don Zimmer and Cerv popped to Reese in short left. The Dodger fans screamed: "Pee Wee! Pee Wee!" as he went out and Gilliam came in and the Dodger captain caught it.

The Yankee supporters applauded Gilliam when he came up to bat in the fifth, one guy screaming: "He's the best man we've got!" Junior didn't get a chance to flub anything else in the outfield because he was moved in to second base after the Brooks got their run in the sixth.

After Reese hit, Snider bunted deftly along the third-base line. Byrne fielded it and threw accurately to first base. Skowron stepped forward to meet the ball, taking his foot off the bag and forcing himself to make a tag play. He swiped at the Dodger runner's back and the ball flew out of his glove for an error.

Walter Alston, winning a World Series in his first try, sensibly ordered Campy to sacrifice and he did. Byrne handled this bunt, too. It seemed that the pitcher had a force possibility on Reese at third, Pee Wee not yet having gone into a belly-whop slide. But Byrne thought otherwise and let Reese make it, tossing to first for the out. Casey Stengel ordered an intentional pass to Furillo and then called in Grim, his relief ace who had saved the first game but was battered as starter in the fifth.

Grim's first batter was Hodges, a tough man with the bases filled. Gil took a strike and then drove a long sacrifice fly to center, Reese scoring. Grim walked Hoak, refilling the lanes, but got George Shuba, a pinch-hitter for Zimmer, on a third-out grounder.

Again the sight of a Dodger run on the scoreboard brought a Yankee threat in the bottom of the inning. This developed into a real big one and also produced the greatest fielding play of the Series—a catch by Sandy Amoros, an outfielder who was held lightly as a prospective regular in the spring because of his shabby fielding and throwing.

Podres, who passed only two, hit a wild streak and walked Billy Martin on four straight pitches. Alston came out to give the youngster a chance to get his breath. With victory so close, he didn't want the Kid to get hysterical. Johnny threw two bad pitches to McDougald, then got one over, which Gil bunted perfectly for a single, Martin taking second.

Then came the key play, the one which probably meant the title. Stengel, disdaining a bunt with Berra up, had Yogi swing away. Podres pitched outside and Berra stroked a long, high fly into the left field corner. Amoros, playing him far over toward center, had to run over 100 feet. The ball stayed up a long time, being held by the wind, and Sandy just reached it, gloving it with his right mitt in fair territory.

Martin and McDougald, not believing a catch possible, were on their horses. Billy suddenly reversed himself when almost to third and Gil was past second base before he found out the ball had been held. Amoros gracefully whirled and fired to Reese, who went into short left for the throw. Pee Wee then made another perfect throw to Hodges, just getting McDougald as he slid back. That was the 12th Brooklyn DP, a new Series record.

Bauer then hit a hopper to short and Reese couldn't get it out of his glove for a frantic portion of a second. When he did, he had to throw a blazer and it just beat the runner, according to first base umpire Frank Dascoli.

Grim was lifted for a pinch-hitter in the seventh, after Howard singled. There were two out, so Stengel sent up his hobbled husky, Mickey Mantle. Podres fooled the Mick with a change-up, Mantle skying the ball to short left where Reese took it, with the Dodger fans again screaming his name.

Podres had a rough time in the eighth, when the Yankees got their second runner to third base. Rizzuto led off with a single to left but Martin flied to Furillo, who came in fast for the looper. McDougald then hit a sharp grounder which bad-hopped off the left arm of Don Hoak, playing third because Jackie Robinson had a sore Achilles tendon in his right foot. Rizzuto got to third as the fluke hit went into left.

The tension was terrific, with Berra and Bauer coming up. Podres really had it, getting Berra to cut under one of his slow curves. The ball went to Furillo in short right and Carl gunned it home, holding The Scooter on third. Then the youngster faced his supreme test in Bauer, who hits lefthanders very well. He took Hank to 2–2 with curves and slow-up pitches, then flung himself off the mound by putting all he could on a shoulder-high fastball which Bauer swung at and missed.

As the Yanks came up, Dodger fans stayed seated. Yankee adherents shouted for a rally.

Skowron cracked a sizzler back at Podres, the hard grounder sticking in his glove web. He was unable to get it out for a second or so, and started to run towards first base to make the putout that way. But he was able to pry it loose and make an underhand toss to Hodges. Cerv then hit a high fly which Amoros took in short left and the Dodgers were one out away from the promised land.

Podres went to 2–2 on Howard and then made him swing off stride at the change-up. Reese took one happy step towards the grounder, aimed it for Hodges and, though the toss was a bit low, Gil kept his foot on the base and the Dodgers had finally arrived in paradise.

1956

Sal Maglie . . .
A Gracious Man

MURRAY KEMPTON

THERE WAS THE CUSTOMARY TALK about the shadows of the years and the ravages of the law of averages when Sal Maglie went out to meet the Yankees yesterday afternoon. It was the first time, after all the years, that he had ever pitched in Yankee Stadium, the home of champions.

He threw that hump-backed let-up pitch that is last in the warm-up, and then for the first time looked at Hank Bauer. He threw the curve in; Hank Bauer made a gesture at bunting; and the strike was called.

The hitter leaned over a little; the pitch was high; Hank Bauer skittered back in haste and the ball went by the catcher's mitt and back to the wall.

"If I know Sal," the old Giant writer in the stands said, "he threw that to tell 'em off. He knows the Yankees probably think he's a little tired. He's saying to them, look fellas, I'm still around. You've got to come and get me."

"The call was for an inside pitch," said Sal Maglie later. "I threw it too high and it got away." He is a gracious man who takes no pride in the legend of special, professional venom.

He worked his arm a little and blew on his hands as though he came from a world no sun could warm. And then Bauer plunked it up to Reese; Maglie looked once at the ball and then at the fielder, and, without needing to see the catch, bent over and worked his long, brown, healer's hand into the resin bag.

He got Joe Collins to hit on the ground to the wrong field; Mickey Mantle went all the way around; Sal Maglie heard the sound and judged it. The left fielder was still circling under it when Sal Maglie crossed the foul line on his way to the dugout. He gives very little and can afford to spend less.

He went that way through the line-up for the first three innings. It seemed a memorable incident when the first pitch to the eighth Yankee batter was a ball. The utility infield of the fifth-place team in the Westport Midget League would have eaten up anything hit by either side in those three perfect eighteen outs. "I figured," said Peewee Reese, "that both you guys weren't giving anybody anything, and we'd have to call it at midnight."

Sal Maglie ended the third for the Dodgers, walking out slowly carrying one bat, digging his spikes in as though anything is possible in this game, driving the first pitch straight to Mickey Mantle and walking over towards third base to change his cap and get his glove.

He threw the warm-up pitches; Roy Campanella was standing up and almost dancing at the plate.

Maglie got the two quick strikes on Bauer who hit to Jackie Robinson; Maglie did not look at the play; he was busy with the resin. He pushed the curve by Joe Collins; it was the third strike. Mantle was back.

The first strike was a curve and called. There were no times intruding upon the memory when he had seemed more sharp. He threw the next pitch outside, and then hit the corner again. He waited awhile, rubbing his fingers on his shirt, wiping the afternoon's first sweat off his forehead. He threw a pitch on the corner that was low by the distance of a bead of sweat from the skin; it was that close and it was called a ball.

Mantle hit a foul; Sal Maglie knew it was out of play; the left fielder was still running and he was working on a new ball. The next pitch he threw Mantle was down the middle a little inside. Roy Campanella said later that it hit his fists. Sal Maglie watched it almost curve and then stay fair in the stands; with the unseeing roar all around him, he walked back to the rubber and kicked it once.

"He'd been fouling off the outside pitches," he said later. "I thought I'd try him inside once." He stopped for a minute, naked and dry beside his locker, the skin showing through the thin hair above his forehead. "That shows what can happen when you're thinking out there and the other guy isn't." That was as close as he came to suggesting that God is too tolerant with the margin of error he assigns the very young.

Then Yogi Berra hit one hard to the wrong field; Duke Snider ran the distance of years, and tumbled with it. Sal Maglie had no reason to know it then, but that was the inning and the run.

In the fifth Enos Slaughter was walked very fast. Billy Martin bunted. Sal Maglie came scuttling onto the grass and snatched the ball and turned around and fired it high and smoky to second just in time, a forty-year-old man throwing out a forty-year-old man and knowing he had to hurry. He was sweating hard by this time. Harold Reese went up half his height, met McDougald's drive and knocked it into the air, and recovered it for the double play. Sal Maglie was watching the way the ball went now; the sound was different; for the first time today he had to think of the fielders.

Don Larsen went on making the rest period painfully short. Sal Maglie took his warm-ups for the sixth; he was throwing the last one in hard now. Andy Carey hit one over his head into center and the old remembered tightrope walk had begun.

Larsen bunted the third strike; Maglie and Campanella scrambled off too late to get the runner at second; they had made their mistake. Carey went far off second; Bauer slapped the ball to left. Sal Maglie drove himself over to back up third, but the run was in and safely in. Walter Alston came out; the conference went on around Maglie. A man in the stands said that if Labine was ready, it was time to bring him in. "Take Sal out?" Campanella said later, "the way he was pitching?" Joe Collins hit a low, hard single; Maglie went over to cover third again and came back slamming the ball into his glove. Mantle was up.

The first pitch was out of control; then he threw two strikes, one called, one swinging. Mantle hit the ball to the first baseman who threw to the catcher, who threw not well to the third baseman, who fell away and threw around Bauer to get him. After the game, Sal Maglie looked at Jackie Robinson, sitting sombre across the dressing room; in a moment of surprise, Robinson's hair was gray. "That was a throw," he said. "Him falling away like that." Maglie saw it, and walked to the third base line and waited for the rundown, so as not to interfere, like a waiter at his station, and then walked slowly back to the dugout.

He was the last to come out after the swift Dodger half of the seventh. That appears in the boxscore to have been all it was, except that in the bottom of the eighth, Don Larsen was the first to bat. Sal Maglie went on with his warm-ups; alone in that great park, he and Campanella were not looking at the hitter. He struck out Larsen; he struck out Bauer; he struck out Joe Collins swinging. When he walked back, the crowd noticed him and gave him a portion of its cheers. It was the last inning of the most extraordinary season an old itinerant, never a vagrant, ever had. "I figured," he said later, "that for me, either way, it was the last inning, and I didn't have to save anything."

"I would like to see him," he said later, "pitch with men on bases." Someone asked him if he had minded Larsen getting his no-hitter. "I might have wanted him to get it," he answered, "if we hadn't had a chance all the time."

They asked him was he satisfied with the game he pitched. "How," said Sal Maglie, "am I to be satisfied? But you got to adjust yourself." To time and to ill-chance, and the way they forgot, you got to adjust yourself. Someone asked if you knew when you had a no-hitter, and he said, of course, you do. You remember who had hit, for one thing. "If you ask me two years from now," said Sal Maglie, "I'll be able to tell you every pitch I threw this year."

He said it, in passing, naked, his body white except for the red from countless massages on his right arm, tearing his lunch off a long Italian sausage.

"They are pros," he said. "The way we are. You make one mistake with them and you're in trouble."

On the other side of the room, somebody asked Campanella if Maglie had made any mistakes out there. "Sal make mistakes?" said Campanella. "The only mistake he made today was pitching." He pulled on his jacket and turned to what was left of the assemblage. Maglie was going now, as losers are required to go, to get his picture taken with Don Larsen in the Yankee dressing room.

"I told you," chided Roy Campanella, as Sal Maglie went out the door, "that there would be days like this."

1960

"Dad Would Have Loved It"

WILL GRIMSLEY

DAD WOULD HAVE LOVED IT—I only wish he could have been here today."

The tears in Bill Mazeroski's eyes were half from joy and half from sad memories as he sought to resurrect the drama of the ninth-inning home run which smashed the New York Yankees, 10 to 9, and brought Pittsburgh its first World Series victory in 35 years.

"Dad always wanted to play big-league baseball himself," Mazeroski reminisced. "He was considered a great prospect. Once he was ready to sign with the Cleveland Indians and then he had a foot cut off in a mine accident.

"From then on, all his hopes and ambitions were wrapped up in me, because I was an only son.

"Dad had to work hard in the mines, but whenever he could he always would try to catch me in a ball game or two. Then a year and a half ago he died of lung cancer."

Mazeroski, who hit the first and last home run of this wild Series, said he remembers tossing a baseball around and swinging a bat ever since he was big enough to walk.

"I was born in Wheeling, West Virginia," he said, "but the family moved to Adena, Ohio. It was a pretty hard life. But Dad was determined that I become a major-league ballplayer and he used to play with me by the hour."

As for the hit itself which won the seventh and climactic game of the Series—a prodigious blow over the 406-foot brick wall in left field—Mazeroski said he never once doubted that it would go all the way.

"I came to bat intending to go for the long ball," he said.

"The first pitch by Ralph Terry was a slider, a ball. The second was a high, fast one.

"I caught it on the fat of my bat. I knew immediately it was a well-hit ball. I watched it sail over the fence as I rounded the bases.

"I touched every base. As I rounded second, I saw people coming out to meet me, but I kept going.

"What did I think? I was too excited and too thrilled to think. It was the greatest moment of my life."

The Pittsburgh second baseman, who homered in the fourth inning of the opening game, said the Pirates never once despaired in the long, up-and-down game which at one stage saw the Yankees lead by 7–4.

"We kept telling each other we could do it. All year we've been a fighting, come-from-behind ball club. We always felt we could pull it out—even after the Yankees tied it up in the ninth—but I didn't think I'd be the guy to do it."

Mazeroski, 24, a slender six-footer, was a right-handed pitcher in high school but his coach converted him into an infielder to take advantage of his hitting.

1962

Tension and Torment

ARNOLD HANO

JACK SANFORD SAT ON A RUBDOWN table, slumped against a wall of the Giants' clubhouse at Candlestick Park. He did not move. He did not talk. A writer leaned over and said something quietly to Sanford, and the big pitcher, not looking up, said, "I do not want to answer questions."

He sat like that, in the trainer's room where ballplayers go to escape the press after a galling ball game, but on this day the press and other people intruded, and there was no escape. So Jack Sanford sat in silence.

Next to him, Jim Davenport talked of playing golf the next day, with Al Dark. Don Larsen sat in a corner of the same rubdown room, and three times he said the famous four-letter obscenity. Chuck Hiller came into the room, and he said to nobody in particular: "How I'd love to see 'em next year! The obscenity Yankees!"

But Sanford didn't move. He didn't talk.

Fifty-five minutes went by. Then Sanford stood and walked through the Giant clubhouse. He went across a brief corridor that separates the Giant clubhouse from the visiting clubhouse—in this case, the New York Yankee clubhouse—and walked inside the Yankee dressing room and over to Ralph Terry. He spoke quietly to Terry and shook his hand, and Terry hugged Sanford and spoke into his ear, and Sanford walked out.

This is the way one man loses.

Jack Sanford had just pitched and lost a 1–0 game to the Yankees, and the 1962 World Series had come to a close. On the last play of the game, with Giants on second and third, Willie McCovey had hit a line drive—into Bobby Richardson's glove. A scream of rising joy had been strangled. A few inches had marked the difference between a winner and a loser. Jack Sanford had become the biggest loser in sport's biggest event. You can't pitch much better than Jack Sanford pitched that day or that Series. You can compare the statistics of Ralph Terry and Jack Sanford for the three tight games they pitched against each other in the 1962 World Series, and you cannot slip a woman's silken hair between them, that is how similar they are. Yet as they so often do, the statistics only tell a partial story. There is a chasm between Terry and Sanford, between winning and losing; it is the difference between a man sipping champagne and a man sitting in a near-catatonic immobility, reliving a bitter memory.

Six days earlier, when Jack Sanford walked from the mound during the fifth game of the Series (seconds after Tom Tresh had hit a three-run home run), the crowd at Yankee Stadium stood and applauded and roared down their sympathy and appreciation. He had pitched magnificently, except for that one pitch. After the game somebody asked Sanford how he felt about the applause.

"I'm losing 5–2," he said bitterly. "Who hears applause?"

Fate is an extraordinary creature. She chooses her victims with a pitiless, macabre sense of humor. Before the first game of the World Series, the San Francisco ballplayers—nearly to a man—said, "This is just another game." After the playoff, how could they get excited, nervous, tense, emotional? They were tired, in physical distress, aching to get the season, the Series, over with.

Yet one man spoke with excitement, no, astonishment. "Another game?" said Jack Sanford. "Of course it's not just another game. It's a World Series game."

And this is the man who wound up the Series' biggest loser.

Nobody lost harder than Jack Sanford that last day. But there was bitterness elsewhere in the Giant dressing room. Matty Alou sat in his cubicle, staring down, unseeing, his shirt unbuttoned, his spiked shoes off. He undressed that far and then he had paused, and now he sat. Finally he stood up and unpeeled his shirt. He shook his head and he said, "Bad." He spat on the floor. He removed his belt. He threw the belt—slam—into a corner of his dressing cubicle. And he kept his back turned. He would keep his back turned, a visitor knew, for a long time.

As a man, the Giant team had trooped into that dressing room—losers—and they shook their heads and some said, "Lucky obscenities!" and others held up two hands a few inches apart— the difference between McCovey's ball being caught and landing fair, driving in the winning runs. The first thing manager Al Dark said to the press was: "A couple of inches! That was twice as hard a line drive as any man can hit!" It was not an alibi; it was not an excuse; it was simply a man's defenses rising up and trying to explain away an unalterable fact.

The 17-year-old batboy, Ernie Reddick, who had been with the Giants for three seasons, found it hard to believe that the long, long season was over. "We'd been through so much," he said, almost pleadingly, as though he were somehow asking for that last pitch all over again, "and to have it end this way! I wouldn't cry. I'd be too embarrassed to cry." So he didn't cry. That is how Ernie Reddick lost.

Willie McCovey—who'd hit that ball, and another ball earlier for a triple—wouldn't complain. He had his chance. Over and over, writers came over to McCovey and they asked the same question: "If the wind hadn't been blowing in so strong, would your triple have gone out?" And McCovey grinned and shook his head and he explained (again and again): "I can't say what would have happened if the wind wasn't blowin', because the wind was blowin' and it always blows." McCovey kept a smile on his face during the grueling interviewing; there was a sense of achievement in McCovey, even in losing. "A man hits the ball as hard as he can," he said. "He can't feel bad about what he does. Of course you want to win; of course you'd rather hit one off the fists and break your bat and have it drop in, but if you hit hard, that is all you can do." There was further pride in McCovey. He felt something had been proved during the World Series. "We are a great team," he said, "and the Yankees know it, too."

But San Francisco had lost.

Perhaps—even in spite of the closeness of the Series—it was inevitable that the Giants would lose. They looked like losers when the Series started. Chuck Hiller's left leg was chinked up the shin bone with raw welts, where he'd been spiked during those last bristling days of the National League pennant race, and then spiked again by Tommy Davis in the sapping, unbelievable three-game playoff. His right ankle was bruised nearly black. Jim Davenport had fought off a bad cold—a flu, probably—and his ulcer was acting up. It hits him in the stomach and gives him butterflies. The tension of it all had gotten to Davenport. He is not supposed to smoke, but by the time the Series had started, he was smoking more than a pack a day. Tom Haller had six stitches in his left forearm (two separate open wounds, each with three stitches in it); Lee Walls had gashed him with his spikes in that second playoff game with the Dodgers. The stitches were frayed black threads growing out of Haller's arm. He swore the wounds didn't hurt.

Jose Pagan was bandaged up his legs. There is a standing joke about Pagan: "Jose doesn't get dressed. He just puts on bandages."

After the first game, they looked worse. In it Felipe Alou raked his arm on the fence trying to catch the ball Roger Maris hit for a first-inning double. There was a four-inch welt on Alou's arm. In the Yankee clubhouse they talked about how Elston Howard had hurt his hand sliding into third base in that first game, but in the Giant clubhouse, Jim Davenport sat with his leg outstretched and a piece of flesh gouged out of it. He'd been on the other end of Howard's slide. A thick glob of white salve lay over the wound;

crusted blood and hair mixed with the salve. "It's nothing," Davenport said.

They looked—when the Series opened, and after the first game—like GIs in Korea.

And yet looking like that, they had come down to a single run difference in the seventh game. The Giants had lost the first game and won the second and lost the third, and it had gone on like that for seven games, spread out over 12 days, two teams so evenly matched the entire Series hung on a line drive in the bottom of the ninth, with two men out and the winning runs on base. The Giants had looked like losers, but they hadn't acted like losers. Perhaps it was the cruel pressures of the pennant race that had elevated them beyond their own physical weakness. "Defeat ennobles and fortifies," Havelock Ellis has said, and the Giants had been a beaten team all season long, until the very end. Losing may have made the Giants winners. Larry Jansen, who does not read Havelock Ellis, said it more simply: "I think we'll be a better team next year. We lost too casually before. Now we know the value of winning."

Winning the pennant, yes. But they then lost the biggest event in all of sports, and though they lost with dignity and courage and an astonishing show of stamina, they still lost. "It was better," Arthur Machen once wrote, "to fail in attempting exquisite things." Don't tell it to the Giants. Don't tell it to Jack Sanford. Don't tell it to Matty Alou.

A writer peels back his memories of the 1962 World Series, this writer, who spent the entire seven games, 12 days, watching the losers. Each game I entered the losing dressing room, and you could see the different ways different men lost. Some were filled with nameless rages—Sanford hurling soap, Matty Alou throwing down his belt and turning his back—and others lose with a near-blasé attitude. After the seventh game Orlando Cepeda strode the Giant dressing room stark naked except for a catcher's glove, laughing. How did he feel? Cepeda stopped, and he said, "Well, it would be better to win, but . . ." He shrugged, and strode on.

Felipe Alou said, "I feel a little bit down. Next year, we try. It was nice to win the pennant. It would be nice to be world champions." Then he shook his head, and the pain struck his face. He winced and said: "To play so long, and to lose . . ." and he too stopped and shrugged and walked away.

But it wasn't only the Giants who had lost. The Yankees were losers, too. Three times. (Perhaps three more times than many of them expected to lose. When the Series started, if I were to use one word to sum up the Yankee attitude toward the Giants, the word would be contempt.)

Contempt. After the first game—won by the Yankees, 6–2—I asked Ralph Houk whether the Giants had impressed him.

Houk paused. It was a long pause, and you could see Houk trying to find a kind word to say about this ragtag team of bloodied men. "Well, naturally—they have men—they have several players who naturally impress you."

After the second game, won by the Giants and Sanford, 2–0, Elston Howard spoke only of the next game, and going against Billy Pierce. "Everybody hits Pierce good," he said, with satisfaction.

But losing shook up the Yankees; at least, a little. Bill Stafford shook his head in the Yankee dressing room, after that Sanford shutout, and he said, "That guy must have thrown a lot of perfect pitches out there. I never saw the Yankees take so many pitches." Stafford was impressed. Yet that is not the lasting memory of the Yankee dressing room after that Giant win. The lasting memory is of Roger Maris holding a hardboiled egg in his hand, and the yolk falling from his hand, rolling away on the floor. Maris looked at the yolk longingly. Then delicately with his big naked toe he flicked it away from him, and walked away for another hardboiled egg. And you remember that same afternoon, Whitey Ford talking about a golf course he owns. The Yankees had lost that day, but you had to struggle to discover it. Roger Maris said pleasantly: "It is already out of my system. You win a few, you lose a few. No game eats me up." And then Ford forgot golf and began talking about a new diet he had discovered: "You lose seven pounds in three days."

"Not if you're on booze," somebody said, and Ford laughed and agreed it helped if you weren't on booze.

That was after the second game. No Yankee sweat. There was some Yankee sweat after the fourth game, won by Chuck Hiller's grand-slam home run off relief pitcher Marshall Bridges. Writers wanted to know why Houk had taken Ford out for a pinch-hitter earlier in the game, with the score 2–2. Had Whitey lost his stuff?

And Houk said, Yes, Whitey agreed his stuff wasn't too good any more, but it didn't matter, because Houk would have taken Ford out even if he still had his stuff. But Houk sounded like a man squirming a bit, a man on a witness chair, and he looked drawn and sweaty himself. The World Series had taken on its true quality by this time, a grim, dirty, roll-in-the-mud sort of quality, with sloppy fielding and superb gutty pitching, and the teams always fighting back when apparently beaten. It was not what Houk had expected, no matter what he said, no matter what the other Yankees said. They simply hadn't expected to lose; they hadn't expected to fight and be fought this way.

Writers asked Houk what kind of pitch Bridges had thrown to Hiller, and Houk said it was a high fast-ball, "a pitch that got away."

What sort of pitch should Bridges have thrown?

"You'll have to ask Bridges that," Houk snapped.

It would be unfair to suggest that this brief exchange typified the Yankee attitude on losing days. Tom Tresh comes closer to typifying it. He said, that afternoon: "Everybody tries his best. Either you win or you lose. You don't try to over-try, either." Did Tresh hold the Giants short?

The young handsome Yankee—who came close to being the No. 1 hero of the Series—was shocked by the question. "Hell, no," he said. "The Yankees never held a team short. Kansas City can beat you. Washington can beat you. Any team can beat you." He didn't hold the Giants short, but the comparisons were to two of the weaker teams in his own league.

And there was occasional flaring anger in the Yankee dressing room, on losing days. A writer suggested to a Yankee pitcher—nameless, here—that one of the team's problems was failure in the bull-pen, relief pitchers coming in and not holding the other ball club. "We won the pennant, didn't we?" the Yankee pitcher yelled. "You want us to win by 15? Maybe the problem is that the home-run hitter didn't hit 60 home runs this year!"

These are the pressures, the tensions. They were not exclusive to the Yankees. Before the fifth game—won by Tresh's three-run homer—the Giants took their batting practice at Yankee Stadium, and at a given time, the regulars yielded the hitting cage to the substitutes. Ed Bailey—who was not to catch that day—stepped in, swinging a bat in his hand, and Willie Mays came up behind Bailey, hoping to sneak in a few extra swings. Bailey's swinging bat nearly hit Mays, and Mays shouted at Bailey (who hadn't known Mays was behind him). Bailey took his stance at the plate, waiting for the practice pitcher to lob in a few, and Mays—still waiting to hit—took his stance across the plate. For a few seconds, neither man moved; finally Bailey deferred to Mays and let Mays have an extra swing. But the practice pitcher threw in the dirt, and Mays picked up the ball and had to fungo it, and as he hit the ball, he said, "Shove the blankety ball up your blankety blank." It was the one ugly moment of the Series, and a minor one at that, and you have to remember that all through the Series, Willie Mays kept saying, "I'm so tired, I can't wait for this thing to end." The phone at Mays' house never stopped ringing; he did not get his rest; the pressures on Mays were physical and psychological. He knew so much depended on him, and it was also typical of this Series that the final game came down to a Giant on base, with two out, and Willie Mays at the plate. And Mays doubled.

Tension. Some rise to it; others are baffled by it, almost para-lyzed by it. Jose Pagan said before the Series started: "I like thees kind of game. I like it tough." And all through the Series, Pagan was not merely a fine ballplayer; he was a great ballplayer, at the top of his talent. "You see," he said after he'd homered in the fifth game, "I like—no, I love the beeg game." And he tapped his chest and nodded and smiled. Not cocky. No. But with an aggressive confidence.

There were other Giants like that, and it is mainly the Giants we are interested in. They lost. In batting practice, one afternoon at Yankee Stadium, Matty Alou slashed a ball foul, into the seats, and Matty muttered, "Keel somebody, keel somebody." It is an instinct, a killer's instinct, if you will, and that is how Matty Alou plays. If I ever were to wander into an alley in the dark, and I needed companions, I'd send Matty Alou out in front of me, and then I'd have Jack Sanford with me. You can have Sonny Liston.

Other men—other Giants—react differently. They are not all killers. Billy Pierce is a dapper, chipper, affable man with a worldly wit. After the Giants had lost the first game, Pierce said, "One game never matters. Besides, we are still living off yesterday." Yesterday was the last game of the Dodger-Giant pennant playoff, and the Giants had won though nobody had thought they'd win, and Pierce still floated with that win.

Most of the Giants felt that way, as a matter of fact, after losing the first. But when they won the second and squared the Series, there was a different attitude. Felipe Alou expressed it in almost classical fashion. "If we lose now," Alou said—and he said it seriously, his brow furrowed, because Alou is a man who says what he means, and means what he says—"if we lose, it is because they are the better team." And how did Alou personally feel, now that he'd had one decent night's sleep.

"I feel good, strong, like the beginning of the season." One win and Alou had come all the way back.

And so the writer moves through the dressing rooms, a different room each game, because no team won two in a row. And you talk about losing. I asked Giant coach Larry Jansen some time during the Series whether he still remembers pitching in the 1951

World Series and losing a game to the Yankees by giving up a home run to Joe Collins. How long did the pitch nag at him?

"I pitched it over and over till the next day," Jansen said. "I had to figure where I goofed. I had to figure what he'd hit and why. I kicked myself in the butt all day. Then I forgot about it."

You forget it, if you can. Ralph Terry was the World Series' No. 1 hero. On the morning of the seventh game, Terry told a writer: "After that Mazeroski home run in 1960, the fact that this team is letting me pitch the seventh game is like a tonic to me." It was two years later and Terry had won more games than any other American League pitcher in the 1962 campaign, and still he needed a vote of confidence to erase the image of Bill Mazeroski, and to wipe out the stigma of being a loser. They said of Ralph Terry after the 1960 Series, after that seventh-game, sudden-death home run, he had not been dismayed, he'd been destroyed.

Perhaps the word was too strong. But surely the memory had lingered. When the 1962 seventh game ended, and Ralph Terry was drinking champagne, Joe DiMaggio came into the Yankee dressing room to congratulate the men on the team he once played for. He looked over at Terry's cubicle, and he called out: "You can forget that Pittsburgh thing now, Ralph." Two years, and a vote of confidence, and still the memory, to be erased.

Some of the losing attitudes are the usual postures. When the Giants were beaten in Yankee Stadium the first time, Jim Davenport complained about batting against the white-shirted crowd. Did the Giants pick up the ball late, while hitting? "Ah did. Ah don't know about the rest of them, but Ah did." The next day the Giants won, and Davenport said he was seeing the ball much better.

On the pitch Willie McCovey hit for a home run in the second game—at Candlestick—Ralph Terry insisted he got the ball exactly where he wanted to. Larry Jansen grins when he hears these things. Says Jansen: "Over two-thirds of balls that are hit for home runs are made when the pitcher goofs, when he throws a ball where he doesn't want to." But Terry insists. "I'd throw that pitch in exactly the same place again," Terry says, "if I had the chance." And now Jansen's grin is broader. "And McCovey would hit it in the same place again," says Jansen, "if he had the chance."

Still, some of the attitudes are surprisingly not usual. Cletis Boyer, surely one of the finest of all defensive third basemen, committed two errors and misplayed another ball or two. His second error occurred at Candlestick Park after the long delay, and a writer asked Boyer whether the infield was in bad shape.

"This is the finest visiting infield I've played in in a World Series," Boyer said. "It's better than Pittsburgh or Cincinnati. It's a fine infield."

Boyer is an admirable young man. He has class. After Billy Pierce had beaten the Yankees in the sixth game, holding them to three hits, and again tying the Series, the writer asked Boyer whether Pierce was throwing the same sort of stuff he'd thrown when the Yankees had beaten him, 3–2, at Yankee Stadium.

"Pierce always throws the same kind of stuff," Boyer said. "You have to admire him. He goes out there and he throws the ball over the plate, and he makes you hit it. You have to admire the old man."

And so you do; you have to admire most of them, most of the losers. You asked Pierce how he felt before he pitched the first time in the Series, and he laughed and said, "There's no place I'd rather be in October than right here." To be here—in the Yankee Stadium—in October meant you were in the World Series, because the Yankees always were.

Which is what it all gets down to. The Yankees are always in the Series—almost always—and they are the winners. By nature, by tradition, by history. It almost didn't work out this time. The ragtag crew—the team that took batting practice after winning the sixth game, the team of bloodied shins and ulcers—came terribly close.

But close is no cigar. Close is losing. And the Giants lost. Walking through the dressing room, on that last day, you saw the signs of losing. In each dressing cubicle stood a bottle of Mumm's extra-dry champagne. Unopened. And walking about the dressing room was a young man named Ernie Bowman. Ernie Bowman was a loser. Before the sixth game of the Series, the Giants and the Yankees worked out on a ball field in Modesto, California, and during the Giant workout, Ernie Bowman ran into Jose Pagan while the two were pursuing a pop fly. Pagan injured his left wrist—more bandages—and Bowman loosened three teeth.

"One is so loose I can pull it out with my fingers," Bowman said before the sixth game.

But that is not what really marks Bowman as a loser. All the Giants were aching. The mark on Bowman was an undershirt he wore around the Giant clubhouse after the seventh game, after the Series was over, and the Giants had lost.

The undershirt was marked: "Yoohoo, the drink of champions, says Yogi Berra."

When the Giants had to wear a shirt of a champion, it had to be a Yankee shirt.

There is a final postscript to this tale of losing. Much of the Giant attitude—much of the near-blasé quality of Orlando Cepeda and of some of the others—may have simply been the result of the exhausting playoff that preceded the Series. It is not really part of the story of losing a World Series—that playoff—but if a man wanted to see the torment of losing, he would have been at Dodger Stadium that ninth inning of that third playoff game, and then he would have been in the Dodger dressing room immediately after.

I was there. Don Drysdale slammed the dressing-room door open with a crash, to go out for a drink of pop or beer or whatever he drank that afternoon after the bitter defeat. And when the door was open, Drysdale reached behind him and slammed it shut. His mouth was a thin blade, and a curse word was wrestled past his tight lips. Willie Davis walked by, and I said softly, "Hello, Willie," and Davis kept on walking, unhearing, unheeding. And finally Walt Alston sat with the press and managed to speak in composed terms of what had transpired. He explained why he hadn't batted for Ed Roebuck and why he hadn't used Larry Sherry, and why he had used Stan Williams, and it was an agonizing experience. Alston's voice was calm, he sat quietly, and he did not reveal with words what was going on inside.

But as he spoke, he broke open a pack of cigarettes, and as the words tumbled out softly and calmly, Walt Alston rolled little silver-paper balls from the cigarette pack, and rolled them in his fingers, rolled them, rolled them, little Queeg balls. Finally, when he had tortured the silver-paper balls long enough, he kept on talking, answering questions, explaining, and the only other sound in the room was Walt Alston's cigarette lighter being opened and snapped shut, opened and snapped shut, and the recurring click was louder than a scream.

These are the ways men lose.

1963

The Last Shovel
(World Series Game IV)

JERRY IZENBERG

THE MORNING OF THE FUNERAL dawned bright and clear and in front of the Statler-Hilton two cars full of kids with musical instruments pulled up next to the Yankee team bus.

One by one, the rapidly expiring champions climbed on board and the kids hooted and jeered and when Mickey Mantle came strolling through the big glass doors of the Statler, the musicians broke into "The Mickey Mouse Club Theme Song."

Then everybody went out to the ball park where Sandy Koufax threw the last left-handed shovel full of earth on the team which used to be the Yankees. And so it ended . . . the calf killed the butcher . . . the missionaries ate the cannibals . . . and the Dodgers beat the Yankees in four straight games.

Yesterday's services took a modest hour and 50 minutes. The thing was handled with exceptional dispatch because the batting orders marched to combat with all the violence of a duel to the death between rival quilting-bee champions.

"Choose your weapons," the man shouted. "Powder puffs at 50 yards," the warriors said. The Dodgers collected two hits, the Yankees six.

For the most part Sandy Koufax and Whitey Ford played their

own ball games. In the fifth inning, Frank Howard put one into the left-field seats and in the seventh Mantle evened it in the same way. These were, at best, rude interruptions.

This was, after all, a war between rival bands of mosquitoes. In the end, therefore, the thing was laid out tenderly with a touch of charity and a burst of speed. It was tied together smartly by the muscular fingers of Mrs. Koufax' son Sanford.

In the seventh inning, Junior Gilliam swung mightily and lined the ball toward the left field but Clete Boyer, moving rapidly upwards with no visible means of support, hauled the ball down after a very large bounce and gunned it over to Joe Pepitone at first.

It was a good throw. It was straight and hard and Pepitone caught it smartly with his wrist. Then he caught it with his forearm. Then he caught it with his chest and the ball rolled and rolled and so did Junior Gilliam.

"When I got to second," Junior said afterwards, "I never thought of stopping, I just wanted to know where the ball was."

Pete Reiser, the third-base coach, knew where the ball was. So did Pepitone. It was rolling off toward the low fence near the dugout and Reiser was waving his arm over his head in great big circles. Pete Reiser is a method school coach and Jim Gilliam is a method school runner and when the ball finally caught up with them, they were both resting comfortably at stage left.

There was nothing left for Whitey Ford but to pitch to Willie Davis, who hit one high enough and far enough to Mantle to get the offense home.

And there was nothing left for Sandy Koufax but to tear the final sheet off the calendar. This was not without drama because Bobby Richardson, first Yankee hitter in the ninth, singled.

So Koufax threw strike three past Tom Tresh and then it was Mantle and on the third pitch, superstar stood there like something by Rodin. "Strike three," yelled Shag Crawford, the umpire.

Mantle did a neat column left and marched for the dugout.

There was only this little bit left and Elston Howard kept it alive by hitting the ball to Maury Wills, who should have had it all but Dick Tracewski dropped the throw at second.

And it came down to Hector Lopez, who tried to check his swing on the very first pitch and succeeded only in ending the death rattle. It went Tracewski to Moose Skowron and then there was a gentle riot out near the pitcher's mound.

Somebody heaved the ball in the upper deck and then people were throwing rented pillows at the Dodgers and the Dodgers were throwing their caps at the people and La Dolce Vita came to Disneyland.

These are hard times for the royalists. When the Yankees left home Thursday night, Pete Sheehy, the clubhouse man, had to go back and get the bats because somebody had forgotten to pack them. It was hardly worth the effort.

And yesterday, an hour after it was over, Lopez emerged from the Yankee dugout in street clothes and took a long, lonely walk through the outfield toward the exit where the Yankee bus waited.

As he reached the midpoint, the Dodger groundskeeper turned on the sprinkling system. It was not a happy thing to be both dry-cleaned and laundered in the same afternoon.

1967

The Knot-Hole Gang
Goes Climbing

BUD COLLINS

WEDNESDAY AFTERNOON'S MATINEE at Fenway Park was over-priced and under-active, but at least it was the most forgettable game of the baseball season. Carl Yastrzemski seldom acts like a dove, but any time he is party to a bombing pause, you can forget it.

Yaz abstained from violence in four times at bat and Our Old Town Team went pacifist, losing 2–1. Although the customers had waited 21 years to witness a World Series here, they were stoic in defeat. Particularly since most of those who bought $12 and $8 seats were involved in some kind of tax write-off.

The occasion had its virtues, though, as a demonstration to the world that American youth has not gone soft. While baseball is a moderately athletic diversion, it inspired extraordinary feats of athleticism outside the park by those youths who were trying to get in and were handicapped by the absence of tickets.

They were not handicapped by a lack of what one harassed policeman called "the return of Yankee ingenuity."

The spirit of Teddy-Green-In-Reverse was rampant outside the walls. Teddy climbed walls to get out of a joint. The kids were climbing, trying to get in, and a few of them probably made it, although the cops said no.

It was the biggest game of cops and risers of the year, as teenagers sought to scale Fenway from all approaches. Those defeated at the walls crossed Lansdowne St. and crawled and scrambled up buildings. Then they made precarious ascents of steel supports to attain the heights of billboards that towered nearly 100 feet with a view of the playing field over the left field wall.

Yastrzemski made a splendid catch of Curt Flood's line drive in the seventh. He also spiked a St. Louis run with a fine throw to the plate in the fourth inning, apprehending Joolie Javier. Yet nothing he did could compare to the exertions of such as a 16-year-old blonde from Dorchester named Cathy Dawson. She mounted a fire escape behind a liquor warehouse on Lansdowne, clambered the rest of the way up the side to the roof along with another 16-year-old, June Pearson. Finally they scrambled up to a perch on a billboard that read "Go Red Sox—John Donnelly & Sons."

"We can out-climb the guys," Cathy said. There were few girls, though, among perhaps 250 kids who forged to the crest of three large signboards with the determination of Edward Whymper conquering the Matterhorn.

The buildings that nestle against the old ball park looked like a castle under siege. Kids were shinnying drainpipes, wooden poles, balancing on window sills and narrow ledges as though Sherpa blood filled their veins. They planned to leap from the buildings onto the bleacher wall at Fenway and disappear into the crowd.

Andy Filaska was clawing his way along a sill, about to pull himself onto the roof when a face appeared over the side. "It's no go, kid," said Patrolman Peter McDonough, "You got to get down." The kids below booed and swore at the cop.

"I don't like to push them around, but I'd hate to see anybody fall and split his head," McDonough said. "We have orders to keep them off the roofs."

Later, in the third inning, the game stopped while McDonough got rid of a kid who had made it, somehow climbing a rope that hung over the wall. For a moment this kid was inside, atop the fence, hugging the left field foul pole. He stood 40 feet above Lou Brock, who was in left for the Cardinals. Bob Gibson, the pitcher, stopped work on the mound and stared at the kid. So did the 34,796 conformists who had paid their way in, probably admiring his daring. In an instant at the cops' insistence he was gone—back down the rope and almost into the jaws of a police dog that was patrolling the wall by that time. From on high, at the summit of a billboard, Eddie Manning of Roslindale, as Gabriel, blew a salute to the young adventurer on a red plastic trumpet.

Until the police dogs showed, the kids were working hard at the adjoining buildings. "They did this Sunday, too," said Chris Pintsopoulos, a beer distributor, whose place is a minor peak in the Fenway range. "They jump from our place to another building, then to the wall. Several kids did it early this morning, before the cops went on duty. Sunday after the game they broke through a skylight and sat in here drinking my beer. It's things like this that cut down on my World Series spirit."

Tommy Hart, a 15-year-old South Bostonian got a boost to a sign projecting from the ball park wall, lifted himself over the wall and onto a concrete beam above the ticket-takers. He was inside Fenway, but still outside the turnstiles. The beam led nowhere, and it was too high above the cement floor to jump.

"Now what?" he yelled down to Tommy Lee, who is 14.

"I'll think of something," said Lee.

Who are you? Lee was asked.

"I'm his agent. I'll get him and me in yet. Maybe," Tommy said, "we'll try the sewers."

The great athletes were outside of Fenway Park Wednesday. Forget about the Sherpas in Nepal. The next time you want guides for climbing Mt. Everest, get in touch with Tommy Lee, Cathy Dawson and the rest of the gang on the Old Grand-Dad sign at Lansdowne St.

1969

Defying Belief

ARTHUR DALEY

WHAT ELSE DID YOU EXPECT? In one final, convulsive rupture of the credibility gap, those darlings of destiny, the Amazing Mets, came roaring from behind in their last three turns at bat to win the championship of the world in the Shea Stadium madhouse yesterday.

For the last two months the Mets made every big play they had to make. They defied the odds to beat the Cubs for the Eastern leadership of the National League. They defied the odds to beat the Braves in the pennant playoff. They defied the odds to beat those proud paladins of the American League, the Baltimore Orioles, in the World Series. From start to finish this ninth-place team of a year ago defied belief. If it seemed at times that providence guided their hands and steered their course, no one would argue to the contrary. In this Series especially, they made no mistakes after they had settled down at the conclusion of a loss in the opener. They then regained their mystique and their magic.

They even had the gremlins working for them yesterday. When the plate umpire ruled that Cleon Jones had not been hit on the foot by an errant pitch, Gil Hodges walked calmly from the dugout where the ball had rolled and showed the ball to His Nibs.

A white spheroid with a smudge of shoe polish on it. Cleon was awarded the base and Donn Clendenon promptly caromed a homer off a corner of the left-field stands. From being behind, 3–0, they had narrowed the margin to 3–2.

ANOTHER HERO

That was in the sixth. An inning later, the unlikeliest slugger in the line-up, Al Weis, slammed the first home run he had ever hit at Shea Stadium. It tied the score. An inning after that, Jones and Ron Swoboda pieced together two doubles for one run and a second score arrived when the jittery Orioles made two errors on one play. It added up to a 5–3 victory that was awaiting the Mets at the end of the rainbow. It was the last Impossible Dream.

Before the game, television cameras focused on Casey Stengel. He was asked to utter one word, which really was short-changing the garrulous old man.

"Amazin'," he said. Why shouldn't he utter it? After all he was the inventor of the catchline, "The Amazin' Mets." He originally meant it in the pejorative sense, but it now is a true description. Ol' Case even sniffed at critics who had termed the Mets lucky.

"You can't be lucky every day," he said with gravel-voiced positiveness. "But you can if you get good pitchin'."

The Mets got it yesterday from Jerry Koosman. He had been rocked in the third by a two-run homer from the feeble-hitting Dave McNally, his opposite number, and a single-0 homer by the authoritative Frank Robinson. But a scratch hit was the only other Baltimore hit the rest of the way.

Although the regular customers are usually shunted aside by the toffs and other influential people for World Series seats, there still were enough New Breeders to display the usual Metsomania when the final out was made. They came tumbling from the stands by the thousands, lit red flares, brandished signs and whooped it up in unrestrained glee. They stole all the bases and home plate and ripped up the turf for souvenir pieces until it was as pockmarked as a battlefield.

CARBON COPY

The freakish Cleon Jones episode with the shoeblack evidence naturally brought to mind the almost identical happening to Nippy Jones of the Milwaukee Braves in the 1957 Series. He also was hit on the foot. He also was a neat man with polished shoes. He also was refused free passage to first base until he displayed shoeblack on the ball. He represented the tying run against the Yankees, as Eddie Mathews won it for the Braves with a home run in that same inning, the 10th.

As they had been doing all through this Series, the Mets fielded beautifully behind Koosman. The hero with a diving catch the day before, Swoboda, came up with a dilly on Don Buford in the fifth. In fact, rugged Ron's Wednesday effort may even have been superior to Tommie Agee's dazzlers of the previous day.

But how does one measure those things? Memory can play such tricks that I'm slightly red-faced, because I hailed Agee's second catch as perhaps the best ever. I had unaccountably forgotten Willie Mays's unforgettable catch on Vic Wertz in the 1954 Series.

"The best I ever saw," said Moe Berg, the baseball sage, "was the one Terry Moore pulled on Joe DiMaggio in the 1942 World Series. Stan Musial slipped in going for the ball. Moore dived over Musial's prostrate body and caught the ball in mid-air with his body parallel to the ground."

It hardly matters now. The Mets won. Ah, those Mets! They are amazing, fantastic, preposterous, stupendous, colossal, inconceivable and wonderful. Take your pick, one adjective or all.

The World Turned Upside Down: The Last Five Series of the 1960s

LUKE SALISBURY

FEW PERIODS IN AMERICAN LIFE have been more interesting or unexpected than the years 1965–1969. This was delightfully true in baseball. The late sixties were a cultural and baseball interregnum. Baseball emerged from the hegemony of the New York Yankees and America from the tedium of the 1950s. Baseball, like college campuses and "people's heads," was joyously free. It was brief; it was turbulent; it was wonderful.

If you went off to college in 1965, you would have told a foreigner the United States had never lost a war, was solving problems like poverty and civil rights, conquering space, winning was the New York Yankees and losing the New York Mets.

You might not have been aware that never had so many great players been in their prime in one league at one time. Before sports medicine, steroids, 70 home runs a year, and padded batters who yelp if pitched inside was the National League in 1965. Willie Mays at thirty-four had his best year hitting 52 homers and winning the MVP. Hank Aaron, thirty-one, was in his prime—that incredibly long prime—and hit .318 with 32 homers. Roberto

Clemente, thirty, won the batting title and made godlike throws from right. Frank Robinson, twenty-nine, was still on the Reds. The secondary stars—Pete Rose, Lou Brock, Willie McCovey, Willie Stargell, Ritchie Allen, Ernie Banks, Billy Williams, Ron Santo, Eddie Mathews, and Maury Wills (Orlando Cepeda was injured and batted only 34 times), were as good or better than the stars of the next two decades. As for pitchers, Sandy Koufax was the best anyone who saw him ever saw, and remains so to this day. The same is true for Willie Mays—no one has seen a better all-around player. Behind Koufax were Juan Marichal, twenty-seven, and Bob Gibson, twenty-nine, who were as good as anyone since, then Don Drysdale and Jim Bunning.

The NL pennant race was a classic to-the-knife four-team frenzy that came down to the clubs who hated each other most—the Dodgers and Giants—and the Dodgers with superb pitching, excellent defense, and a run-scratching offense, somehow beat the power-laden Giants. After the NL pennant race, the Series seemed anticlimactic.

The Minnesota Twins, the former Washington Senators, a prototypical, hard-hitting American League club modeled on the 1950s Yankees, met the light-hitting, NL-hardened Dodgers. LA's lineup of Maury Wills, Junior Gilliam, Willie Davis, Lou Johnson, and Wes Parker met slugging Harmon Killebrew, Bob Allison, Don Mincher, Earl Battey, and a terrific young hitter, Tony Oliva.

Koufax didn't pitch the first game, because of a Jewish holiday—he didn't make a big deal of it, he just didn't pitch. Today, it's all ethnicity all the time, and this would be The Story. In 1965, it was *a* story. The Twins beat Drysdale in game one and the Master in game two. Suddenly the Series wasn't anticlimactic. The league whose all-stars were Harmon Killebrew, Al Kaline, and Carl Yastzremski was poised to beat the champion of a league with Mays, Aaron, Clemente, and Koufax. This is the glory of the World Series. Underdogs with pitching can bottle the post-season lightning.

The Dodgers had to win game three and Claude Osteen

pitched a shutout. LA won game four behind Drysdale, won game five with Koufax, then lost game six, setting up Koufax for the finale on two days' rest. Koufax, so tired he could only throw fastballs, shut out the hard-hitting Twins 2–0, proving there may or may not be a God, but there is Sandy Koufax.

By 1966 you would have done pot, heard of hippies, LSD, the Jefferson Airplane, and the Baltimore Orioles. The Orioles traded Milt Pappas for Frank Robinson and got National League grit, not just one man. Baltimore was a mixture of young and old talent. Frank Robinson joined Luis Aparicio, Brooks Robinson, and an extraordinarily young pitching staff, and beat the Dodgers at their own game—low-run games. After Jim Lefebvre homered in the second inning of game one, and Moe Drabowsky, who relieved Dave McNally, walked in a run in the third, the Dodgers scored no more runs in the Series. Drabowsky, a journeyman ex-Cub, had the six and two-thirds innings of a lifetime and fanned 11—one of the great long relief jobs in Series history. Jim Palmer, Wally Bunker, and McNally followed with shutouts. The Dodgers' scratch-a-lead-for-Sandy-and-Don finally came up short. Koufax lost game two on errors by Willie Davis and game four on a solo homer by Frank Robinson. Jim Palmer was twenty, Dave McNally twenty-three, and Wally Bunker twenty-one. Youth was about to be served all over the country.

By 1967, you perhaps had done LSD, were a hippie, had benefited from the sexual revolution, and had a strong opinion about the Vietnam war. It was the year the world got turned upside down, or "on," if you will. Sex, drugs, underdogs, and a new kind of rock and roll were everywhere. *Sgt. Pepper's Lonely Hearts Club Band* changed music; so did Jimi Hendrix, the Doors, and Otis Redding. A gathering of bands at Monterey, California, introduced the rock festival and the idea of a generation united by peace, love, and music—or as Governor Ronald Reagan said of public higher education in California: "Four years of sex, drugs, and treason." The antiwar demonstration at the Pentagon in October changed the political climate. Wilt Chamberlain beat Bill Russell and won an NBA championship.

And the Red Sox.

As if God's bounty hadn't already been showered on young America, 1967 was the most intense American League race since 1908—four teams were still in it on the last weekend—and the least likely, a 75–1 shot, ninth-place finisher the previous year, the Boston Red Sox, the country club of losers, won the pennant on the last day of the season.

The Series was David and Goliath. The St. Louis Cardinals were an excellent club. The best fielding team in baseball, they had speed with Lou Brock and Curt Flood, power with Orlando Cepeda, and the incomparable competitiveness of Bob Gibson. David had used every conceivable stone in the pennant race but, on the arm of Jim Lonborg who threw a one- and three-hitter to win games two and five, and with the hitting of Yastzremski and the rest of an unlikely crew, took the fight to seven games. Lonborg faced Gibson on two days' rest in the final game and got bombed, but the moral was clear—anything could happen! New England fandom, which had slumbered like Arabia before the coming of the Prophet, awoke with a frenzy of rooting and desire which persists to this day. A new energy had been released. Life, for a brief while, passed into the "realms of gold," as Keats said.

By 1968, you probably expected a revolution, knew someone in Vietnam, had given up on the two-party system, and wondered if anyone would ever hit 50 home runs or bat .350 again. It was the year of the Tet Offensive, assassinations, riots, the Chicago Convention, Richard Nixon, and the pitcher. Everything that went right in '67 went wrong in '68.

The baseball season was dull. In this year of the pitcher, no one could hit. Only one man in either league hit 40 homers. Carl Yastzremski led the AL hitting .301, the lowest ever, including the Dead Ball era. The dominance of two clubs and two pitchers was uncontested. The Tigers ran away with the AL with Denny McLain winning thirty-one games. No one had won thirty since Dizzy Dean in 1934. In the NL, the Cardinals were never challenged. Bob Gibson pitched thirteen shutouts and had an ERA of 1.12, the lowest of the Live Ball era. Five AL pitchers had ERAs under 2. Between them, pitchers in both leagues pitched 349 shutouts. Winning thirty-one games or achieving an ERA of 1.12 is amazing. It's like Ted Williams hitting .400. It hasn't been done since. Both figures are unapproachable as baseball is now played.

Two powerhouses met in the Series. Each had a great starter, power, and defense. The Cardinals could run. Detroit manager Mayo Smith made an audacious gamble—he played center fielder Mickey Stanley at short in place of weak-hitting Ray Oyler, which allowed Al Kaline and Jim Northrup to play in each game. No manager has tried anything like it since.

Gibson beat McLain in the first game and fanned a Series record 17, as the Cards won 4–0. Mickey Lolich, an overweight lefty who said his fastball sank better as he tired, beat St. Louis in game two. Lolich, one of the worst-hitting pitchers in baseball history, hit a home run. The Cardinals won the next two—McLain lost again to Gibson in game four.

Down three games to one, the Tigers trailed 3–2 in the fifth inning of the sixth game, when Lou Brock, the best base runner of his era, tried to score standing up and was thrown out by left fielder Willie Horton, who despite a left fielder's arm made a great throw. Brock told posterity he didn't slide because he was safe. Kaline knocked in the winning runs in the seventh and Detroit was down three games to two. The Tigers won game six 13–1 as McLain finally won, but Detroit had to face Gibson in game seven. It was unthinkable that Gibson could lose. He had won seven straight World Series games, beaten the Tigers twice, set the strike-out record against them, and was arguably the greatest pitcher in World Series history. Lolich, like Lonborg the previous year, was pitching on two days' rest. It was unthinkable, but this was the sixties, when the unthinkable (How could another

Kennedy be assassinated? How could little guys in the black pajamas, as Eldridge Cleaver said, defeat the US?) could and did happen. In the seventh inning of a scoreless game, Curt Flood, the best defensive center fielder in baseball, misjudged Jim Northrup's fly ball, two runs scored, and the Tigers went on to win. Lolich had beaten the great Bob Gibson. Like Harry Brecheen in '46 and Lew Burdette in '57, a number-two starter was Series hero.

It was also the last World Series with league, not division, champions. You had to beat everyone over 162 games. No stumbling in with an 82–79 record. No BS.

Think about that.

In 1969, you were 1-Y, teaching school, in Canada, boot camp, or San Francisco, lamenting the breakup of the Beatles, and rooting for the Mets.

The New York Mets had defined losing, as the New York Yankees defined winning. The Mets were Casey Stengel falling asleep in the dugout, Marv Throneberry committing comedy at first, and Jimmy Piersall hitting his one hundredth career home run and running around the bases backward at the Polo Grounds. They were not only awful, they were the icon of awful.

By 1969, if one looked closely, the Mets were strong up the middle with Jerry Grote at catcher, Bud Harrelson at short, and Tommy Agee in center. They had two outstanding young pitchers, Tom Seaver and Jerry Koosman, two excellent prospects in Gary Gentry and Nolan Ryan, a solid veteran in Don Cardwell, and another, Ron Taylor, in the bullpen. The Mets had been so bad that the idea they could win anything, let alone get to the World Series, was, to use a word from the time, revolutionary.

But get there they did, only to face a newly assembled Baltimore mini-dynasty. The Orioles had power, the best defensive team of both the sixties and seventies, and their own young pitchers, but it was the sixties, and the turbulent underdog decade ended with a phenomenal upset. After the Birds won the first game, the Mets won four straight. Tommy Agee and Ron Swoboda each made a great catch at a crucial moment. J. C. Martin was ruled safe when he ran in foul territory after a bunt. Koosman won two games; Seaver pitched a 1–0 shutout. Al Weiss, with eight home runs in his career, hit one in game five for the tie. It was magic. It seemed if you wished hard enough, if "your head was together," the world was changeable. Changeable and wild with possibility.

Neither life nor baseball stays wild. Baseball and America would return to business as usual soon enough. For baseball—mini-dynasties and the return of capital as the defining force in the game. For the country—Republicans, money as God, selfishness as patriotism, and winnable wars. The baseball legacy of the sixties would be free agency, which for a while would break the Yankee monopoly, then guarantee it.

After Koufax, Gibson, the '67 Red Sox, and '69 Mets, real pennant races—after the hope and liberation and energy of the sixties, what else?

We'd seen it all.

1973

The Game They Invented for Willie

RED SMITH

OAKLAND, 1973

WHEN WILLIE GOT THE HIT, Ray Sadecki and Harry Parker were watching on television in the clubhouse of the New York Mets. For a moment there was silence. Then Sadecki, who had pitched an inning and one-third, turned to Parker, who had pitched one inning. "He had to get a hit," Sadecki said. "This game was invented for Willie Mays a hundred years ago."

It was the longest day in the long, long history of World Series competition, and for Willie Mays it was eternity. It was the second match in the struggle with the Oakland A's for the baseball championship of creation. It was the nineteenth such game for Willie in a span of twenty-two years. In the forty-third year of his life, this may have been the final bow for the most exciting player of his time. So he lost the game in the ninth inning, won it in the twelfth, came perilously close to losing it again—and walked away from disaster grinning.

Never another like him. Never in this world.

"Yesterday," a man told him, "you said you were going to let the kids win it the rest of the way. What do you say about the old folks now?"

Willie took a sip from a can of Coke. He lounged on a platform behind a microphone, one leg slung over a television receiving set. His jaw worked rhythmically on a cud of gum.

"What old folks you talkin' about?" he asked.

Strictly speaking, Willie never lost the game and never won it. It only seemed that way. When the Mets had the decision in hand, 6–4, in the last of the ninth, Mays fell down chasing a drive by Deron Johnson and the two-base hit that resulted started a rally that tied the score.

Willie had gone into the game as a pinch-runner and had fallen down rounding second, but that had been only an embarrassment without effect on the score. For the most spectacular outfielder of an era, though, that pratfall in center was catastrophic.

"I didn't see the ball," he said, and he wasn't the only one dazzled in the sun field of Oakland-Alameda County Stadium. "I tried to dive for it the last second. We had a two-run lead and I shoulda played it safe."

His chance for redemption came in the twelfth with the score still tied, two out and two Mets on the bases. The game had already gone on longer than any World Series match before, longer than the one between the Cubs and Tigers that consumed 3 hours 28 minutes in 1945.

Rollie Fingers, fifth of the six pitchers who worked for Oakland, threw a strike and Willie slashed at it, missing. Fingers threw another and Willie slapped it straight back, a bounder that hopped high over the pitcher's head and skipped on into center field, sending Bud Harrelson home with the run that put New York ahead.

"I think it was a fastball, up," Willie said. "I'd seen Fingers a lot on television and he likes to work inside and outside, up and down. Yesterday was the test. He threw me a fastball, then gave me a breaking pitch and came back with a fastball, so I knew he'd feed me 80 percent fastballs."

Waxed mustache twitching angrily, Fingers flipped his glove away in disgust. One play later the Oakland manager, Dick Williams, sent Fingers away, too, but more in sorrow than in anger. By that time Cleon Jones had singled to load the bases, and errors soon would let in three more runs.

With New York in front, 10–6, Reggie Jackson opened the rebuttal. He drove a mighty shot high and deep toward the wall in center. Willie went back to the fence, set himself and saw the ball drop in front of him.

"I saw it," he said afterward, "and in a close game I might have had a chance on it, but we had a four-run lead then and I didn't want to kill myself because we got a lot more games to play."

"But Willie," a man said, "you fell down in center field. What happened out there?"

"Two balls come out there," he said. "That's most of it." His voice dropped, took on a comforting tone. "You've seen me play enough. I wasn't out there long today. You know when I play regular. . . . But I'm not a player that makes excuses."

Excuses? Some of those who heard him could remember the catch he made off Cleveland's Vic Wertz in the World Series of 1954, the time he ran down Carl Furillo's drive, spun completely around and threw out Billy Cox at the plate, the impossible chance he grabbed off Roberto Clemente of Pittsburgh. To be sure, this time Jackson scored and the A's went on to fill the bases. But excuses? Not for Willie, ever.

1975

The Sixth Game

PETER GAMMONS

BOSTON, OCTOBER 22, 1975—Then all of a sudden the ball was suspended out there in the black of the morning like the Mystic River Bridge. Carlton Fisk broke forward for a step, then stopped and watched. He later remembered none of the clumsy hula dance that NBC made famous, only that "it seemed like the wait for Christmas morning" as he watched to see on which side of the fine line it would land: home run/victory or foul ball/strike one.

When it finally crashed fair off the mesh attached to the left-field foul pole, Fisk raised his fists above his head in applause in the midst of his convulsive leap, and as if conducted by Charles Munch, the reaction unfurled. Fenway Park organist John Kiley boomed the opening notes of Handel's "Hallelujah Chorus," Fisk gamboled his way around the bases, teammates passionately staggered to home plate, and from the bleachers to Presque Isle people looked at one another as the first shock warmed into reality. In Raymond, New Hampshire, an Episcopal minister named James Smith burst out of his house, ran across to St. Bartholomew's Church, grabbed the rope, and began ringing the church bell about the same time that, in Yardley, Pennsylvania, the wife of another Episcopal minister, Gretchen Gammons, ran across the street to St. Andrew's and did the same.

It had been back in the tenth inning that Pete Rose had turned from his place in the batter's box and said to Fisk, "This is some kind of game, isn't it?" At 12:34 A.M., in the bottom of the twelfth inning, Fisk's histrionic, 304-foot home run brought Red Sox shortstop Rick Burleson running to home plate saying to teammate Rick Miller, "We just might have won the greatest game ever played."

So it seemed at the moment, frozen in time. Judged soberly, rationally, there are undoubtedly dozens and hundreds and thousands of baseball games staged from Old Orchard Beach to Los Angeles that one would have to say had more technical brilliance. But this one had captured all that baseball could be. Fisk's home run had virtually altered the autumnal equinox. By the time the ball had caromed off the screen and thirty-five thousand people had stood to sing "Give Me Some Men Who Are Stout-Hearted Men" as Fisk galavanted across the field to an interview room, the entire emotional scale had been played.

After three days of rain, the Red Sox had begun this fight for survival with a three-run, first-inning homer by wonderchild Fred Lynn. Then they watched in resigned silence as, slowly but surely, the heavily favored Reds chipped away at the mortality of a hero named Luis Tiant. When Cincinnati center fielder Cesar Geronimo homered in the top of the eighth inning, El Tiante left, trailing 6–3, to heartfelt but polite applause that accepted the finality of the situation.

If some clock had been allowed to run out at that point, the sixth game of the 1975 World Series would have been no more, no less than a game from the, say, 1961 World Series or 1969 National League Championship Series. But, turn after hairpin turn, it became the Sixth Game. First, in the bottom of the eighth, Bernardo Carbo hit a stunning two-out, three-run homer that tied it. In the ninth, when Boston had the bases loaded and none out, Cincinnati left fielder George Foster caught Lynn's fly ball and threw Denny Doyle out at the plate to kill what was apparently a certain game-winning rally. In the eleventh, Dwight Evans made a catch that Reds manager Sparky Anderson insisted was "given its significance, one of the two greatest catches ever made" to rob Joe Morgan of a game-winning double, triple, or homer and turn it into a double play. Then, in the twelfth inning, against Pat Darcy, the record twelfth pitcher in the 241-minute game, came Fisk's shot, the cherry on the top of this all-time banana split of a game.

The Sixth Game was an abridgment of the entire splendid series in which Boston led in all seven games and lost the lead in five of them, in which five games were decided by one run, two were decided in extra innings, and two others in the ninth inning. But there was much more to this game, and this series, than statistics, however dazzling they might be. Baseball was coming out of an era of five consecutive vanilla-bland World Series won by teams from Baltimore, Pittsburgh, and Oakland, hardly centers of media excitement. Immediately preceding those five World Series were the years when no one could score runs, which came just a few years after an era in which a team from New York or Los Angeles had been in the World Series for twenty consecutive Octobers. Nineteen seventy-five was the year television coverage of baseball came of age, with the split image of Fisk's rhumba and the ball suspended against the morn, a fitting symbol of TV's ascendancy.

There, too, like a Christmas carol service, at the end of a decade that decried all customs and history, were all the traditions of a sport whose lineage is steeped in history. Cincinnati and Boston, in fact, were the first two professional baseball cities. Fenway Park, with its nooks and crannies and its promise that no two games will ever be alike, is the romanticists' ideal. The matchup of the two teams presented emotional extremes: the IBM image of the Big Red Machine, the best team in baseball, with its short hair and the kind of puissance that earns the Pete Rozelle Trophy, against the Olde Towne Teame, the last great white team, which had come out of nowhere that year with the only rookie ever to be Most Valuable Player (Lynn), an institution (Carl Yastrzemski), a Brahmin New Englander (Fisk), and some characters named Tiant and Carbo and Bill "Space Man" Lee. Riverfront Stadium, which could have been ordered from a Sears catalogue, as contrasted with the idiosyncratic Fenway Park.

The Reds' characters were submerged in and by a team perfection, and in the end, they won the series because they simply played the game more perfectly than Boston, for whom Doyle was the sixth runner in six games tagged out at the plate. It was the Red Sox who did the spectacular in the series, the Red Sox who did so much to bring individualism and personality back into the sport. "When tonight is over," Lee was credited with saying before he pitched the seventh game, "Don Gullett is going to the Hall of Fame, and I'm going to the Eliot Lounge."

What few remember about the Sixth Game was that despite its days of dramatic rainout buildup, it was seven outs from having all the drama of the Astros playing the Giants in August, from a routine conclusion of the Reds defeating the Red Sox in six games. It had begun with Lynn's three-run homer off Cincinnati starter Gary Nolan—who, like all the Reds starters that year, would be gone within three years—in the first inning. That was the final, dramatic blow of what was one of the greatest rookie seasons in baseball history. There was a Joe Hardy air about Lynn, a private, loping kid a year and a half out of the University of Southern California. One week into the season, which the Red Sox had started after a horrible September 1974 collapse, the inability to deal (in the wake of the Yankees getting Bobby Bonds, the Orioles Lee May, and the Tigers Nate Colbert), and a 10–21 spring training, Yankee manager Bill Virdon said, "Don't bother talking about Bonds. Fred Lynn may be the next DiMaggio." Virdon completed his statement with an "I told you so" when Lynn's spectacular diving, bouncing, ninth-inning catch in Shea Stadium in August saved a 1–0 Boston victory that marked the Yankees absent the remainder of the season. Lynn batted .331. He drove in 105 runs, scored 103, rapped 47 doubles and 21 homers, and made one tumblers' catch after another en route to being named both Rookie of the Year and his league's Most Valuable Player. In the fifth inning of the Sixth Game he banged into the center-field fence leaping for Ken Griffey's triple, slid to the ground in a heap, and lay there. The stands fell silent as if witness to a presidential assassination, and Red Sox owner Tom Yawkey turned to scouting director Haywood Sullivan and said, "Those walls must be padded before next season."

For more than a month, it had been Tiant—likened by the *Boston Globe*'s Leigh Montville to the old man in *The Old Man and the Sea*—who had pulled the Red Sox together. El Tiante was listed at thirty-four and rumored to be closer to forty, but he was the central nervous system of the team. He had been sidelined for weeks with a bad back, and when September came (Baltimore manager Earl Weaver kept promising his team's annual comeback and one Baltimore columnist labeled the Red Sox the Boston Chokers), it was Tiant who stepped forth. On September 11, he returned from a three-week absence, took a no-hitter into the eighth, and beat Detroit 3–1. Four days later, with what Red Sox officials later admitted was a crowd in excess of forty-five thousand (prior to standing-room fire laws), he rode the home runs of Fisk and Rico Petrocelli to a 2–0 win over the Orioles' Cy Young Award winner, Jim Palmer, on the night that the chant "LOO-EEE, LOO-EEE" came into being. He shut out Cleveland on the final Friday night of the season to all but clinch the pennant. When the A's began the playoffs as the experienced favorites, he shut them out in the first game and began a three-game sweep. When the Reds began the World Series as heavy favorites, he shut them out, and comically out of place at bat but somehow effective, he started the winning six-run, seventh-inning rally. When, in Cincinnati, the Red Sox were down 2–1 in games, he pitched the game by which he always said he'd like to be remembered: 163 pitches, a 5–4 lead in the fourth, two runners on in each of the last five innings, and a 5–4 victory that was as gutsy as John Garfield in *Body and Soul.*

But this night, El Tiante's marionette abracadabra could carry them no more. A walk to designated bunter Ed Armbrister began a three-run fifth inning that not only broke Tiant's skein of forty consecutive scoreless innings in Fenway but tied the game. Foster made it 5–3 with a line drive off the center-field fence in the seventh, and when Cesar Geronimo angled his homer inside the right-field foul pole leading off the eighth, Tiant left as *Sport* magazine editor Dick Schaap began collecting the MVP ballots in the press box. No one much noticed when the Red Sox got two on leading off the eighth; Cincinnati's prized rookie reliever Rawlins Eastwick III came in and struck out Evans, got Burleson to fly out, and had only to get the pinch hitter, Carbo, to bring the Reds to within an inning of their first championship in thirty-five years.

Bernardo Carbo. He was a cartoon character of sorts, a frizzy-haired kid who traveled with a stuffed gorilla dressed in a Cardinals uniform and named Mighty Joe Young. After running into the bullpen wall to save a home run in the crucial June series with the Yankees, Carbo delayed the game for ten minutes while he scoured the warning track for the chaw of tobacco that had popped out of his mouth; when he found it, he put it back in his mouth and the game continued. Carbo was a streak hitter who, in both of the two years since being obtained from the Cardinals, had hit spectacularly for the Red Sox until mid-May, then ended up relegated to the bench. He never accepted that, once charging up to general manager Dick O'Connell's office immediately before a game to protest Evans's presence in the lineup. Bernardo always had trouble accepting authority, which is why Sparky Anderson and the Reds had traded him to St. Louis in the first place. He had hardly played at all in the second half of the season, but in game three had pinch-hit a homer, and with two outs in the bottom of the eighth of game six, he got his second chance.

With two strikes, Eastwick threw him a fastball that befuddled Bernardo as if it were the Pythagorean theorem. He pulled his bat up in self-defense, deflecting the third strike off to the left. "That might have been the worst swing in the history of baseball," Fisk would tease Carbo later, but it wasted the pitch. Eastwick came in with another fastball and Carbo drove it into the center-field bleachers. "The crowd willed it up into the seats," claims Rose.

6–6. "Bernie," said Lee, "is the only man I know who turned fall into summer with one wave of his magic wand."

The Red Sox had a chance to win it in the ninth, with the bases loaded and none out. When Lynn lofted a fly ball down the left-field line halfway between third base and The Wall and George Foster settled under it 170 feet from home plate, third-base coach Don Zimmer yelled to base runner Denny Doyle, "No, no."

Doyle, however, thought Zimmer was saying "Go, go." He took off, Foster's throw to Johnny Bench cut him down easily, and the threat passed. Then with Griffey on first, one out in the eleventh, Red Sox reliever Dick Drago pitched to Joe Morgan.

When the series was over, Anderson was to say that the Boston player who had impressed him most was Evans. Dwight was only twenty-three at the time, but his three-year major-league career had been a struggle to approach others' expectations. He arrived in September 1972 with the promise of superstardom, but youth, two serious beanings, and personal problems and insecurities had complicated his baseball life. Once the Gold Dust Twins, Fred Lynn and Jim Rice, arrived in 1975, it was Evans who the media constantly suggested should be traded for a pitcher or a power-hitting third baseman. That only added to his problems. But, whether he hit .223 as he did as a rookie or .274 as he did in '75, Evans never wavered in the field. He was at that point in his career a defensive offensive player and an offensive defensive player, the premier defensive right fielder in the American League, playing the most difficult right field in baseball. In this series it was his dramatic ninth-inning, two-run homer off Eastwick that took the third game into extra innings and to the Armbrister interference controversy.

As Red Sox reliever Dick Drago went into his stretch, Evans tried preparing himself for all possibilities. "In all important situations, Doyle would give me a signal if Drago were throwing a breaking ball to a left-handed hitter so I could be leaning for him to pull," Evans said. "One of the great things about playing the outfield with Fisk catching was that he moved so much you could tell the location of the pitch. Knowing the pitching and seeing Fisk set up, I was thinking that the worst thing that could happen would be that Morgan could pull a line drive directly over my head, so I was mentally leaning in that direction." Morgan indeed smashed the worst, a line drive directly over Evans's head. But, breaking as the ball was hit, Evans scrambled backward, stabbed the ball at full stride as he crossed the warning track, ricocheted off the wall, whirled, and fired back to the infield; Yastrzemski, the first baseman, grabbed the throw halfway between the coach's box and the dugout and tossed to Burleson—who'd raced across from shortstop—to complete the double play. "It probably wouldn't have been in the seats," said Evans, "but it would have been the game." As it turned out, it was a catch that shares a place in World Series history with such other historic defensive plays as Willie Mays's in 1954, Al Gionfriddo's in 1947, and Harry Hooper's in 1912.

Pat Darcy, the seventh pitcher, began the bottom of the twelfth by running a sinker down and in to Fisk's wheelhouse. "He's a lowball pitcher, I'm a lowball, dead-pull hitter, so I was looking for that one pitch in that one area," said Fisk. "I got it, then drove it." He chopped his woodcutter's swing and sent his line drive searing toward the foul pole. The problem was keeping the ball in fair territory, as with that short, chopping swing Fisk had spent much of his career setting unofficial records for foul homers. But this was Fisk's season of retribution—after a knee injury that nearly ended his career in 1974, he had broken his arm in the first exhibition game of 1975 and came back in June to bat .331 the remainder of the season. So he found retribution for game three. That night he impaled his mask onto the screen as Morgan's game-winning line drive soared over Lynn's head and Geronimo danced across the plate in front of him; it had been Geronimo whom Armbrister was trying to advance with his bunt attempt, but after the controversial collision as Fisk tried to pounce on the ball, his off-balance throw to start what could have been a double play sailed into center field to launch what would be a long winter's argument with and torment for home-plate umpire Larry Barnett.

But this twelfth-inning drive crashed against the mesh attached to the foul pole, and as Fisk was madly running and skipping and clapping around the bases, George Frederick Handel echoed across the Back Bay and church bells pealed out for both the New England town team and baseball itself.

No seventh game was really necessary, at least from the romanticist's viewpoint, and that encompassed much of the audience, since so much of baseball and its tradition from Abner Doubleday to Babe Ruth to Fernando Valenzuela is romance. "Instead of playing a seventh game, they should spread tables and checkered tablecloths across the outfields and just have a picnic, a feast to a glorious World Series, and toast one another until dawn," suggested television journalist Clark Booth. There was a seventh game, of course, which served to put it on the record that the Cincinnati Reds won—albeit by one run in the ninth inning—and that the Boston Red Sox still had not been world champions since 1918, when Ruth was their best pitcher and Yawkey was a fifteen-year-old student at the Irving School in Tarrytown, New York.

The deciding game was dotted with essences of both teams. Once again, the Red Sox had a 3–0 lead, forged from Gullett's sudden wildness in the fourth inning. Once again, the Red Sox could not put Cincinnati away, either with their bats (Burleson had struck out with the bases loaded to end the fourth) or with their pitching or with their defense. Once again, it was the Hun, Rose, who lead their charge, as he'd led it from the first at-bat of the first game when he snarled, "Tiant is nothing," a declaration he continued to make for two weeks.

With his beloved moon staring down over his left shoulder, Bill Lee had cruised along into the sixth inning with the 3–0 lead. No one entertained America during the series more than The Space Man, as he happily discussed Vonnegut ("In nonsense is strength"), organic gardening, violence ("I'd have bitten Barnett's ear off—I'd have Van Goghed him"), and Boston politics with any journalist who would listen—and most of them did. That he was even on the October stage was surprising: after August 24, when he shut out the White Sox in the rain throwing Leephus bloopers and had a 17–6 record, he did not win another game, finishing the season lost in the bullpen until the Boston scouting reports suggested that his screwball and off-speed stuff would be more effective against Cincinnati's potent lineup than the conventional hard sinker-slider repertoire of late-season Reggie Cleveland. He'd pitched brilliantly in the rain-delayed second game, coming within an inning of a 2–1 victory that would have done in the Reds. But Johnny Bench, showing his experience, looked for the screwball, got one inches off the outside corner on the first pitch of the ninth, and drove it into the right-field corner. Then a David Concepcion infield hit and a Griffey double off Drago took the Reds home to Cincinnati 3–2 winners.

By the sixth inning of the final game, Rose was stomping around the dugout like a whiffling Che Guevera. He screamed, hollered, and slapped his teammates, then stomped up to the plate and led off the inning with a single, one of the extraordinary eleven times he reached base in his final fifteen plate appearances. An out later, Bench pulled a Lee sinker into the ground for what appeared to be an inning-ending double play to Burleson. "There are some things you just can't allow to happen," said Rose. "At that moment, a double play was one of them." He sent himself into a kamikaze orbit toward Doyle. "He saw me coming for ten feet in the air," Rose later chortled. "I made sure of it." He wanted his take-out slides to go to Cooperstown with his base-hit records.

Doyle had another problem besides Rose. The baseballs used then were made in Haiti, and once in a while the force of the bat would literally tear the cover off a ball. "The cover had almost entirely torn off when Bench hit it," Doyle revealed the next spring. "When I went to get rid of it to first, it just flew out of my hand." Utility infielder Bobby Heise retrieved the ball in the dugout, an unenviable trophy that Doyle would keep. The only postseason opportunity of Doyle's career was not one bathed in heroics, for he had lost another Bench double-play ball in the whiteness of Bench's uniform in game five.

So, instead of being out of the inning, Lee then had to face Tony Perez. For the first four games, Perez had been mired in a hitless slump. But in game five he walloped two tremendous home runs off Cleveland to provide Gullett the margin for the 6–2 victory. The scouting reports told Lee not to throw Perez, a deadly off-speed hitter, any junk. But The Space Man did what he wanted to do whenever he wanted to do it—which is how he became one of baseball's first and foremost counterculture idols—and he insisted on throwing Perez one of his Moon Curves or Leephus pitches. A blooper ball. He had thrown three earlier, two for strikes, one for a pop-up, and had even thrown one to Perez that was taken for a strike. "Lee was throwing that hard screwball so well, I never thought he'd throw another one of those bloopers," said Perez. "Sure, I was surprised, but I was geared up for the fastball, and that's so slow it's easy to adjust to." Rumor has it that the ball ended up in Kokomo, Indiana, having landed on a truck in the westbound lane of the Massachusetts Turnpike. Fact had the Red Sox lead cut to 3–2, and an inning later Lee developed a blister. "All of a sudden I found myself pitching to Griffey and I couldn't get the ball to go anywhere near where I wanted it," explained Lee, and when he walked Griffey, manager Darrell Johnson had to bring in left-hander Rogelio Moret. Griffey stole second, and after an out and a walk, Rose slapped another single that tied it. Right-hander Jim Willoughby, a tall, floppy sinker-baller who looked as if he were falling out of a tree when he pitched, came on to retire Bench with the bases loaded, pitched a one-two-three eighth, and looked forward to the ninth. He had pitched six and a third series innings without allowing an earned run.

After Evans led off the bottom of the eighth with a walk,

Burleson failed to put down a bunt, grounding into a double play that would have brought Willoughby, the most effective reliever of the series, to the plate. Johnson sent up Cecil Cooper. Thus was another link in the chain of Boston's problematic baseball legacy forged.

Three months later, a man sat in the Abbeyfeale Café in Inman Square in Cambridge, drinking fifty-cent shots with twenty-five-cent drafts, blankly staring at the television mounted up in the corner of the bar. He had been there for nearly four hours, watching, when he turned for the first time to a group of three men down the bar. "Why," he stammered, "did Johnson bat for Willoughby?"

"Where were you," replied one of the men, "when you heard Denny Galehouse was pitching against the Indians?"

"How," asked another, "could Slaughter have scored from first?"

At the time, Cooper was going through what Gil Hodges had experienced in 1952, and what Eddie Murray and Willie Wilson and Dave Winfield would later have to face. He had gone into a dreadful slump that at that point had reached one-for-eighteen, a dour ending to what had been an emerging (.311) season before he had been hit in the face by a pitch thrown by Milwaukee's Billy Travers September 7.

Manager Johnson, too, was experiencing a public flogging of sorts. Lee, ired at being passed over for the sixth-game start when rain allowed Tiant to come back, said, "Darrell's been falling out of trees and landing on his feet all season." Johnson was a quiet man, whose inability to articulate had made him the butt of press conference jokes by the national media. He'd been the minor-league manager who helped direct most of the extraordinary young talent to Boston, and he'd organized and expertly handled a pitching staff to get as much out of it as one ever could have asked. But Johnson also was nearly fired in June, when, as the team went on a 9–4, job-saving road trip, the front office talked to

Detroit officials about luring away Tigers manager Ralph Houk. Second baseman Doug Griffin, replaced by Doyle in mid-June, stated, "We're going to win this thing in *spite* of the manager." Such fragments of disrespect clouded the season. Fisk and Lee walked out of a meeting in the manager's office in Baltimore, claiming Johnson was incoherent. When the Red Sox clinched the division championship the last Saturday, Johnson refused to grant Yastrzemski permission to fly home to Florida and miss the final day of the season and the next couple of workouts prior to the playoffs; Yastrzemski went anyway. When they won the playoffs in Oakland, Johnson never went in and joined in the clubhouse celebration, instead sitting in his tiny office a few feet away, sipping champagne with Oakland outfielder Joe Rudi, his off-season hunting companion.

Replacing Willoughby, Cooper went out, and rookie left-hander Jim Burton came in to pitch the top of the ninth, since Drago had pitched three innings the night before. Burton promptly walked the man he was brought in to face, the left-hand-hitting Griffey leading off. Two outs later, Griffey was on second. Burton wisely walked Rose and pitched to the National League's Most Valuable Player, Morgan. It doesn't matter how the ball got out there, that Burton threw a pitch Morgan described as "a breaking ball on the outside corner that two years earlier I couldn't have handled," or that Morgan's bloop barely carried the infield into shallow left-center. The Reds had scored what would be the winning run in the ninth inning of the seventh game, and when Will McEnaney finished off the bottom of the ninth and watched Yaz—who in 1967 had made the last out of his only other World Series—hit a gentle fly to Geronimo, they had completed a task that most everyone in America had figured they'd accomplish with considerably greater ease.

THE SIXTH GAME, OCTOBER 21, 1975

CINCINNATI	AB	R	H	RBI	BOSTON	AB	R	H	RBI
Rose, 3b	5	1	2	0	Cooper, 1b	5	0	0	0
Griffey, rf	5	2	2	2	Drago, p	0	0	0	0
Morgan, 2b	6	1	1	1	Miller, ph	1	0	0	0
Bench, c	6	0	1	2	Wise, p	0	0	0	0
Perez, 1b	6	0	2	0	Doyle, 2b	5	0	1	0
Foster, lf	6	0	2	0	Yastrzemski, lf-1b	6	1	3	0
Concepcion, ss	6	0	1	0	Fisk, c	4	2	2	1
Geronimo, cf	6	1	2	1	Lynn, cf	4	2	2	3
Nolan, p	0	0	0	0	Petrocelli, 3b	4	1	0	0
Chaney, ph	1	0	0	0	Evans, rf	5	0	1	0
Norman, p	0	0	0	0	Burleson, ss	3	0	0	0
Billingham, p	0	0	0	0	Tiant, p	2	0	0	0
Armbrister, ph	0	1	0	0	Moret, p	0	0	0	0
Carroll, p	0	0	0	0	Carbo, ph	2	1	1	3
Crowley, ph	1	0	1	0					
Borbon, p	1	0	0	0					
Eastwick, p	0	0	0	0					
McEnaney, p	0	0	0	0					
Driessen, ph	1	0	0	0					
Darcy, p	0	0	0	0					
TOTALS	50	6	14	6		41	7	10	7

Cincinnati   000 030 210 000—6
Boston   300 000 030 001—7

LOB-Cincinnati 11, Boston 9. 2B-Doyle, Evans, Foster. 3B-Griffey. HR-Lynn, Geronimo, Carbo, Fisk. SB-Concepcion. S-Tiant.

	IP	H	R	ER	BB	SO
Nolan	2	3	3	3	0	2
Norman	2/3	1	0	0	2	0
Billingham	1 1/3	1	0	0	1	1

Carroll	1	1	0	0	0	0
Borbon	2	1	2	2	1	1
Eastwick	1	2	1	1	1	2
McEnaney	1	0	0	0	1	0
Darcy (L)	2	1	1	1	0	1
Tiant	7	11	6	6	2	5
Moret	1	0	0	0	0	0
Drago	3	1	0	0	0	1
Wise (W)	1	2	0	0	0	1

Tiant pitched to one batter in the eighth. Borbon pitched to two batters in the eighth. Eastwick pitched to two batters in the ninth. Darcy pitched to one batter in the twelfth.

HP-By Drago (Rose). T-4:01. A-35,205

Rose, Morgan, and company had won the 1975 World Series. But when the Sixth Game had ended with that ball suspended out in the black of the morning like the Mystic River Bridge, Carlton Fisk, Bernardo Carbo, Luis Tiant, and the Red Sox *were* the 1975 series.

Baseball had seized the imagination of the entire country; the excitement and color of that World Series marked it immediately as one of the greatest ever. It seemed inevitable that the Red Sox would dominate their league for years, and that baseball was entering a golden era in which this most traditional of sports would enjoy unprecedented tranquility, prosperity, and popularity.

FINAL AMERICAN LEAGUE STANDINGS AND RED SOX STATISTICS, 1975

EAST	W	L	PCT	GB	R	HR	BA
BOS	95	65	.594		796	134	.275
BAL	90	69	.566	4.5	682	124	.252
NY	83	77	.519	12	681	110	.264
CLE	79	80	.497	15.5	688	153	.261

MIL	68	94	.420	28	675	146	.250
DET	57	102	.358	37.5	570	125	.249

WEST

OAK	98	64	.605		758	151	.254
KC	91	71	.562	7	710	118	.261
TEX	79	83	.488	19	714	134	.256
MIN	76	83	.478	20.5	724	121	.271
CHI	75	86	.466	22.5	655	94	.255
CAL	72	89	.447	25.5	628	55	.246
LEAGUE TOTAL					**8281**	**1465**	**.258**

MANAGER	W	L	PCT
Darrell Johnson	95	65	.594

POS	PLAYER	B	G	AB	H	2B	3B	HR	R	RBI	BA
REGULARS											
1B	Carl Yastrzemski	L	149	543	146	30	1	14	91	60	.269
2B	Doug Griffin	R	100	257	69	6	0	1	21	29	.240
SS	Rick Burleson	R	158	580	146	25	1	6	66	62	.252
3B	Rico Petrocelli	R	115	402	96	15	1	7	31	59	.239
RF	Dwight Evans	R	128	412	113	24	6	13	61	56	.274
CF	Fred Lynn	L	145	528	175	47	7	21	103	105	.331
LF	Jim Rice	R	144	564	174	29	4	22	92	102	.309
C	Carlton Fisk	R	79	263	87	14	4	10	47	52	.331
DH	Cecil Cooper	L	106	305	95	17	6	14	49	44	.311
SUBSTITUTES											
2B	Denny Doyle	L	89	310	96	21	2	4	50	36	.310
3B	Bob Heise	R	63	126	27	3	0	0	12	21	.214

Pos	Player	B	G	AB	R	2B	3B	HR	RBI	BB	AVG
DH	Tony Conigliaro	R	21	57	7	1	0	2	8	9	.123
3B	Dick McAuliffe	L	7	15	2	0	0	0	0	1	.133
1D	Deron Johnson	R	3	10	6	0	0	1	2	3	.600
2B	Steve Dillard	R	1	5	2	0	0	0	2	0	.400
3B	Butch Hobson	R	2	4	1	0	0	0	0	0	.250
2B	Kim Andrew	R	2	2	1	0	0	0	0	0	.500
2B	Buddy Hunter	R	1	1	0	0	0	0	0	0	.000
OF	Bernie Carbo	L	107	319	82	21	3	15	64	50	.257
UT	Juan Beniquez	R	78	254	74	14	4	2	43	17	.291
OF	Rick Miller	L	77	108	21	2	1	0	21	15	.194
C	Bob Montgomery	R	62	195	44	10	1	2	16	26	.226
C	Tim Blackwell	B	59	132	26	3	2	0	15	6	.197
C	Tim McCarver	L	12	21	8	2	1	0	1	3	.381
C	Andy Merchant	L	1	4	2	0	0	0	1	0	.500

PITCHER	T	W	L	PCT	ERA	SV
Luis Tiant	R	18	14	.563	4.02	0
Bill Lee	L	17	9	.654	3.95	0
Rick Wise	R	19	12	.613	3.95	0
Reggie Cleveland	R	13	9	.591	4.43	0
Roger Moret	L	14	3	.824	3.60	1
Dick Pole	R	4	6	.400	4.42	0
Dick Drago	R	2	2	.500	3.84	15
Diego Segui	R	2	5	.286	4.82	6
Jim Burton	L	1	2	.333	2.89	1
Jim Willoughby	R	5	2	.714	3.54	8
Steve Barr	L	0	1	.000	2.57	0
Rick Kreuger	L	0	0	–	4.50	0
TEAM TOTAL		95	65	.594	3.99	31

Instead, the new era was quietly ushered in a few short weeks later in the office of arbitrator Peter Seitz, who ruled that Andy Messersmith and Dave McNally were, as they had claimed, free agents not bound to their respective teams forever through the option clause in their contracts. Though no one suspected it on that glorious October night, the Sixth Game and the 1975 World Series marked the end of an old era, not the beginning of a new one.

1977

The Right-Field Sign Says "REG-GIE, REG-GIE, REG-GIE"

Thomas Boswell

Some say there isn't enough mustard in the world to cover Reggie Jackson. Tonight, there wasn't enough glory as the New York Yankees defeated the Los Angeles Dodgers, 8–4, to win the World Series.

"Reg-gie, Reg-gie, Reg-gie," says the sign in right field in Yankee Stadium, once the home of the mighty Ruth and now the residence of the prodigious Jackson. Tonight the sign was right all three times.

Jackson, the man who has swung New York between delight and exasperation since the day he was bought at modern auction for $3 million, hit three home runs in the sixth and final game of the Seventy-fourth World Series.

This Yankee victory over the Dodgers will go down as one of many milestones in this ancient rivalry. But Jackson's evening may in time be regarded as the single most dramatic slugging performance in Series history. "Nothing can top this," said Jackson, who saw only three strikes in his four at-bats tonight and hit each farther than the last. "Who in hell's ever again going to hit three home runs in a deciding World Series game. I won't.

"Babe Ruth, Hank Aaron, Joe DiMaggio . . . at least I was with them for one night."

Jackson was wrong there. He was ahead of them. If numbers tell any fraction of the truth, Jackson wrapped up the greatest statistical Series in history tonight.

Jackson became the first man to hit five home runs in a Series. In fact, he hit them in his last nine at-bats.

Jackson hit four of the homers on his last four swings. He connected on his final swing Sunday. After a four-pitch walk in the second inning tonight, Jackson hit the first pitch in each of his last three appearances.

His final blow in the eighth inning—the shot that made his achievement unique—was a truly Ruthian, 500-foot swat halfway up into the black bleachers in dead center off a Charlie Hough knuckleball.

Jackson scored four runs and drove home five tonight. His dozen total bases in the game tied a record, while his 25 bases for the Series broke the record of 24. His 10 runs scored for this October feast passed the old standards of Ruth and Gehrig by one.

Babe Ruth twice hit three homers in a Series game, the last time in 1928. No other man had. Until tonight.

Needless to say, Jackson, with his .450 batting average and his 1.250 slugging mark, won his second World Series MVP award. His other was in 1973.

On Jackson's night, Mike Torrez and Chris Chambliss carried spears with dignity. Chambliss tied the game, 2–2, with a homer after Jackson's walk in the second. Torrez struggled through a nine-hitter, his second triumph of this title affair.

Nevertheless, all the memorable theatrics tonight belonged to Jackson, the player above all others in baseball who longs for the spotlight and plays to it.

Jackson's first two homers were almost instant replays of each other—and both, though they traveled no more than 370 feet, were the sort that few other players have hit. In the fourth and fifth innings, each time with a man on first, Jackson crashed a low-inside fastball on a low, hooking line toward the right-field wall.

For other hitters the balls might have barely reached the warning track. In fact, right fielder Reggie Smith, who hit a solo homer of his own tonight, had his back to the plate preparing to field both balls when they banged off the wall. They never did.

Both plunged into the first row of seats perhaps 30 feet right of the 353 sign.

The first blast put the Yankees ahead, 4–3, and knocked out starter and loser Burt Hooton, whose curves were well-knuckled tonight. The second put the Yanks in front, 7–3, and knocked out reliever Elias Sosa, who in truth, was only so-so. Two Jackson swings, two pitchers sent to the showers.

If homers No. 1 and 2 decided this last Series game, giving the determined Torrez more cushion than he needed, it was the third homer that probably will live in legend longest.

In future years those who were here will say that Jackson's record-setter hit the Marlboro sign 650 feet away in center. Perhaps they will say it cleared everything and never came down.

In reality, if this game stayed within that boundary, Jackson's third blow looked like a gigantic pop-up. The crowd's cheer stuck in its throat for a second. Could a ball so high possibly reach the black bleachers, that no-man's-land attained by so few, behind the 417 sign?

But Jackson knew. He stood at the plate and watched. Why should he miss what other millions were admiring?

The fourth homer in four swings finally landed—pay attention, posterity—on the first row of backless seats above the exitway on the right side of the empty ebony bleachers. The first huge bounce hit the black wall beneath the Marlboro sign. Estimated distance: near 500 feet. With hop: close to 600.

Jackson leaped on second base with an enormous stride, pumped both fists between second and third, then clutched his chest with both hands, pulling his uniform away from his body to show how his heart was bursting, as he headed for home.

As Jackson took his home-run trot, one Dodger was awestruck. The L.A. first baseman, Steve Garvey, who had knocked home two first-inning runs with an opposite-field triple, said, "As he went around I was applauding into my glove.

"I have never seen anything like that in a championship game situation," the Dodgers first baseman said of Jackson's stunning performance.

"He beat us single-handedly. And actually that's exactly what he did. He knocked in five runs and we only scored four.

"I sure wish that I'd had a chance to talk to him at first base. But he didn't stay there long enough for conversation."

A saddened Dodger manager Lasorda called Jackson's performance the greatest he's ever seen in a World Series.

"We lived by the long ball all year and we got killed by the long ball tonight," said Lasorda.

The fans who had withheld their love so long poured it out in standing cheers that lasted and lasted.

When Torrez caught the final L.A. pop-up, Jackson ran for his life—faster by far than Ruth ever had, or ever needed to. Taking a great-circle route through center field, Jackson built a head of steam worthy of his 9.6 dashman's speed. He careened through bodies like a wild linebacker, then flew into the Yankee dugout bench so hard that he almost knocked himself senseless.

Jackson rose and staggered toward the waiting champagne, toward the tears of Yankee joy and relief. He staggered toward a place next to Ruth in the Yankee's World Series pantheon. He was New York's best-loved son at last.

1981

Brooklyn No Longer Place to Be When Dodgers Win

JOE SOUCHERAY

IT IS NEW YORK AND IT IS LATE at night, and from all you have ever heard and read on the subject, you should go to Brooklyn in the hours after the Dodgers beat the Yankees in the World Series.

It used to mean something, a World Series in Brooklyn when the Yankees were the other guys; it used to mean real despair and real hope and once, in 1955, it meant real joy because that autumn the Bums beat the Yankees in seven games in the tournament between subways.

You have read somewhere, something by Roger Kahn probably, that after the 1955 Series victory by the Dodgers the Brooklyn Eagle blocked out new type for its traditional banner headline. "Next Year Is Now," it said. In 1941, 1947, 1949, 1952, 1953 and back again in 1956, the Eagle always set the same type, "Wait Til Next Year," after the World Series. And it was always the Yankees who had done the Dodgers in.

Maybe they have remembered that in Brooklyn. Maybe they have gotten over the broken hearts they suffered after the 1957 season when Walter O'Malley neatly packed his club into a carpetbag and fled to Los Angeles, all the way across the world. Maybe there are a few of them still, Brooklyn Dodger fans dancing in old saloons and honking their horns up and down the avenues in 1981.

"Maybe in your imagination," Danny said.

This is Danny from Brooklyn, Danny the hack driver. This is Danny at the wheel of an automobile that has a life expectancy of perhaps two more hours before it falls into a heap on the street, like some jalopy from a Bowery Boys film. This is Danny who can't possibly risk having his last name appear in print, even in Minneapolis. But this Danny is perfect for the trip to Brooklyn because this Danny hates the Yankees the way a real Dodger fan should, this Danny was one of the shocked when the Dodgers evacuated westward.

"It ain't the same, rooting anymore," Danny is saying. "It ain't the same rooting for any of the sports. It's just a feeling that none of it is the same."

He is rattling uptown through Manhattan along the FDR Expressway, to the Brooklyn Bridge, which is beautiful, its suspension cables glowing like harp strings on a dark stage, its light reflecting off the black waters of the East River below.

From the bridge, off to the right, you can see the towers of the World Trade Center and the Wall Street district and the Statue of Liberty in the harbor and the whole city of Manhattan lights in the background. Yankee lights to a Brooklyner, as Danny calls his people.

"The Brooklyn Eagle is gone," Danny says, "and so is Ebbets Field. It's a housing project now on Bedford Avenue."

He is going up the Brooklyn Heights side of the East River, up the Brooklyn-Queens Expressway. The clock on the tower of the Bon-Ton Potato Chip factory reads 2:59 a.m., but in some spots they have forgotten to turn back the clocks in Brooklyn. Danny pulls off finally and motors the heap into Bay Ridge. It is quiet. O'Sullivan's is closed. So is Hobnails and the Golden Dove and Manar's. And there is no honking of horns or dancing in the wide streets. The real, modern Dodger celebration was taking place at that moment on the team's jetliner at 30,000 feet. But there is a joint that Danny knows of and there will be people there who remember the Dodgers from Brooklyn.

Irish music is spilling out the doors of Danny's place, a joint called Peggy O'Neill's, which actually is a very new place and not full of much memory except for the people inside. A guy named Timmy O'Donnell is behind the bar and when you mention the Dodgers and the kinds of feelings that his patrons must have on a night like this, he points to his friend at the bar. It is like a beam of light has come on this guy, Bob, a policeman, 45, working on a drink and a cigarette and 25 years' worth of sorrow over his absent Bums.

"It broke my heart when the Bums left here," Bob is saying, "and I will take it a step further. You will never find fans in your life like Dodger fans. The Dodgers were bums."

"Why?"

"Because they were bad and they let the Yankees beat them," Bob says. "But I will take it a step further. The Dodgers were the hope of all the people that were struggling in Brooklyn. It used to be this way: People thought New York State was New York City and they thought New York City was Brooklyn. The team made us."

They were all taking it a step further now. It seems that when the Dodgers beat Montreal for the National League pennant, and folks in Brooklyn knew the Dodgers would be coming to Yankee Stadium again, a petition drive was started to ask the Dodgers to change their name in Los Angeles, that the O'Malleys had no business hanging on to that name.

"The name comes from people in Brooklyn having to dodge trolley cars," Bob says. "What are they doing with our name in Los Angeles?"

Bob did not root for the Yankees on this night. But he didn't feel cheer for the Dodgers, either. Most Brooklyners have retained allegiances in the National League and bestowed a cautious affection on the Mets when that team was born in 1962. But it isn't the same, the Mets aren't tucked into the borough the way the Dodgers were. The Mets aren't family the way the Dodgers were.

"And I will take it a step further," Bob is saying now. "Look at all your old war movies. When they really wanted to test a guy's loyalty, who do they bring up? They bring up the Dodgers. The Dodgers were the hope of all the people who were struggling in Brooklyn."

Part of that image, of course, was the work of script writers and comedians and those of us who find affection for the underdogs on the sporting fields. Part of that image is real, if for no other reason than the nostalgic memories that the pairing of the words Brooklyn and Dodgers creates in all of us.

A fire burned in the hearts of men for a baseball team in Brooklyn. That much is certain. It made no difference that the club was considered "hapless" more often than not. The club belonged to Brooklyn and in a few hearts the longing still exists, but there can be no cheer in the longing.

"That's what's different," Danny is saying, retracing the route back toward the lights of Manhattan. "Teams don't seem to belong to a place anymore. Not the way they did. The teams now, they belong to themselves."

1985

In the World Series, Any Buddy Can Be a Hero

TONY KORNHEISER

BIANCALANA. DOESN'T THAT HAVE a nice lilt to it? Go ahead. Divide it into syllables and say it out loud: Bi-an-ca-la-na. Sounds like a crisp, white wine. Excuse me, but might I have a bottle of Biancalana, please? Buddy Biancalana. That's a great name, isn't it? You want to know his real name? Roland Americo Biancalana Jr. How can someone named Anthony Irwin Kornheiser not root for someone named Roland Americo Biancalana Jr.?

You know, it hasn't always been easy on the Biancalana Bus, no sir. Buddy hasn't exactly been Kansas City's answer to Honus Wagner. In his brief major league career—156 games over slivers of two seasons and chunks of two more—Biancalana's batting average is .194, a nifty number for a weekend bowler, but more or less underwater for a major league baseball player. This season, he jolted the old horsehide at a .188 clip. Numbers like that tend to make a brief career briefer. Excuse me, but have you considered getting a day job?

When players slam long home runs, they say they dialed 8 (for long distance). Biancalana had to dial 0 and ask for an outside line just to dial 9. When Pete Rose broke Ty Cobb's record, David Letterman, who first showed his baseball savvy by calling Terry

Forster "a fat tub of goo," began the Buddy Biancalana Watch, telling people how many hits Buddy needed to catch Pete in case they wanted to plan ahead. Let's put it this way: if you're thinking of visiting Hawaii anytime in the next 35 years, book the trip.

So guess what?

With hitters such as George Brett, Willie McGee, Tommy Herr, Willie Wilson and Lonnie Smith to choose from, who do you think has the best on-base percentage of any regular in the World Series?

Biancalana.

(Well, now that you mention it, maybe one glass, thanks. And a breadstick.)

Eight for 16. Fifty percent. Four hits, four walks.

"We've been pitching Biancalana like he's Babe Ruth," groused Whitey Herzog.

And if you find that hard to believe, how about this? The battle of shortstops in this World Series matched Biancalana against Ozzie Smith, which was sort of like matching Pablo Picasso against Earl Scheib. Not that Buddy isn't a good fielder, he certainly is. But Ozzie may wind up in Cooperstown, and Buddy may wind up in siding. So not only is Biancalana hitting 270 points higher than the Wizard of Ahhhs, but with the same number of fielding chances, Buddy is 18 for 18, and Acrobatic Ozzie has one error.

Cue Dom DeLuise: "Surprised?"

Buddy, baby, talk to us.

"Am I surprised?" Biancalana said, repeating the question and grinning. "I'm not going to say I'm surprised, but I'm pleased." Looking out at all the reporters who had gathered around his locker after Thursday night's game in St. Louis, he said, "You guys are surprised. Maybe the Cards are surprised. Maybe my manager is surprised. I'm not."

Can you do a back flip?

"I can do a somersault. I'll save it for Game 7," Buddy said, giggling and having a heck of a time. "I'm feeling real good about myself now. I'm having a good Series, and it feels good after the way people got on me during the season. Don't misunderstand me, it was justified—my numbers speak for themselves. But I took this as a second chance after the year I've had, and I may have opened some eyes and shut some mouths."

At 25, he still looks young enough to be carded, and when he took a small furtive sip of the beer he was holding, he might have been a teen-ager from an S.E. Hinton novel. Except that far from feeling alienated, Biancalana felt more secure than ever. "I don't think it can feel any better than this," he said, thinking it over. "I guess maybe I could hit a home run to win a game." He laughed. "Maybe that's in the cards for the sixth game." Everywhere he looked, all he could see was blue sky and candy. "It's been very satisfying. It's going to be a nice winter to walk around in, if we win the Series."

And if the Royals didn't, could he still enjoy the walk?

"Yes. As of now, yes I could."

As of now—and believe me, I never thought I'd be writing this—Buddy Biancalana is in the hunt for the car. And he knows it. "I thought about it a little before the Series—could it *possibly* be me? But to be honest with you, it crossed my mind (Thursday) when I got on three times."

Wouldn't it be something if he won it. How long do you think it would take Letterman to call and invite him onto the show? Fifteen seconds?

"I'd go," Biancalana said happily. "But I'd need some of you guys to write me some lines. I'm not very creative."

Dick Howser, who has to be almost as happy at Biancalana's blossoming as Biancalana is, was in another room, delightedly telling people that the key move in turning Biancalana from beep-beep to boom-boom was batting eighth in this DH-less Series. "They're pitching around him to get to our pitchers," Howser said jokingly.

And so it was asked of Howser if Biancalana is this good moving up one spot in the order, when are you going to bat him cleanup?

Howser laughed. "Not within the next two days, I can assure you."

May I propose a toast then to Kansas City's new star. This, Buddy, is for you.

1986

Game Six, World Series

ROGER ANGELL

THE METS ARE NOT LOVED—not away from New York, that is. When the teams moved up to the Hub, with the Mets behind by two games to none, there was a happy little rush of historical revisionism as sportswriters and baseball thinkers hurried forward to kick the New York nine. Tim Horgan, a columnist with the Boston *Herald,* wrote, "Personally, I don't think anything west of Dedham can be as marvelous as the Mets are supposed to be. I wouldn't even be surprised if the Mets are what's known as a media myth, if only because New York City is the world capital of media myths." Bryant Gumbel, on NBC's *Today* show, called the Mets arrogant, and ran a tape of Keith Hernandez' bad throw on a bunt play in Game Two, calling it "a hotdog play." Sparky Anderson, the Tigers manager, declared over the radio that the Indians, the traditional doormats of his American League division, put a better nine on the field than the Mets, and a newspaper clip from the heartland (if San Diego is in the heart of America) that subsequently came my way contained references to "this swaggering band of mercenaries" and "a swaying forest of high fives and taunting braggadocio." Much of this subsided when the Mets quickly drew even in the games, and much of it has nothing to do with baseball, of course; what one tends to forget is that there is nothing that unites America more swiftly or happily than bad news in Gotham or a losing New York team. Some of these reflections warmed me, inwardly and arrogantly, as Game Six began, for I was perched in a splendid upper-deck-grandstand seat directly above home plate, where, in company with my small family and the Mets' mighty fan family, I gazed about at the dazzlement of the ballpark floodlights, the electric-green field below, and the encircling golden twinkle of beautiful (by night) Queens, and heard and felt, deep in my belly, the pistol-shot sounds of clapping, the cresting waves of "LETSGOMETS! LETSGOMETS! LETSGOMETS!," and long, taunting calls—"Dew-eee! DEW-EEEE!" and "Rog-errr! ROG-ERRRR!"—directed at some of the Bosox below: payback for what the Fenway fans had given Darryl Strawberry in the last game in Boston. And then a parachutist came sailing down out of the outer darkness and into the bowl of light and noise—a descending roar, of all things—of Shea. "GO METS," his banner said as he lightly came to rest a few steps away from Bob Ojeda in midinfield and, encumbered with minions, went cheerfully off to jail and notoriety. We laughed and forgot him. I was home.

Game Six must be given here in extreme précis—not a bad idea, since its non-stop events and reversals and mistakes and stunners blur into unlikelihood even when examined on a scorecard. I sometimes make postgame additions to my own scorecard in red ink, circling key plays and instants to refresh my recollection, and adding comments on matters I may have overlooked or misjudged at the time. My card of Game Six looks like a third grader's valentine, with scarlet exclamation points, arrows, stars, question marks, and "Wow!"s scrawled thickly across the double page. A double arrow connects Boggs, up on top, to Spike Owen, down below, in the Boston second—a dazzling little hit (by Wade)-and-run (by Spike) that set up Boston's second score of the game. Two red circles are squeezed into Jim Rice's box in the Boston seventh—one around the "E5" denoting Ray Knight's wild peg that put Rice on first and sent Marty Barrett around to third, and the other around the "7–2" that ended the inning, two outs and one run later, when Mookie Wilson threw out Jim at the plate. A descendant arrow and low-flying exclamation points mark

Clemens' departure from the game after the seventh (the Red Sox were ahead by 3–2, but Roger, after a hundred and thirty-one pitches, had worked up a blister on his pitching hand), and an up-bound red dart and "MAZZ PH" pointing at the same part of the column denote Lee Mazzilli's instant single against Schiraldi, while the black dot in the middle of the box is the Mazzilli run that tied the score. But nothing can make this sprawling, clamorous game become orderly, I see now, and, of course, no short-hand can convey the vast encircling, supplicating sounds of that night, or the sense of encroaching danger on the field, or the anxiety that gnawed at the Mets hordes in the stands as their season ran down, it seemed certain, to the wrong ending.

The Red Sox scored twice in the top of the tenth inning, on a home run by Dave Henderson ("Hendu!" is my crimson comment) and a double and a single by the top of the order—Boggs and then Barrett—all struck against Rick Aguilera, the fourth Mets pitcher of the night. Call it the morning, for it was past midnight when the Sox took the field in the bottom half, leading by 5–3. Three outs were needed for Boston's championship, and two of them were tucked away at once. Keith Hernandez, having flied out to center for the second out, left the dugout and walked into Davey Johnson's office in the clubhouse to watch the end; he said later that this was the first instant when he felt that the Mets might not win. I had moved down to the main press box, ready for a dash to the clubhouses, and now I noticed that a few Mets fans had given up and were sadly coming along the main aisles down below me, headed for home. My companion just to my right in the press box, the *News'* Red Foley, is a man of few words, but now he removed his cigar from his mouth and pointed at the departing fans below. "O ye of little faith," he said.

It happened slowly but all at once, it seemed later. Gary Carter singled. Kevin Mitchell, who was batting for Aguilera, singled to center. Ray Knight fouled off two sinkers, putting the Red Sox one strike away. (Much later, somebody counted up and discovered that there were *thirteen* pitches in this inning that could have been turned into the last Mets out of all.) "Ah, New England," I jotted in my notebook, just before Knight bopped a little single to right-center, scoring Carter and sending Mitchell to third—and my notebook note suddenly took on quite a different meaning. It was along about here, I suspect, that my friend Allan, who is a genius palindromist, may have taken his eyes away from his set (he was watching at home) for an instant to write down a message that had been forming within him: "Not so, Boston"—the awful truth, no matter how you look at it.

Schiraldi departed, and Bob Stanley came on to pitch. (This was the Steamer's moment to save what had been an unhappy 6–6 and 4–37 season for him, in which his work as the Sox' prime right-handed stopper had received increasingly unfavorable reviews from the Fenway bleacher critics; part of me was pulling for him here, but the game was out of my hands—and evidently out of his as well.) Mookie Wilson, batting left-handed, ran the count to two-and-two, fouled off two more pitches, and then jumped away, jackknifing in midair, to avoid a thigh-high wild pitch that brought Mitchell flying in from third, to tie it. Wilson fouled off two more pitches in this at-bat of a lifetime and then tapped a little bouncer down toward first, close to the baseline, that hopped once, hopped twice, and then slipped under Buckner's glove and on into short right field (he turned and stared after it in disbelief), and Knight thundered in from around third base. He jumped on home plate with both feet—jumped so hard that he twisted his back, he said later—and then disappeared under an avalanche of Mets.

The post mortems were nearly unbearable. "This is the worst," Bob Stanley said.

"I'm exhausted," Ray Knight said. "My legs are trembling."

"As close as we came . . . " whispered John McNamara. "As close as we came, I can only associate it with California."

"It's baseball," said Dave Henderson. "It's baseball, and we've got to live with it."

Questions were asked—they always are after major accidents—

and some of them must be asked again, for this game will be replayed, in retrospect, for years to come.

Q: Why didn't Davey Johnson double-switch when he brought in Jesse Orosco to get the last out of the eighth inning? Without an accompanying substitute at some other slot in the order, Jesse was forced to depart for a pinch-hitter an instant later, in the Mets' half, thus requiring Johnson to wheel in Aguilera, who was a much less certain quantity on the mound, and who quickly gave up the two runs that so nearly finished off the Mets. A: I still don't know, for Davey is a master at the double switch—a textbook maneuver in National League tactics, since there is no designated hitter—and a bit later on he made a much more questionable switch, which removed Darryl Strawberry from the game. It came out all right in the end, but I think Davey just forgot.

Q: Why didn't McNamara pinch-hit for the creaking Buckner in the tenth, when another run could have nailed down the Mets for sure? And, having decided against this, why didn't he at least put the much more mobile Stapleton in to play first base in the bottom half—perhaps to gobble up Wilson's grounder and make the flip to the pitcher? More specifically, why didn't he pinch-hit Baylor, his designated hitter, who batted in the No. 5 slot throughout the regular season and in the playoffs but rode the bench (no D.H.) almost to the end during the games played at Shea? A: Johnny Mack has defended himself strongly against both of these second-guesses, citing Buckner's excellent bat (a .267 year, with eighteen home runs and a hundred and two runs batted in) and Buckner's glove ("He has good hands," he said), in that order. His answer to the Baylor puzzle is to say that Baylor never pinch-hits when the Red Sox are ahead—sound strategy, one can see, until a game arrives when they might suddenly fall behind at the end. McNamara also claims that Stapleton normally substitutes for Buckner at first base only if there has been an earlier occasion to insert him as a pinch-*runner* for Buckner; this is mostly true (it wasn't the case in Game Five), but the fact remains that Stapleton was playing first base in the final inning of all three games that the Sox did win. My strong guess is that McNamara is not beyond sentiment. He knew the torments that Buckner had gone through to stay in the lineup throughout the season, and the contributions he had made to bring the club to this shining doorstep (he had mounted a seventeen-game hitting streak in mid-September, and at one stretch drove in twenty runs in a span of eight games) and he wanted him out there with the rest of the varsity when the Sox seemed certain to step over it at last.

We need not linger long on Game Seven, in which the Mets came back from a 3–0 second-inning deficit and won going away (as turf writers say), 8–5. It was another great game, I suppose, but even noble vintages can become a surfeit after enough bottles have been sampled. A one-day rainout allowed us to come down a little from the sixth game and its astounding ending, but then we came to the last day of all, and the sense of that—a whole season rushing to a decision now—seized us and wrung us with almost every pitch once play resumed. Ron Darling, who had given up no earned runs in the Series so far, surrendered three in the second inning (Evans and Gedman whacked home runs on successive pitches) and was gone in the fourth. Hurst, for his part, permitted only a lone single in five full innings, but ran dry in the sixth, when the Mets evened the game. They had specialized in this sleeping-dragon style of play all through the championship season, and this last time around they showed us once again how dangerous they really were: nine hits and eight runs in their last three innings of the year. Somehow, the anguish of the Red Sox mattered more than the Mets' caperings at the very end, because it was plain by now that it could have just as easily gone the other way. In the Boston clubhouse, Al Nipper, who was badly battered during his very brief appearance in the New York eighth, sat at his locker with his back turned and his head buried in his hands. Dennis Boyd, who had not been called on in the Sox' extremity, rocked forward and back on his chair, shaking his head in disbelief. Friends of mine said later that they had been riveted by a postgame television closeup of Wade Boggs sitting alone in the dugout with tears streaming down his face, and a couple of them who are not fans asked me how it was possible for grown men to weep about something as trivial as a game. I tried to tell them about the extraordinary heights of concentration and intensity that are required to play baseball at this level, even for a single trifling game in midseason, but I don't think they believed me. Then I remembered a different moment on television—something I saw a couple of years ago on a trip abroad, when the captain of the Australian cricket team was interviewed over the BBC just after his eleven (I *think*) had lost a protracted test match to the West Indies. I listened to the young man's sad recapitulations with predictable American amusement—until I suddenly noticed that there were tears in his eyes. He was crying over *cricket!* I suppose we should all try to find something better or worse to shed tears for than a game, no matter how hard it has been played, but perhaps it is not such a bad thing to see that men can cry at all.

The acute moment in Game Seven was produced in the Mets' sixth, when Keith Hernandez came up to bat against Hurst with the bases loaded and one out and the Red Sox still ahead by 3–0. Anyone who does know baseball understood that this was the arrangement—this particular batter and this precise set of circumstances—that the Mets wanted most and the Red Sox least at the end of their long adventures. It was the moment that only baseball—with its slow, serial, one-thing-and-then-another siftings and sortings—can produce from time to time, and its outcome is often critical even when reexamined weeks later. I think the Red Sox would have won this game if they had got Hernandez out. As it was, he took a strike from Hurst (a beautiful, dipping off-speed breaking ball) and then rocketed the next pitch (a fastball, a bit up) to deep left-center for a single and the Mets' first two runs and the beginning of their championship comeback. I'm not sure that anyone remembered at the time, but we should remember now that Hernandez, then a member of the Cardinals, hit a crucial two-run single up the middle in the sixth inning of the seventh game of the 1982 World Series, to start that team on its way to a comeback 6–3 victory over the Milwaukee Brewers.

Many fans think of Gary Carter as the quintessential Mets player, while some may see Lenny Dykstra or Wally Backman or Dwight Gooden, or even Ray Knight (who won the Series M.V.P. award), or perhaps Mookie Wilson in that role (Mets-haters despise them all, for their exuberance, their high-fives, their cap-waving encores, their vast publicity, their money, and their winning so often: winning is the worst mannerism of all), but for me the Mets are Keith Hernandez. His game-long, season-long intensity; his classic at-bats, during which the contest between batter and pitcher seems to be written out on some invisible blackboard, with the theorems and formulas being erased and rewritten as the count progresses; his style at the plate, with the bat held high (he is mostly bare-armed), and his pure, mannerism-free cuts at the ball; and, above all, his demeanor afield—I would rather watch these, I think, than the actions of any other player in the game today. Watching him at work around first base—he is sure to earn his ninth consecutive Gold Glove for his performance at the position—you begin to pick up the little moves and glances and touches that show what he is concerned about at that instant, what dangers and possibilities are on his mind. Holding a base runner close, with a right-handed pull hitter up at bat, he crouches with his left foot planted on the baseline and toeing to right—a sprinter's start, no less—and he moves off so quickly with the pitch that he and the runner appear to be tied together, one mass zipping along the base path. When there's a left-handed batter in the box under the same circumstances, Keith leaves his post just as quickly once the pitcher lets fly, but this time with a crab-like backward scuttle, quicker than a skater. He makes the tough 3–6 peg down to second look easy and elegant, and he attacks bunts with such assurance that he sometimes scoops up the ball on the third-base side of the invisible pitcher-to-home line (I have seen only two or three other first basemen pull this off even once; Ferris Fain, of the late-nineteen-forties Athletics, was one of them) and then gets off his throw with the same motion. If you make yourself notice where Hernandez has stationed himself on the field, you will sometimes get a sudden sense of what is really going on down there. Wade Boggs, the best hitter in baseball, usually raps the ball up the middle or to left, even though he is a left-handed swinger, but his failure to pull even one pitch up the line to right in the course of the World Series allowed Hernandez to play him more and more into the hole as the Series went on, and contributed to Boggs' problems at the plate in these games. Even one pulled foul would have altered his positioning, Keith said after the Series ended; he was amazed that Boggs hadn't attacked him in this way.

Hernandez is probably not an exceptionally gifted athlete, but his baseball intelligence is remarkable. Other Mets players say that he always seems to be two or three pitches ahead of the enemy pitcher and catcher, and that he almost seems to know the other team's coaches' signals without looking, because he understands where they are in their heads and what they hope to do next. He shares all this with his teammates (keep count in a game of the number of different players he says something to in the course of a few innings), and the younger players on the club, including Darryl Strawberry, will tell you that Keith's counsel and patience and knowledge of the game and its ways have made them better ballplayers, and winners. All this comes at a price, which one may guess at when watching Hernandez chain-smoke and put away beers (there is a postgame ice bucket at his feet by his locker) in the clubhouse as he talks and comes down after the game. The talk is a season-long seminar that Mets writers attend, day after day, taking notes and exchanging glances as they write. The man is in the game.

Davey Johnson also has some baseball smarts, and in this last game he showed us, if we needed showing, how far ahead he had been all along. Sid Fernandez, the Mets' dumpling left-handed strikeout pitcher—their fourth starter this year, and during some stretches their best—came into the game in the fourth inning, with the Mets down by 3–0, and stopped the Sox dead in their tracks: a base on balls and then seven outs in succession, with four strikeouts. "That did it," Keith said afterward. "When Sid was in there, we began to feel that we might win this game after all. He was the necessary hero." Johnson had passed over Fernandez as a starter in the Series (he is streaky and emotional), but he had brought him along, all right. Fernandez had pitched a shaky one-third of an inning in Game Two, surrendering three hits and a run late in a losing cause; in Game Five, which the Mets also lost, he had pitched four shutout innings, with five strikeouts. He was Series-tested by the end, and he became Johnson's last and best move.

The Sox, for their part, mounted a courageous rally in their eighth inning, when three successive solid blows accounted for two runs and closed the score to 6–5 before Orosco came in and shot them down for good. By this time, the Mets hitters had done away with Schiraldi and were loose in the Boston bullpen—John McNamara's worst dream come true. Strawberry's homer and the cascade of Mets runs at the end released the fans at last, and their celebrations during the final outs of the year—the packed thousands together chanting, roaring out the Freddie Mercury rock chorus "We will, we will . . . ROCK YOU!" while pointing together at the Boston bench—were terrific fun. There was a great city party there at Shea, and then all over town, which went on into the parade and the ticker tape (it's computer paper now) the following afternoon, but when it was all over I think that most of us, perhaps all of us, realized that the victory celebration didn't come up to the wonderful, endless sixteen innings of Game Six, back during the playoffs. As one friend of mine said later, "For me, that night was the whole thing. Whatever there was to win had been won."

There was a surprise for me, there at the end. I am a Mets fan. I had no idea how this private Series would come out, but when the Mets almost lost the next-to-last game of the Series I suddenly realized that my pain and foreboding were even deeper than what

I had felt when the Red Sox came to the very brink out in Anaheim. I suppose most of my old Red Sox friends will attack me for perfidy, and perhaps accuse me of front-running and other failures of character, but there is no help for it. I don't think much has been lost, to tell the truth. I will root and suffer for the Sox and the Mets next summer and the summers after that, and if they ever come up against each other again in the World Series—well, who knows? Ask me again in a hundred and sixty-seven years.

1988

It's Never Happened Before in the World Series

THOMAS BOSWELL

LOS ANGELES, OCTOBER 16, 1988—It's never happened before in the World Series.

That's what you wanted to know, isn't it? Now don't you feel better? That's why you, and everybody else who watched Kirk Gibson's home run on Saturday night, felt so perplexed with amazement.

Nobody—now let's word this exactly right—had ever before hit a ninth-inning home run to turn defeat into victory in the World Series. Let alone with two out. Let alone with two strikes. Let alone with injuries to both legs so bad he could barely limp around the bases.

In eighty-five Series, you'd figure everything has transpired. Don Larsen's perfect game and the Black Sox' imperfect fix. Bill Wambsganss's unassisted triple play and the 10th-inning, final-game fly Fred Snodgrass dropped to blow the 1912 Series. The Athletics' 10-run inning to wipe out an 8–0 lead. Reggie Jackson's five home runs.

From Mickey Owen's passed ball to Bill Buckner's boot; Mazeroski's homer to Don Denkinger's blown call; the Babe's called shot to Fisk's foul pole polka; the Big Six's three shutouts to the pebble that finally gave the Big Train a Series win, baseball has consistently suspended disbelief in October.

But only one man knows how Gibson feels: Cookie Lavagetto. His two-run double with two out in the ninth inning of Game Four in '47 ended Yankee Bill Bevens's bid to pitch the first Series no-hitter and gave Brooklyn a 3–2 win.

Which Dodger was better? Kirk or Cookie? Both had two-out, two-run hits to turn a loss into a win. They're the only pair to do that in the last inning. Is a homer by a star better than a double by a journeyman? Is breaking up a no-hitter better than dragging yourself out of an ice bucket, shot up with Xylocaine and cortisone, to beat a pitcher with 45 saves?

Take your pick.

Lavagetto's hit tied his Series, but the Dodgers lost in seven games. Maybe that gives Gibson a potential edge.

Nobody's saying that Gibson's homer is on the short list of Greatest Series Moments. It was only Game One—though it certainly seemed to carry weight into Game Two. The Dodgers waltzed so blithely—6–0 behind Orel Hershiser—that Gibson stayed frozen in carbonite for an extra day, hoping to play in Oakland.

Other famous game-winning, last-inning homers in the Series have all come with the score tied. Sorry, Casey Stengel (inside-the-park in '23), Tommy Henrich ('49), Dusty Rhodes ('54), Eddie Mathews ('57), Bill Mazeroski ('60), Mickey Mantle ('64) and Carlton Fisk ('75), that's not quite the same.

Those in Dodger Stadium on Saturday night, especially the Athletics, know the difference. Some mortal Dodger, in the grip of hero worship, wrote "Roy Hobbs" above Gibson's locker. However, even *the Natural,* dedicated to the proposition that mythic excess is art, would not have dared to pull a stunt like Gibson, who is baseball's halt and lame Un-natural. Only real life can end this way and get an Oscar.

Gibson's homer did not short-circuit a light tower and burn

Chavez Ravine to ash. It just scorched Dennis Eckersley, Tony LaRussa and an Oakland team that would like to get its foot out of its mouth and Gibson's boot off its neck.

Even now, a day and a game later, what Gibson did bestrides this World Series, just as his two game-winning homers within thirteen hours against the Mets defined the National League playoffs.

"I don't think I'll ever see anything like that again for as long as I live," said Dodger Dave Anderson.

"Excited? I was going to run around the bases with him," said Mickey Hatcher, king of the L.A. Stuntmen. "I figured they'd have to get a wheelchair out there for him. My first reaction was to go out and kiss him. But the guy doesn't shave."

It's impossible not to acknowledge the Hollywood-script quality of the whole evening. Gibson was a mystery man all night, back in the clubhouse getting shots and ice. He hadn't even been able to bear taking practice swings in his living room in the morning, with the pain in his bum right knee far surpassing that of his healing left hamstring.

"I didn't even think the guy could walk," said Brian Holton. "I'd forgotten all about Kirk," added Hatcher. "I didn't even see him all night," said Steve Sax.

But Gibson was still hoping. When broadcaster Vin Scully said on TV that Gibson was gone for the night, Gibson growled, "Bullshit," and broke out of his ice wrap like the Thing coming to life.

Gibson, reduced to "visualizing" his swing for three days, started hitting off a tee and, as the ninth inning began, had the bat boy fetch Tommy Lasorda. "I told him, 'If you get [Mike] Davis to hit for [Alfredo] Griffin, I can hit for the pitcher.' He took off for the dugout. I guess it was what he wanted to hear."

With Davis, a home run threat and former Athletic, at bat, Lasorda deked Oakland nicely by sending the weak Anderson out on deck. Eckersley pitched too carefully and walked Davis, assuming the Dodgers had no power left. "You can't walk the tying run," said Eckersley; ". . . that's why I lost."

As Gibson did a jig of pain after each lunging swing, and even tried a half-speed jog to first on one foul dribbler, the A's continued to pour fastballs at the outside corner. "He didn't look too good on his swings," said Hassey, the catcher, yet he kept ticking off fouls.

But the Dodgers adapted by running. On the first steal attempt, Gibson finally had a decent swing, poking a foul to left. Oh, so that's their game, thought the A's. Can't allow a hit-and-run double to the opposite field.

So they changed plans. On the first slider, Davis stole second and the count ran full. Suddenly, LaRussa had to face a decision with historic overtones. In the 1985 playoffs, in this ballpark, Lasorda pitched to Jack Clark in just such a spot, top of the ninth, with first base open. Next pitch, home run. Season over. However, in 1947, the Yankees intentionally walked Pete Reiser, whom they feared, to get to Lavagetto. The Reiser run beat them.

With hindsight, the A's may remember Game Five of the '84 World Series, when Goose Gossage talked Dick Williams into letting him pitch to Gibson with Detroit ahead, 5–4, in the eighth. "Ten bucks says they pitch to me," yelled Gibson to Sparky Anderson. "Ten bucks says they don't," yelled back the Tigers' manager.

They did. Gibson went into the upper deck for three runs and the icing on a world title.

Now it is easy to say you should let Eckersley pitch to right-handed Steve Sax. But, at the moment, Hassey thought "we can freeze Gibson" with a backdoor slider—a pitch that looks like a low outside fastball for a semi-intentional walk, then snaps back to nick the corner and end the game, unhit.

"I tried to make a nasty pitch," said Eckersley. Instead, it proved to be "the only pitch he could hit out."

Already, the home run, probably not a 400-footer, is growing by the hour. Now Sax says Gibson "hit it with one hand." There's a palm tree, about 500 feet from home plate. If it ever dies, folks here will swear Gibson killed it. That won't be true. But if the burly A's somehow lose this Series, there won't be much doubt who killed them.

1991

As Series Go, '91 Is
One to Remember

DAVE KINDRED

THE WORLD SERIES OF 1991 stands alone. There is no need to thumb through record books. No need to ask historians for perspective. Anyone lucky enough to have seen this one knows what it was. It was baseball as good as baseball gets. It's just too bad the Twins and Braves quit so soon.

Commissioner Fay Vincent said to Ted Turner, "Why don't we play all winter and make it the best of 90?" Atlanta's little hero Mark Lemke said, "I wish this season would never end."

One soft and beautiful autumn night, the Orlando baseball poet Russ White sat in the upper deck along Atlanta's right-field line. He heard the fans, as one, sing low and sweet an Indian hymn. He saw diamonds in the sky above him. He saw Steve Avery on the diamond below. Pretty sure he wasn't in Iowa, Russ White asked, "Am I in heaven?"

For a week and more, to baseball folks, the answer was yes, spoken loudly. Minnesota and Atlanta, last-place teams a season ago, had been transformed, as if by divine touch, into champions who gave us a World Series so good that it can be called the best ever.

About such bold judgment there is room to quibble. The Hall of Famer Johnny Bench quibbled about some poor baserunning and flawed fielding. "The fans were the best thing of all," Bench said. He liked the hankies and tomahawks. As for the games, he said, they were not so well played.

One begs to differ with the distinguished Mr. Bench. His Cincinnati Reds of 1975 created a classic Series. Oakland's dynasty began in the '72 Series that gave us six one-run games. And who didn't like it in '55 when Brooklyn's beloved Bums finally beat the Yankees?

All were good Series. But none, it says here, ever had all the right stuff of this one.

"Every pitch, every strike, every ball, every inning—everything mattered in every game," said Terry Pendleton, the Atlanta third baseman.

"Tomorrow," said Minnesota's Kent Hrbek, "I'm going to the doctor to fix my ulcer."

Never in 87 years had a World Series given us three games decided on the last pitch. This one gave us not three such games but four.

Five games were won by one run and that run scored in the home team's last at-bat.

Two games were won by sudden home runs, lightning bolts of drama. And two nights in a row, a baserunner's gambling sprint and wonderful slide carried home the winning run a heartbeat ahead of an outfielder's throw. Never before had any team won two nights in a row in its last at-bat.

We saw three runners tagged out at the plate by catchers so resolute they accepted collisions and rose from the dust to do it some more. Dan Gladden of Minnesota, spikes Ty Cobb–high, knocked over Greg Olson. The catcher was seen standing on his left ear, an exclamation point turned upside down. Did Olson straighten up with his fists balled, looking for a fight? No, he simply rose and handed Gladden his cap. This is the show. It's hardball up here.

We saw 16 home runs, at least two in each of the first six games. Someone should look that up to see if it has ever been done. (It hasn't.) In Game 5, Atlanta scored 14 runs, the most ever by a

National League team. The Braves that night racked up a record 34 total bases. That's two more than the Yankees of '28 managed with Babe Ruth and Lou Gehrig.

We saw players who may be in the Hall of Fame someday, and we saw why. What Kirby Puckett did to Ron Gant in Game 6 was astonishing. Willie Mays outrunning Vic Wertz's long fly in '54 was no more sensational and certainly less meaningful than Puckett's flight to Gant's line drive.

Jack Morris, of the thick and villainous red mustache, rendered helpless Atlanta's good offense. He went 10 innings to win Game 7 and threw more effectively the later the hour became. Someone asked him afterward how much longer he could have pitched and Morris allowed himself a little smile.

"A hundred and 12 innings," he said.

Atlanta couldn't score against Morris in the eighth after putting men at second and third with none out. Minnesota loaded the bases with one out in the eighth and couldn't score. In the ninth, the Twins had runners at first and second with none out— and couldn't score.

As Pendleton came to bat in the 10th inning, Minnesota catcher Brian Harper said to him, "Why don't we just quit and call it a tie?" Pendleton laughed aloud and then grounded out to shortstop, the last out of Atlanta's season.

Minnesota would win it in their part of the 10th, doing it with a hit delivered by an obscure infielder named Gene Larkin. He'd driven in only 19 runs all year. He'd been to bat only three times in this Series. Perfect.

It was perfect because for a week and more, in this day of the jaded millionaire slugger, we saw the pure heart of baseball, a kid's game.

Greg Olson loved it. The Atlanta catcher is no one's fool. He understands his worth. In April, after all, he was not Atlanta's starting catcher.

"This year could be the last year when I know I'll be an impact player in a World Series," Olson said one sweet afternoon. He spoke to his ghost writer who took notes for "Greg Olson's Diary," appearing in the Atlanta Constitution. The pay: $100 a piece. A guy making minimum wage takes a buck wherever he finds it.

"So I'm having fun right now because I may never have this chance again," Olson said. "I enjoy baseball, period. I can't tell you with a straight face that it's a job."

We might grouse about the Metrodome. It distorts the game as surely as the designated-hitter rule distorts it. Lonnie Smith may be roasted for what some will call a baserunning mistake in Game 7, but he deserves the benefit of our doubt. If Pendleton says it's hard to see the ball against the white roof, it's hard to see it. Smith did the careful thing, waiting until he saw the ball bouncing, and Atlanta still had men at second and third with none out. Not Smith's fault. Blame it on the Dumbdome.

Otherwise, it was a Series made fascinating by the ways it thrilled us. Even now anyone who saw it can see it still: Puckett on the run toward left center. Gant's shot is out of reach. Surely it is out of reach. But Puckett is on the run. He catches most everything that stays inside Minnesota's borders. He is on the warning track. He gathers his stubby little self for an Air Puckett leap. Bumping high against the wall, he snatches the baseball out of the air.

A night later, Puckett is off the ground again. His Twins have won the World Series. Chili Davis has Puckett in his arms. Davis has lifted Puckett high above the celebrants clamoring around the pitcher's mound. Puckett throws wide his arms. His cap is in one hand. There is on his face a little boy's smile of pure joy.

1994

Game Is Too Young to Die

JIM MURRAY

ONCE UPON A TIME IN THIS COUNTRY there was a game called baseball.

You would have loved it.

Green grass, bright sunshine, hot dogs, Cracker Jack. The cares of the world you left at the door. "Outta the lot, Hack!" "We're wit ya, Carl, baby!" You were a kid again. No matter what age you were.

You brought the kids. It was an heirloom sport. Passed on from fathers to sons. Generation after generation. The baseball gene ran in families.

And the ballparks! You should have seen the ballparks! Lovely old Fenway Park. That left-field fence! The Monster! The Creature that ate pitchers. Ted Williams hit here.

You ever been to Fenway Park? A pity! Everyone should spend an afternoon at Fenway Park. It's a part of Americana.

Then there was Yankee Stadium. The house that Ruth built. Opera lovers had La Scala. Balletomanes had the Bolshoi. Playgoers had the Old Vic. We had Yankee Stadium. There's a monument to Babe Ruth in the outfield. "How about that!" Mel Allen would say.

The game had stars. Walter Johnson had a fastball you could only hit by Braille. Ruth hit more home runs himself than any team in the league some years. Nolan Ryan threw two no-hitters a year.

You loved to hear the infield chattering. "No hitter up there, Sandy! Throw him the deuce! Make him be a hitter, babe!"

Some of the best afternoons of your life were spent in a ballpark. The poet said the time spent in a ballpark, like fishing, didn't count against your life span. No one could age in a ballpark. You got younger, not older. You could live forever in a ballpark. Someone once complained the game was too slow. Not for us. I never went to a ballpark in a hurry in my life. If you're in a hurry, go to an airport, I'd tell them.

It was a game that Yogi Berra—ah, Yogi Berra!—once said ain't over till it's over. Not so dumb, at that. It's a game without a clock, is what he's saying. A football game can be over before it's over. Not a baseball game. The gun doesn't go off on you. You never run out of time, just outs.

What happened to this happy hunting ground, this magic isle in life? Where did all those summers go?

Well, it might have died in the summer of 1994. By its own hand.

No one could ever figure out quite why. It was the picture of health to the end.

It didn't run out of sluggers, southpaws, speed burners, shortstops. It ran out of love. It didn't die of old age, lack of interest, neglect. It died of a disease for which there is no known cure—stubbornness.

They all said they weren't trying to kill baseball, they were trying to save it. Meanwhile, the patient died on the operating table. The tombstone should read, "Here Lies Baseball—Negotiated to Death." It was an inglorious end for such a glorious tradition.

It was the victim of the oldest feud in the annals of sport—owners vs. players. It doesn't matter what the issue is—salary cap, pensions, revenue sharing. If the owners are for a salary cap, the players are against it. If the players are for revenue sharing, the owners are against it. If the owners were against the man-eating shark, the players would be for it.

It's nothing new. It's as old as the game.

Owners were always rich men. Ownership was a hobby. But they couldn't help applying business principles—if that phrase is not an oxymoron—to their hobby. They tried to make a profit. They were, after all, capitalists.

They managed to move the game outside the Constitution of the United States early on—1876, to be exact—when they instituted the "reserve clause," which bound the services of five players to the parent club in perpetuity. Eventually, they expanded it to include all players. The players' resistance was token at first. After all, it wasn't considered a profession then. Most of them kept their day jobs.

But the players countered by trying to form a new league—in 1890 and again in 1914. Both leagues went spectacularly broke.

The owners held unbroken sway from 1920 to the mid-1960s when the players brought up a can't-miss rookie.

Marvin Miller couldn't hit the change-up, couldn't bat .300, field .900, throw, catch or hit the curve, but he had what all the great ones from Cobb to Robinson had—a searing resentment of the Establishment verging on hatred.

The game was never the same after he joined it. Baseball's were probably the last workers of the world to unite. Miller put together a union equivalent of the '27 Yankees. They never lost a strike. Or a lockout.

Other factors played a part—most notably binding arbitration, which the owners put in themselves—but the bare facts of the matter are that, when Marvin Miller undertook to organize the players, the average big league salary was $19,000. Today, it is $1.2 million.

The even stranger truth is, even though it cost them astronomically more money to run the game, the owners ended up making more.

Most of them anyway. A whole cannot be greater than the sum of its parts and baseball is no exception. Historically, whenever a part began to threaten, the whole had a solution: Move it. There were always bright-eyed, bushy-tailed new towns slavering for big league baseball.

A lot of them have since managed to make do with pro basketball or pro football franchises. And moving doesn't always prove a solution in the long run. The portable franchise started with Boston, which moved to Milwaukee in 1953 after its attendance bottomed out at 281,276. The Boston Public Library drew more.

The Braves went to Milwaukee, where they were to draw 2,131,488 two years later. However, 13 years later, after new ownership had announced a move to Atlanta as soon as was legally possible, they bottomed out at 555,586 and headed southeast. And there were times in Atlanta when that franchise was put in the window with a "make-offer" tag on it.

It was a great game. It's too young to die. But those who love it were not consulted, the ones who collected the bubble gum cards, peeked through knotholes, bought the jackets, ate the Wheaties, waved the pennants and said, "Say it ain't so, Joe," and introduced sons to the game. Who cared about them?

But what's October without a World Series? Italy without a song? Paris without a spring? Canada without a sunset?

Once upon a time in this country, we had World Series. You would have loved them. Ruth pointing. Sandy Koufax curving. Pepper Martin stealing. Kirk Gibson homering.

You shoulda been here.

2000

Roger & Out

TOM VERDUCCI

A DANGEROUS HAIR-TRIGGER REACTION BY ROGER CLEMENS AND A BLUNDER ON THE BASES SET THE TONE AS THE YANKEES GOT A 2–0 SUBWAY SERIES JUMP ON THE METS

FORTITUDE WEARS A NEW YORK YANKEES cap. That was obvious last weekend to anyone who strolled past the New York Public Library, where the northernmost of the twin marble lions that guard the building's main entrance, Fortitude and Patience, sported a Bombers hat. It was just as obvious, too, to anyone who watched the Yankees, once again calling upon a reserve of cool under fire deep enough to shame a Navy SEAL, seize Games 1 and 2 of the World Series against their intracity rivals, the Mets.

This was an all–New York World Series, all right. While the first two games were played in the St. Patrick's Cathedral of baseball, Yankee Stadium, they had the gritty texture of Times Square before Disney-fication. They were raw, emotional, edgy, a bit dangerous, bizarre and ultimately tighter than a streetwalker's spandex. You knew this was not going to be your properly dignified Fall Classic when Mets relief pitcher John Franco showed up for

Game 1 riding shotgun in a police cruiser. This was the World According to Garp Series.

Through the madness the Yankees remained Fortitude's favorite sons. Their two wins, each by a margin as uncomfortably thin as your typical vehicular following distance in Manhattan, made the Yankees of manager Joe Torre the only team in baseball history to win 14 straight World Series games. Over five years Torre's Yankees have never lost a one-run postseason game in the Bronx. Going into Tuesday's Game 3 at Shea Stadium, they also had outscored their opponents from the seventh inning on, 98–44, during a 44–14 run through Octobers that has made them more synonymous with the month than Elvira is. The Mets became the latest team to learn that the Yankees are that trick candle on a birthday cake. You simply can't put them out. "This team is as mentally tough as any team I've ever had," gushed Yankees owner George Steinbrenner after Sunday's 6–5 victory, which followed a 4–3 extra-inning thriller on Saturday. "It has as much heart as any team I've ever had."

Steinbrenner was a power station of static electricity, a regular Con Edison in loafers as he paced the clubhouse carpet during the two games. No one, though, set off more charged ions into the loaded atmosphere than Yankees righthander Roger Clemens, the Game 2 winner. He was a spark-throwing bundle of intensity when he arrived at Yankee Stadium for his outing. He hadn't pitched in seven days, since his one-hit domination of the Seattle Mariners in the American League Championship Series. The last four of those days had been filled with New York media buzz about his facing Mets catcher Mike Piazza for the first time since beaning him on July 8, during one of the teams' interleague series. "I was anxious all day," Clemens said after Sunday's game. "I felt I couldn't go up and in, which I normally do on Mike, because what if one got away? All the talk really wore me down. I kept telling myself, You've got to get ahold of your emotions."

There was more to think about. Pitching coach Mel Stottlemyre stopped by to chat with Clemens in the clubhouse before Game

2. Stottlemyre hasn't been with the Yankees this postseason because of stem-cell treatments he's receiving to fight blood-plasma cancer. Clemens also knew that his mother, Bess, would be at the game, seated in the wheelchair section behind home plate. She had come last year to watch her son pitch in the World Series, but she bolted after five innings because she couldn't stand the tension, and she missed seeing him close out the Fall Classic with a 4–1 win over the Atlanta Braves.

The seven days of rest had seemed like forever to Clemens. All the waiting, all the anxiety—he couldn't wait to unleash it. He spoke to almost no one in the clubhouse before the game. Minutes before he took the mound, he stretched out over a padded table in the training room. A trainer rubbed hot liniment all over his body, even between his legs. Clemens said nothing. He just let out loud, rhythmic blasts of air through his nostrils, in the manner of a wild bull in the last moments before the wooden door of the holding pen swings open to the possibilities of danger. "I don't remember ever being more ready for a start," Clemens said. "But I also knew I had to control it somehow."

On the eve of the Series, Yankees righthander David Cone, a wizened elder of New York baseball (he pitched for the Mets from 1987 to '92), noted, "More than ever guys know they'll be remembered forever by what happens in this Series. One incident, one play, one gaffe, and it will be remembered forever."

In that morning's newspapers, Brooklyn Dodgers catcher Mickey Owen was still—59 years later—dropping that third strike to allow the Yankees to win Game 4 of the '41 World Series. The Series is a spin of the roulette wheel. What Cone could not know was that the wheel would stop on the number 6 of Mets right-fielder Timo Perez in Game 1 and the number 22 of Clemens in Game 2.

Fifteen Mets players and about a dozen front-office workers dined together on the evening before the Series opener at a Manhattan steakhouse, consuming slabs of beef the size of bread boxes. Owners Nelson Doubleday and Fred Wilpon each toasted the players, wishing them luck and expressing pride at having the Mets in their first Series in 14 years. There is, after all, a reason that Patience, the other library lion, wears a Mets cap.

New York percolated. The Subway Series was the toughest ticket in New York this side of one for jaywalking. A fellow Clifton (N.J.) High '63 alum telephoned Mets media relations director Jay Horwitz looking for tickets. It gave the man no pause that he and Horwitz hadn't seen or spoken to each other for 37 years.

The Mets made the 9.1-mile trip from Shea Stadium to Yankee Stadium in two chartered buses under police escort, with Franco in the lead car. A crowd 15 people deep, kept at bay by police barricades, jeered the team as it entered the ballpark; one Yankees fan held a sign that read WE NEVER TRADED NOLAN RYAN. Mets first baseman Todd Zeile and outfielder Darryl Hamilton pressed camcorders to their faces to record the carnival.

As Perez discovered, sometimes posterity is bigger than 8 mm. He and the other Mets had appeared loose, with third baseman Robin Ventura giving new meaning to the term by taking batting practice sans undergarments. With two outs in the sixth inning and the game scoreless, Zeile smacked a fly ball deep to leftfield off Yankees lefty Andy Pettitte. Perez, the dynamic rookie who had reached first on a single, unwisely ran in low gear, thrusting an arm in the air to signal that Zeile had homered. Zeile, too, pumped a fist in celebration, while rounding first base. One problem: The ball didn't leave the park. It hit the top of the padded wall and caromed to leftfielder David Justice. "Where's Jeffrey Maier when you need him?" Zeile would crack later, referring to the 12-year-old boy whose reach turned a fly ball out by Yankees shortstop Derek Jeter into a home run in the Yankees' win over Zeile's Baltimore Orioles in Game 1 of the 1996 American League Championship Series.

The 5'9" Perez tried to outrun his blunder, but Jeter would not allow him to get away with it. He took a throw from Justice and, wheeling toward the plate and throwing off one foot (think Joe Montana to Dwight Clark), fired a strike to catcher Jorge Posada to nail Perez. "I'll gain experience from it," the humbled Perez said. "If I'd left at full throttle, I would have scored easily." The new Lonnie Smith (Smith's baserunning blunder cost the Atlanta Braves Game 7 of the 1991 Series) was chastised by several teammates, who told him never to be so careless again.

The missed run loomed large in the ninth inning, when the Mets asked closer Armando Benitez to protect a 3–2 lead. Benitez did get one out and came within one strike of the second, but rightfielder Paul O'Neill, in the most important and stubborn at bat of the young Series, drew a 10-pitch walk. Not even the IRS takes as much as the Yankees; they outwalked the Mets in the first two games 15–1.

Then lefthanded-hitting pinch hitter Luis Polonia laced a single off Benitez with a bat on which he had written A. BENITEZ and T. WENDELL in anticipation of facing Benitez and Turk Wendell, the Mets' top righthanded relievers. Another single, by second baseman Jose Vizcaino, set up a game-tying sacrifice fly by designated hitter Chuck Knoblauch.

It wasn't until the 12th inning that the Yankees won, on a bases-loaded single by Vizcaino off Wendell. New York had waited 38 years for a Mets-Yankees Subway Series, and Game 1 seemed to take just as long. At four hours, 51 minutes, it was the longest of the 560 World Series games ever played and only five minutes shorter than the two previous Subway Series games combined, in '56 between the Yankees and the Dodgers. Not even Torre's Yankees had won a game like this. The franchise had been 0–54 when trailing after eight innings in World Series games since . . . Owen dropped that third strike.

Game 2—and a piece of Series history—belonged to Clemens. His pregame intensity exploded in an angry spray of 98-mph fastballs. He whiffed the first two batters, all the while spitting and snarling and huffing and puffing. "My feet were flying off the ground," he said.

Then, in a blip of time, all his tightly strung circuitry went haywire. On a buzz saw of a fastball, Piazza's bat shattered in three pieces. The largest part, the barrel, bounced to Clemens, who fielded it with two hands as if it were the baseball—which, unbeknownst to both Clemens and Piazza, had fallen foul wide of first base. In this instant the synapses became overloaded. Clemens heaved the daggerlike piece of wood toward the Yankees' on-deck circle. ("I didn't even know [Piazza] was running," Clemens would say.) The bat, its sharp end tumbling end over end, cartwheeled only about a foot in front of Piazza. "What's your problem?" Piazza yelled.

Clemens at first indicated that he thought he had fielded the baseball. Piazza kept yelling for an answer—fishing for Clemens to defuse the situation by passing it off as an accident—but Clemens would not address him. Clemens stalked toward home plate umpire Charlie Reliford, wanting only to get another baseball and get back on the mound. Both benches emptied, though without incident.

On the next pitch Clemens retired Piazza on a grounder. He ducked into the clubhouse, where he ran into Stottlemyre. "You've got to settle down," Stottlemyre told Clemens.

He did. The Mets went down meekly thereafter. Clemens faced 28 batters over eight innings, and only five of them put the ball out of the infield, just twice for hits. The Mets did hang five runs in the ninth on the Yankees' bullpen, but that was one short of the six the Yankees had scratched out off skittish lefty Mike Hampton and a succession of leaky relievers.

The Mets absolved Clemens of intent in the bat incident, and Piazza described himself as "more shocked and confused than anything." In the interview room after the game, Clemens said, "There was no intent there." Torre, normally the stoic sage, blew up at repeated questions from reporters about the incident. Clemens was astonished at Torre's outburst. Later, after he'd showered and put on his black shirt and leather jacket, Clemens telephoned a friend while walking to his black SUV. "Boy, they really got Skip fired up!" said Clemens.

As he arrived at the SUV, his wife, Debra, hopped down from

the passenger seat. There was one thing he had to know. "Did Mom make it?" he asked.

"Yes," Debra replied. "She made it through, all the way until you came out."

Clemens smiled. It was 2 A.M., and only now did he put himself at ease. He had stared down the Mets with the help of a fastball straight out of his youth and a will straight from his mother. It was a night in which he became, in the parlance of the territory, a made Yankee.

2001

New York Stories

GLENN STOUT

CLEMENS'S STANDOUT PERFORMANCE and Rivera's expected spectacular one forced Arizona's hand. Diamondback manager Bob Brenly decided to bring back Curt Schilling in game four on three days' rest, a decision that lit up the airwaves for the next day. Torre stayed the course as usual, sticking with El Duque.

But Torre also did something else. He tweaked his batting order and lineup, leaving Shane Spencer in left, moving Jeter to leadoff and Paul O'Neill to second, playing matchup baseball again, putting each man in the right place at the right time.

For much of the game it made no difference. Schilling was, incredibly, even better and more efficient than before, but Spencer sliced a rare mistake into the stands in right to give the Yankees a 1–0 lead. Mark Green then answered with an upper-deck shot off El Duque in the fourth. But Hernandez, growing stronger as the game went on, kept pace with Schilling. In the fifth, after Tony Womack doubled and moved to third, Luis Gonzalez lofted a ball to left and this time Spencer needed no help from Derek Jeter with his throw. He hit Posada on one hop, perfect, and the catcher—so often overlooked for his defense—made another great stop, spinning and tagging Womack, first with his empty glove and then with the ball out of his bare hand,

and then as he fell turning his palm up to keep the ball from falling out. The game remained tied.

El Duque finally tired in the seventh, and in the eighth a single by Gonzalez and a long double by Erubiel Durazo put Arizona ahead. Moments later, with the infield in, Arizona went ahead when Jeter's throw home went to the wrong side of the plate. With six outs to go, Arizona led 3–1. The Yankees, with only three hits off Schilling, were down and nearly out.

But Brenly pulled a shocker, removing Schilling after only 88 pitches—his last a 98-mile-per-hour fastball that punched out Justice—to save him for a potential game seven, as if he didn't expect to put the Yankees away before then. Submarining closer Byung-Hyun Kim struck out the side in the eighth—all on 3–2 counts—and the game entered the bottom of the ninth with the Yankees still down 3–1.

Jeter tried to bunt for a hit but was thrown out by Matt Williams. Then, with the Who's "Baba O'Riley" wailing, the crowd gave Paul O'Neill his now-obligatory ovation. It was an open secret that the Yankee right fielder, age 38, who had said earlier that "I'm tired of waking up in the morning and finding out what doesn't work," would retire after the Series.

But not tonight, not yet, for Paul O'Neill would play hard to the end. He punched the ball into left field for a single, giving the Yankees a chance. Tino Martinez stepped to the plate, the tying run.

Kim threw one pitch, and Martinez swung. And time stopped.

It was high, it was deep, and it was gone.

And as Martinez's blast dropped over the fence in right center, the Stadium moved again, and what was beyond belief was made real. The game was now tied, remarkably, incredibly, improbably, 3–3, the first time in the World Series since 1947—Lavagetto versus Bevens—that a team had come back after trailing by two in the ninth. Everything suddenly seemed tilted New York's way.

Kim wiggled out of the inning after the Yankees loaded the

bases, and then Torre gave the ball to Rivera in the tenth. Thirteen pitches and three broken bats later and it was time— midnight and November, a month for veterans and Thanksgiving. Derek Jeter stepped in against Kim.

Since taking his tumble into the stands against Oakland, Jeter, limping and wrapped and ending each game packed in ice in the clubhouse, had slumped. He was only one for fifteen in the Series and hadn't gotten the ball out of the infield. The rest of the Yankees weren't doing much better.

But Jeter's childhood dreams had included all of this, every imagined possibility, and he was now the veteran, and it was his month. He'd stayed loose all game, joking with Torre, reminding him that his contract expired at midnight, and asking bench coach Don Zimmer whether he was going to take over. As he prepared to step to the plate to lead off the 12th inning, he went up to his manager—still "Mr. Torre" to Jeter—and told him, "You've only got five minutes."

Then Jeter stepped to the plate. He took a ball low, and then fouled two pitches. The next two drifted wide, and Jeter watched, then stood in, 3–2, bat held high. Kim wound up and threw again . . .

. . . and they all came pouring out—the Yankees from their dugout, the hoarse cheers of fans—when Jeter swung and created another incredible memory for New York, a snapshot of a state of mind that New York needed and pleaded for like no place else. The ball sliced off his bat to right, just long enough, just high enough not to need the help of Jeffery Maier or any other pair of hands into the stands and out of time and into the arms of history. Jeter raised his right arm and ran open-mouthed around the bases—his first walk-off home run ever—then disappeared, lost in the pinstriped mass that always seems to mean the same thing at the end of the year, something almost beyond words, that on this night meant a 4–3 Yankee win and much, much more. Even "cathartic" seemed too small a word to explain the feeling.

Somehow, incredibly, the Yankees were still playing baseball in

November, and Sinatra was singing again. But only moments after striking the home run, while standing on the field being interviewed, Jeter was already warning, "This game means nothing if we lose tomorrow." The player they were calling "Mr. November" was right, and he was already starting to regroup, focusing on what lay ahead, anticipating what might come next.

But not even Jeter could foresee that. Game five unfolded in rough approximation of game four, an extended, improbable setup. Arizona starter Miguel Batista kept New York's virtually hitless wonders off balance all night. Mike Mussina, much better than in game one, was similarly successful, but in a five-minute span in the fifth inning Steve Finley and Rod Barajas both homered and put Arizona ahead 2–0. The Yankees threatened in both the seventh and eighth, but each rally ended short, the first with a fly ball by Brosius, the second with a fly by Martinez. In the top of the ninth the crowd seemed resigned to defeat, cheering Paul O'Neill wildly in what seemed to be his last appearance in the Stadium, calling him out in right field with a syncopated "Paul O-Nee-ul, Paul O-Nee-ul" chant. When the Diamondbacks went down, he entered the dugout and tipped his hat, a good-bye that seemed symbolic, a farewell not only to the game and the season but to the era that in many ways began the day he joined the team.

The ninth inning began with the Diamondbacks poised on the dugout steps for the second night in a row and closer Byung-Hyun Kim on the mound. Yankee fans tried to muster a cheer, but voices still hoarse from the night before had lost their thunder.

Only ten minutes shy of midnight Jorge Posada woke them up with a sharp double to right, the first hard-hit ball for New York since Jeter's home run earlier that morning. Perhaps Kim, who'd thrown 62 pitches the night before, was weakening.

But Spencer grounded to third, and Knoblauch, who'd pinch-run for Justice in the eighth, struck out. All that stood between the Yankees and a 3–2 deficit in the Series was Scott Brosius.

Everyone watching thought about it, but no one dared put

words to the thought. Not even Brosius. The 1998 World Series MVP said later that he thought only of trying to hit the ball hard.

He took a ball. Then, with one swift swing, he took the ball, and the game, and sent it up where all could see it, white against the black of night growing small. He raised his arm, and the Stadium moved and heaved again and spoke with one voice as the ball crashed into the stands in left. For the second night in a row, with two out in the ninth inning, when hope lay dormant, another Yankee rose to the occasion. The score was tied, 2–2.

The Yankees almost won it then, loading the bases afterward before Spencer struck out, then turned to Rivera again. He broke three bats on thirteen pitches in the tenth, but Mike Morgan shut down the Yankees as well.

In the eleventh Rivera, working his third night in a row, proved relatively human, giving up two singles, a sacrifice, and an intentional walk to load the bases with Reggie Sanders coming to bat.

Torre, he admitted later, rolled the dice. He brought the infield in at the corners but left Jeter and Soriano at normal depth, hoping for a bang-bang double play.

But Sanders hit a rocket, and the sharp sound said "base hit."

But there was Soriano, horizontal, diving to his right, with the ball in his glove.

And on the game went. Grace grounding out to Brosius to end the inning, the Yankees going down in order again, then Sterling Hitchcock setting down Arizona in the 12th and Albie Lopez coming on in relief for the Diamondbacks in the bottom of the inning, the tension excruciating, night turning into morning again.

Fundamentals won it. Knoblauch hit his first pitch into center for a single. Brosius bunted his third pitch for a sacrifice, bringing up Soriano. He took two balls, then fouled one off, then swung again.

The ball sliced into right field, landed, and bounced once, then twice away from Reggie Sanders, who scooped it up and turned and fired home. Knoblauch, running hard, saw third-base coach Willie Randolph, who had only two runners thrown out at the plate all year, waving him home.

The ball hit short of the plate and careened off Barajas as Knoblauch slid, bounding free.

Then it all poured forth once more. Clemens picked up Soriano. Knoblauch leapt in the air.

In 1951, following Bobby Thomson's home run, long considered the most dramatic moment in baseball history, Red Smith had written: "Now it is done. Now the story ends. And there is no way to tell it. The art of fiction is dead." Over the course of two improbable mornings, playing baseball in a month and at a time unlike any other, with three home runs and one solid single, the Yankees killed off nonfiction too and created a whole new genre, a place where "back to normal" meant the incredible, where the implausible became routine, and where nothing seemed impossible for this city and this team.

"I can't be surprised," said Torre afterward. "It just happened the day before." Perhaps Yogi had been right all along. It really *wasn't* over till it was over. It *was* déjà vu all over again.

Yet it was not the end of the World Series, even though after these three days in New York the World Series somehow seemed a lesser championship than the victory the Yankees had just earned. The end would come in Arizona, where the Diamondbacks fashioned their own version of the implausible.

Acknowledgments

Thanks to all the people who told me about good World Series writing they recalled, especially Dan Shaughnessy, Bob Ryan, Champ Atlee, Bill Heinz, and Eliot Asinof.

Thanks also to Pete Fornatale, Shana Wingert Drehs, and Dorianne Steele at Crown, and to my friend Richard Johnson, a most tireless and dedicated associate.

—Bill Littlefield

Thanks to Michele Lee Amundsen for the suggestion of the book title, Mary and Richard Thaler for help in New York, to the late Jerry Nason of *The Boston Globe* for donating his amazing sports library to the Sports Museum of New England, to Glenn Stout for his timely and helpful advice, and to Mary, Bobby, and Lizzie, for their patience and love. A sincere thanks to Pete Fornatale and Shana Wingert Drehs for their superb editorial stewardship, and finally to Bill Littlefield, friend and host of *Only a Game*, America's most literate sports radio program.

—Richard A. Johnson

Credits

Grateful acknowledgment is made to the following for permission to reprint previously published material:

The Associated Press: "Dad Would Have Loved It" by Will Grimsley. Reprinted by permission of The Associated Press.

Black, Inc: "Damon Runyon" by Jimmy Breslin. Copyright © by Jimmy Breslin. Reprinted by permission of Black, Inc. on behalf of the author.

Conde Nast Publications: "Game Six, World Series" by Roger Angell (*The New Yorker,* 1986). Copyright © 1986 by Roger Angell. All rights reserved. Reprinted by permission of Conde Nast Publications.

Copyright Clearance Center: "The Knot-Hole Gang Goes Climbing" by Bud Collins (*The Boston Globe,* October 3, 1967). Copyright © 1967 by Globe Newspaper Co. (MA). "The Sixth Game" by Peter Gammons (*The Boston Globe,* October 24, 1975). Copyright © 1975 by Globe Newspaper Co. (MA). Reprinted by permission of the Globe Newspaper Co. (MA) in the form of a trade book via the Copyright Clearance Center.

Charles Einstein: Excerpt from *Willie's Time* by Charles Einstein. Copyright © 1979 by Charles Einstein. Reprinted by permission of the author.

Arnold Hano: "Tension and Torment" by Arnold Hano (*Sports Magazine,* December 1962). Reprinted by permission of the author.

Henry Holt and Company, LLC: Excerpts from *Eight Men Out: The Black Sox and the 1919 World Series* by Eliot Asinof. Copyright © 1963, 1991 by Eliot Asinof. Reprinted by permission of Henry Holt and Company, LLC.

Houghton Mifflin Company: Excerpt from "New York Stories" from *Yankee Century: 100 Years of New York Yankees Baseball* by Glenn Stout and Richard Johnson. Copyright © 2002 by Glenn Stout and Richard Johnson. All rights reserved. Reprinted by permission of Houghton Mifflin Company.

King Features Syndicate: "New York Giants 5, New York Yankees 4" by Damon Runyon (October 12, 1923). Copyright © 1923 by King Features Syndicate. Reprinted by permission of King Features Syndicate.

The Los Angeles Times: "Game Is Too Young to Die" by Jim Murray (*Los Angeles Times,* August 21, 1994). Copyright © 1994 by

Los Angeles Times. Reprinted by permission of *The Los Angeles Times*.

McIntosh and Otis, Inc.: "Chapter 26" of *Maybe I'll Pitch Forever* by Leroy Paige as told to David Lipman. Copyright © 1962 by David Lipman. Reprinted by permission of McIntosh and Otis, Inc.

New York Daily News L. P.: "Tiger Triumph" by Jimmy Powers (*New York Daily News,* October 11, 1945); "Dodgers 3, Yankees 2" by Dick Young (*New York Daily News,* October 4, 1947); "Paradise at Last" by Joe Trimble (*New York Daily News,* October 5, 1955). Reprinted by permission of the New York Daily News, L.P.

The New York Post: "Sal Maglie: A Gracious Man" (*New York Post,* October 1956). Copyright © 1956 by NYP Holdings, Inc. Reprinted by permission of the *New York Post.*

The New York Times: "Washington Senators 4, New York Giants 3," previously published as "Washington Wins Its First World series . . ." by Bill Corum (*The New York Times,* October 11, 1924). Copyright © 1924 by The New York Times Agency. "Boy Regains Health as Ruth Homers" (*The New York Times,* October 8, 1926). Copyright © 1926 by The New York Times Agency. "St. Louis Cardinals 11, Detroit Tigers 0," previously published as "Cards Win 4–3 Even Series as Paul Dean . . ." by John Drebinger (*The New York Times,* October 10, 1934). Copyright © 1934 by The New York Times Agency. "Winning by Striking Out," previously published as "Yanks Win in 9th, Final 'Out' Turns into 4 Run . . ." by Red Smith (*The New York Times,* October 6, 1941). Copyright © 1941 by The New York Times Agency. "Defying Belief," previously

About the Editors

Bill Littlefield is the host of National Public Radio's weekly show *Only a Game*, produced at WBUR in Boston. He has written articles, reviews, and essays for a number of publications, most recently the *Boston Globe*. Bill's commentaries, written and voiced, have won numerous Associated Press Awards. He lives in Massachusetts with his wife, Mary Atlee, and their two daughters, Amy and Alison. He is the author of several books, including the baseball novel *Prospect* and, most recently, *The Circus in The Woods*.

Richard A. Johnson is the curator of the Sports Museum at the Fleet Center in Boston and is author of *A Century of Boston Sports* and *The Boston Braves*. He is coauthor with Glenn Stout of *Red Sox Century* and *Yankees Century* as well as biographies of Ted Williams, Joe DiMaggio, and Jackie Robinson.

About the Contributors

Roger Angell has been writing for *The New Yorker* since 1962. His baseball pieces for that magazine have been collected into several books, including *The Summer Game, Late Innings, Season Ticket,* and, most recently, *Game Time.*

Eliot Asinof, the author of *Eight Men Out,* has written several other books, among them two novels set in baseball: *Off Season* and *Man on Spikes.*

Paul Bauer, a rare book dealer specializing in baseball, lives in Kent, Ohio.

Thomas Boswell has been a columnist at the *Washington Post* since 1984. He has written several books about baseball, including *Why Time Begins on Opening Day* and *How Life Imitates the World Series.*

Brendan Boyd coauthored *The Great American Baseball Card Flipping, Trading and Bubble Gum Book,* with Fred C. Harris, and wrote the text for *Racing Days,* a collaboration with photographer

Henry Horenstein. The Boston native also wrote the novel *Blue Ruin,* from which this excerpt is gleaned.

Jimmy Breslin was awarded the Pulitzer Prize for distinguished commentary in 1986. Through the last five decades, his columns have appeared in various New York City newspapers and have been syndicated nationwide. He is the author of *Damon Runyon: A Life* and several bestselling novels, among them *The Gang That Couldn't Shoot Straight.*

Heywood Broun was a Harvard colleague of Walter Lippman and John Reed who first found work as a sports reporter for the *New York Morning Telegraph.* Two years later he joined the *New York Tribune* and during the First World War worked as a foreign correspondent in France. Upon his return he began writing a column entitled "It Seems to Me." Over the next few years Broun campaigned against censorship and racial discrimination and for academic freedom. He also supported those such as Margaret Sanger, John T. Scopes, and D. H. Lawrence, who were persecuted in the United States for their political and social views.

Bud Collins is best known for his tennis commentary on television and in the *Boston Globe.* He is the author of several books, including *My Life With the Pros,* and was inducted into the Tennis Hall of Fame in 1994.

Bill Corum was a graduate of the University of Missouri and Columbia University Journalism School. Corum was also a major in the AEF in the First World War. He joined the *New York Times* in 1920 and moved to the *New York Journal* in 1925 and the *Detroit Evening Times* in 1935. He was a columnist for the *New York Journal-*

American at the time of his death in 1958. Well liked and respected among writers, he was named president of Churchill Downs racetrack in 1949.

Arthur Daley was a fixture at the *New York Times,* where he wrote his column "Sports of the Times" for thirty-one years, starting in 1942. In 1973 he was the first sportswriter awarded the Pulitzer Prize.

John Drebinger was a high school track star and son of a violinist in the Metropolitan Opera orchestra. Drebinger was the oldest writer traveling the baseball circuit when he retired at age seventy-three. He began his newspaper career with the weekly *Staten Island Advance* and joined the *New York Times* in 1923. He covered every World Series for the *Times* from 1929 to 1963. In 1973 he received the J. G. Taylor Spink Award from the Baseball Hall of Fame.

Charles Einstein, whose work has appeared in San Francisco newspapers and *Sport* magazine, has published four books with or about Willie Mays, and has also coauthored books with Orlando Cepeda and Juan Marichal.

Peter Gammons is a studio analyst for ESPN's *Baseball Tonight*. He began his career as a baseball writer for the *Boston Globe* and has also worked for *Sports Illustrated*. He was voted national sportswriter of the year in 1989, 1990, and 1993.

Will Grimsley was the chief national and international sports correspondent for the Associated Press. He reported on seven

Olympic Games and innumerable Davis Cup and grand slam tennis and golf tournaments.

Arnold Hano's books include *A Day in the Bleachers, Willie Mays, Roberto Clemente: Batting King,* and *Muhammad Ali: The Champion.*

Jerry Izenberg joined the *Newark Star Ledger* in 1963. He has published several collections of columns and essays and produced over thirty television programs, including documentaries on Roberto Clemente and former New York Mets manager Johnny Keane.

Murray Kempton, known for his political and social commentaries, won a Pulitzer Prize in 1985. His books include *Part of Our Time* (1955) and *The Briar Patch* (1973), which won a National Book Award.

Dave Kindred is a columnist for *The Sporting News.* His books include *Glove Stories* and *Heroes, Fools, and Other Dreamers.*

Tony Kornheiser is a columnist at the *Washington Post.* His books include *I'm Back for More Cash (Because You Can't Take Two Hundred Newspapers into the Bathroom), Bald As I Wanna Be,* and *Pumping Irony: Working Out the Angst of a Lifetime.*

Ring Lardner was regarded as unusual when he made the switch from writing baseball humor to being the prolific author of witty essays and short stories. His book *You Know Me Al* is considered an American classic. Lardner was also a skilled reporter; he suspected the White Sox of throwing the 1919 World Series from the start and walked through the team's train car during the Series singing a self-penned ditty, "I'm Forever Blowing Ball Games," to the tune of "I'm Forever Blowing Bubbles," a popular song of the day.

Lloyd Lewis wrote for the *Chicago Daily News* and other newspapers in a long journalistic career.

Christy Mathewson won 373 games for the New York Giants and Cincinnati Reds before serving in World War One. He later served as president of the Boston Braves and died in Saranac Lake, New York, in 1925, as a result of the effects of being subjected to a poison gas attack in the war. Despite recording an amazing 1.26 earned run average in the 1912 World Series, he lost two games with no wins.

Tim Murnane was a baseball man of many talents. He played in the National Association and National League in the 1870s. In the 1880s he helped form the Union Association and was cofounder of the Brotherhood of Baseball Players. Following his playing career he was the chief baseball reporter for the *Boston Globe*. Following his death in 1917 an All-Star contingent of major leaguers played a benefit game in his honor at Fenway Park.

Jim Murray, who wrote for the *L.A. Times* and helped found *Sports Illustrated,* won the Pulitzer Prize for general commentary in 1990 and said he thought a winner should have "to bring down a government or expose major graft or give advice to prime ministers. Correctly quoting Tommy Lasorda shouldn't merit a Pulitzer Prize."

Satchel Paige, who pitched in the major leagues at the age of fifty-nine or thereabouts, is alleged to have shrugged and said: "Age is a question of mind over matter. If you don't mind, it doesn't matter."

Jimmy Powers worked in Oklahoma, Milwaukee, and Cleveland before joining the *New York Daily News* in 1928. His column, "The Powerhouse," ran until 1957, and he was sports editor of the *Daily News* from 1935 until 1957.

Frazier "Slow" Robinson played professional baseball in parts of four decades, beginning in the 1920s. He caught for Hall of Fame pitchers Satchel Paige and Leon Day. He died in 1997.

Damon Runyon is best known for the movies and plays based on his short stories about Broadway characters and sporting types. Runyon joined the *New York American* in 1911, covering the Giants until 1920. Even after leaving the baseball beat Runyon covered big events such as championship fights and the World Series.

Luke Salisbury is the author of the highly acclaimed book *The Answer Is Baseball* as well as three novels, including *The Cleveland Indian*. He is a past vice president of the Society for American Baseball Research.

Marshall Smelser is professor of history at the University of Notre Dame and author of *The Life That Ruth Built, American History at a Glance, The Winning of Independence,* and *The Democratic Republic, 1801–1815.*

Red Smith's *New York Herald Tribune* column, "Views of Sport," began appearing in 1945. He joined the *New York Times* in 1971. Smith won a Pulitzer Prize in 1976, and his columns have been collected in five books.

Joe Soucheray writes for the *Minneapolis Tribune* and has written biographies of speed skater Sheila Young and decathlon champion Bruce Jenner.

Tris Speaker, a Hall of Fame centerfielder, batted .300 in the 1912 World Series and socked the tenth-inning single that tied the decisive eighth game. Speaker batted .344 for his career and holds the major league records for both outfield assists and doubles.

Glenn Stout is the series editor of the annual *Best American Sports Writing* series, editor of the collections *Impossible Dreams,* on the Red Sox, and *Top of the Heap,* on the Yankees. He is the coauthor, with Richard A. Johnson, of books on Ted Williams, Joe DiMaggio, and Jackie Robinson, as well as *Red Sox Century* and *Yankees Century.* He also is a frequent guest on national news and sports programs and coedited *The Best American Sports Writing of the Century* with David Halberstam.

Joe Trimble played baseball for the Falcons in the Brooklyn Amateur League. He played under the tutelage of baseball historian and scholar Dr. Harold Seymour, then started a writing career that led him to the *New York Daily News,* where he served as Yankees beat reporter for four decades.

Tom Verducci writes about baseball for *Sports Illustrated* and appears on CNNSI.

Heinie Wagner was captain of the 1912 World Champion Boston Red Sox. He started his career in Boston in 1906 when the lowly team was still known as the Americans or Pilgrims and ended up as one of only two players, with Harry Hooper, to play on four Red Sox world champion teams in 1912, 1915, 1916, and 1918. He batted only .167 in the 1912 World Series.

Dick Young received the J. G. Taylor Spink Award from the Baseball Hall of Fame in 1979. He worked for the *New York Daily News* for forty-five years, and moved to the *New York Post* in 1982.